D1756496

St Antony's Series

General Editor: **Jan Zielonka** (2004–), Fellow of St Antony's College, Oxford

Othon Anastasakis, Research Fellow of St Antony's College, Oxford and Director of South East European Studies at Oxford

Recent titles include:

Håkan Thörn
ANTI-APARTHEID AND THE EMERGENCE OF A GLOBAL CIVIL SOCIETY

Lotte Hughes
MOVING THE MAASAI
A Colonial Misadventure

Fiona Macaulay
GENDER POLITICS IN BRAZIL AND CHILE
The Role of Parties in National and Local Policymaking

Stephen Whitefield (editor)
POLITICAL CULTURE AND POST-COMMUNISM

José Esteban Castro
WATER, POWER AND CITIZENSHIP
Social Struggle in the Basin of Mexico

Valpy FitzGerald and Rosemary Thorp (editors)
ECONOMIC DOCTRINES IN LATIN AMERICA
Origins, Embedding and Evolution

Victoria D. Alexander and Marilyn Rueschemeyer
ART AND THE STATE
The Visual Arts in Comparative Perspective

Ailish Johnson
EUROPEAN WELFARE STATES AND SUPRANATIONAL GOVERNANCE OF
SOCIAL POLICY

Archie Brown (editor)
THE DEMISE OF MARXISM-LENINISM IN RUSSIA

Thomas Boghardt
SPIES OF THE KAISER
German Covert Operations in Great Britain during the First World War Era

Ulf Schmidt
JUSTICE AT NUREMBERG
Leo Alexander and the Nazi Doctors' Trial

Steve Tsang (editor)
PEACE AND SECURITY ACROSS THE TAIWAN STRAIT

James Milner
REFUGEES, THE STATE AND THE POLITICS OF ASYLUM IN AFRICA

Stephen Fortescue (editor)
RUSSIAN POLITICS FROM LENIN TO PUTIN

St Antony's Series
**Series Standing Order ISBN 978-0-333-71109-5 (hardback) 978-0-333-80341-7
(paperback)**
(outside North America only)

You can receive future titles in this series as they are published by placing a standing order.
Please contact your bookseller or, in case of difficulty, write to us at the address below with
your name and address, the title of the series and the ISBNs quoted above.

Customer Services Department, Macmillan Distribution Ltd, Houndmills, Basingstoke,
Hampshire RG21 6XS, England

Institutions, Ideas and Leadership in Russian Politics

Edited By

Julie Newton
Visiting Fellow, Russian and Eurasian Studies Centre, St Antony's College Oxford, UK

William Tompson
Senior Economist, Economics Department, OECD, France

In Association with St Antony's College, Oxford

First published 2010 by
PALGRAVE MACMILLAN

Palgrave Macmillan in the UK is an imprint of Macmillan Publishers Limited,
registered in England, company number 785998, of Houndmills, Basingstoke,
Hampshire RG21 6XS.

Palgrave Macmillan in the US is a division of St Martin's Press LLC,
175 Fifth Avenue, New York, NY 10010.

Palgrave Macmillan is the global academic imprint of the above companies
and has companies and representatives throughout the world.

Palgrave® and Macmillan® are registered trademarks in the United States,
the United Kingdom, Europe and other countries

ISBN 978-0-230-55147-3   hardback

This book is printed on paper suitable for recycling and made from fully
managed and sustained forest sources. Logging, pulping and manufacturing
processes are expected to conform to the environmental regulations of the
country of origin.

A catalogue record for this book is available from the British Library.

Library of Congress Cataloging-in-Publication Data
    Institutions, ideas and leadership in Russian politics / edited by Julie M.
Newton, William J. Tompson.
        p. cm. – (St. Antony's series)
    ISBN 978-0-230-55147-3 (hardback)
        1. Russia (Federation)–Politics and government–1991–   2. Political
leadership–Russia (Federation. 3. Post-communism–Russia (Federation)
I. Newton, Julie M., 1961–   II. Tompson, William J.

    JN6695.I585 2010
    320.947–dc22   2010010819

10   9   8   7   6   5   4   3   2   1
19 18 17 16 15 14 13 12 11 10

Printed and bound in Great Britain by
CPI Antony Rowe, Chippenham and Eastbourne

*We dedicate this book to Archie Brown
and the example he embodies.*

Contents

Notes on Contributors

J. Paul Goode is an Assistant Professor of Political Science at the University of Oklahoma, where he lectures on Russian and comparative politics. He received a BA from the University of Texas, an MA in politics from the University of Wisconsin-Madison, and an MPhil from the University of Oxford, where he also earned his DPhil in 2005 under the supervision of Archie Brown. Prior to his current post, he was Visiting Lecturer at the Royal Holloway, University of London. He has published articles in *Europe-Asia Studies*, *Post-Soviet Affairs*, and *Russian Analytical Digest*, and he is currently finishing a book on regionalism in Russia.

Jeffrey Kahn is an Assistant Professor of Law at Southern Methodist University, where he teaches and writes on American constitutional law, Russian law, comparative human rights and national security law issues. He earned a BA from Yale University, an MPhil and DPhil from St Antony's College, University of Oxford, and a JD from the University of Michigan School of Law. Prior to academia, he served as a trial attorney in the United States Department of Justice. His doctoral dissertation, completed under the supervision of Professor Archie Brown, was published as *Federalism, Democratization, and the Rule of Law in Russia* (2002). His scholarship on Russian politics and law has been published in *Post-Soviet Affairs*, the *Review of Central and East European Law*, the *Michigan Journal of Law Reform*, the *Georgetown Journal of International Law*, the *Georgia Journal of International and Comparative Law*, and several edited volumes.

Tomila Lankina is a Senior Research Fellow and Lecturer at De Montfort University, Leicester. She received an MA in international relations from the Fletcher School of Law and Diplomacy in Massachusetts and a DPhil in politics from the University of Oxford in 2001 under the supervision of Archie Brown. Prior to her current post, she was Research Associate at the World Resources Institute in Washington, DC, Faculty Fellow with American University, Senior Research Fellow with the Institute for the Social Sciences of the Humboldt University in Berlin, Visiting Woodrow Wilson Fellow at the Woodrow Wilson International Center for Scholars in Washington DC and Post-Doctoral Fellow at Stanford

University. She co-authored, with Anneke Hudalla and Hellmut Wollmann, *Local Governance in Central and Eastern Europe: Comparing Performance in the Czech Republic, Hungary, Poland, and Russia* (2008); and is the author of *Governing the Locals: Local Self-Government and Ethnic Mobilization in Russia* (2004). She has also published in *Europe-Asia Studies, Post-Soviet Affairs, Journal of Communist Studies and Transition Politics, World Politics* and other journals.

Julie Newton is an Associate Professor in both the Department of International and Comparative Politics at the American University of Paris and the Master's Programme in Conflict Resolution, International Affairs and Civil Society Development, run jointly by the Institut Catholique and the American University of Paris, where she has taught since 2004 and won the Distinguished Teaching Award. In addition, she has been a Visiting Fellow at St Antony's College, University of Oxford, since 2006. With a BA from Princeton University and an MA from Columbia University, she received her DPhil from St Antony's College, Oxford, under the supervision of Archie Brown and Alex Pravda. From 1989 to 1990, she was one of two first-ever International Fellows for the US Fund for Peace/Compton Scholarship, created by the US Congress, to study within the Soviet Academy of Sciences. She is the author of *Russia, France, and the Idea of Europe* (2003); has a chapter in *Russia and Europe in the Twenty-first Century: An Uneasy Partnership*, Jackie Gower and Graham Timmins, ed. (2007); and is currently writing a book on Russia and Europe since 1980, with particular attention to Russia, Britain, Germany and France.

Thomas F. Remington is Goodrich C. White Professor of Political Science at Emory University, where he has taught since 1978. A graduate of Oberlin College, he has an MA and PhD from Yale University. In 2007–2009 he was Senior Fellow at the Davis Center for Russian and Eurasian Studies and Visiting Professor of Government at Harvard University. Professor Remington is author of numerous books and articles on Russian politics. Among his publications are two books on the Russian parliament: *The Russian Parliament: Institutional Evolution in a Transitional Regime, 1989–1999* (2001) and *The Politics of Institutional Choice: Formation of the Russian State Duma* (co-authored with Steven S. Smith) (2001). Other books include *Politics in Russia* (fifth edition, 2007); *Parliaments in Transition* (1994); and *The Truth of Authority: Ideology and Communication in the Soviet Union* (1988).

Peter Rutland is the Colin and Nancy Campbell Professor in Global Issues and Democratic Thought at Wesleyan University in Middletown,

Connecticut, where he has taught since 1989, and an Associate of the Davis Center for Russian and Eurasian Studies at Harvard University. He graduated with a BA from the University of Oxford in 1976, where he took a Soviet politics tutorial with Archie Brown, and received his DPhil from the University of York. Prior to his current post, he taught at the University of Texas at Austin, University of York and London University in the UK, and has been a visiting Fulbright Professor at the European University in St Petersburg. He is the author of *The Myth of the Plan* (1984) and *The Politics of Economic Stagnation in the Soviet Union* (1992) and editor of *Business and the State in Contemporary Russia* (2000).

Alfred Stepan is the Wallace Sayre Professor of Government at the School of International and Public Affairs (SIPA), Columbia University, Founder/Director of the Center for the Study of Democracy, Toleration and Religion, SIPA, Columbia University, and Co-Director of the Institute for Religion, Culture and Public Life at Columbia. He holds degrees from University of Notre Dame and Balliol College, Oxford, and received his PhD from Columbia University in 1969. He has served as Dean of Columbia's School of International and Public Affairs, founding Rector and President of the Central European University, and Gladstone Professor of Government, University of Oxford. He is also the Chairman of the Social Science Research Council Advisory Committee on Religion and International Affairs. Professor Stepan is the author of 13 books and edited volumes on such subjects as democracy, authoritarianism, and religion, and his works have been translated into more than a dozen languages including Chinese, Farsi, and Indonesian. Currently, he is working on a book on the world's religious systems and democracy with particular attention to countries such as Indonesia, India, France, Korea, Brazil, Senegal, Iran and the United States.

William Tompson is a Senior Economist in the OECD Economics Department, where he has worked since 2003. In addition, he lectures on political economy at the Institut d'Études Politiques de Paris. Holding a BA and MA from Emory University, Dr Tompson received his DPhil from Oxford University, where he was supervised by Archie Brown and Alex Pravda. He has taught at Birkbeck College, University of London, as well as at Oxford. He has written three books: *Khrushchev: A Political Life* (1995); *The Soviet Union under Brezhnev* (2003); and *The Political Economy of Structural Reform* (2009). He has also been lead author of four OECD country surveys, including the *OECD Economic Survey of the Russian*

Federation (2004, 2006) and the *OECD Economic Assessment of Ukraine* (2007), and has published numerous articles in journals and edited volumes in Europe and North America.

Kenneth Wilson is an Assistant Professor in the Department of Political Science, Dongguk University in Seoul, South Korea. With top honours from the University of Edinburgh and an MA from the University of Glasgow, he received a DPhil from St Antony's College, Oxford, under the supervision of Professor Archie Brown in 2005. Dr Wilson's research focuses on party-system development in Russia and its implications for democratisation. His doctoral thesis was a case study of party-system development under Vladimir Putin, with a particular focus on the party-system reforms passed during the Putin presidency. Recent publications on this theme have appeared in such journals as *Post-Soviet Affairs, Europe-Asia Studies,* and *Government and Opposition.* He also contributes an annual essay on contemporary developments in Russia to the Europa Regional Surveys of the World volume on Eastern Europe, Russia and Central Asia.

1
Introduction: Explaining Political and Economic Change in Post-Soviet Russia

Julie Newton

|That Russia in the post-Soviet era became increasingly *super*-presidential within a semi-presidential political structure is beyond dispute. It is far less clear how to characterise the state of Russia's political and economic institutions – including, parliament, political parties, the legal system or elections and even the executive itself. In the wake of the Yeltsin and Putin presidencies, the degree to which the Russian polity is institutionalised beyond the institution of the presidency is not obvious; nor is the nature of those institutions unambiguous. Is Russia de-institutionalised, or is it weakly institutionalised? Were other political institutions transformed via co-optation or political emasculation into mere supports for the presidency? Or, on the contrary, have certain institutions other than the presidency been strengthened – perhaps even endowed with hidden potential for the development of serious counterweights to the presidency for the future? Much of the ambiguity is symbolised in the person of Vladimir Putin himself. On the one hand, Putin once cried 'anything but institutions!'[1] and worked for eight years to centralise power in the presidency, causing some to warn that the 'centralisation of power [can]not compensate for the absence of political institutions'.[2] On the other hand, Putin unequivocally called for the consolidation of a genuinely competitive party system. Moreover, he initiated reforms to political parties that could, inadvertently, lead to the rise of a consolidated party system capable of *checking* presidential power, as both Thomas Remington and Kenneth Wilson point out in this volume. So it is not certain that institutions other than the presidency were (or are) as good as 'absent'. It is not even certain that the presidency itself is as powerful as its over-development might suggest. Despite Putin's success at vertical restructuring, his presidency did not 'match the institutional power to be found in the Soviet Union up until 1989'.[3] In these contradictory circumstances,

1

what can we confidently conclude about the state and nature of Russia's political institutions at the end of the Putin presidency and the beginning of the Putin/Medvedev tandem?

Still more difficult is the question of *why* Russia's institutions have evolved as they have. Why did post-Soviet political institutions evolve away from the democratic purposes that Gorbachev had set for them? Single-factor explanations focusing on interests, via rational choice theory, offer insufficient understanding of Russia's political and economic evolution. Even double-focused explanations can come up short. Some works, for example, focus on culture and institutions, with little attention to leadership. Others concentrate on leadership and institutions, with little concern for political culture. We need a richer analytical framework that better resembles the eclectic and multifaceted dynamic of real life, despite the difficulties of doing so. To that end, this book explores the *interaction* between institutions, ideas, leadership, as well as interests, in an effort to explain institutional change in post-Soviet Russia. It brings together writers who, taken together, stress all these factors, since it is the complex interaction between such factors that is the source of political change in the real world. In so doing, this book builds on the scholarship of Archie Brown, who over the course of his rich academic life, has contributed significantly to our understanding of each of these dimensions of Soviet/Russian politics, and whose meticulous work, often dissecting the ways in which institutions, ideas, leadership and interests interrelate, has offered some of the most compelling and enduring explanations of Soviet and post-Soviet political change for four decades.[4] All of these contributors were students and/or are friends of Archie, and all are admirers of his excellent ability to combine richness *and* rigour to improve our grasp of political reality and sources of change in Russia.

The goal of this introduction is to highlight points of intersection between these factors in order to learn three things: the ways in which these various elements interacted during the traumatic era of post-Soviet transition, the kinds of institutions that have resulted from those interactions, and what all this might mean for Russia's future.

Analytically, institutions are the natural springboard for thinking about the nature and scope of political change. Not only do institutions represent the building blocks of politics, but 'political thinking has its roots in the analysis and design of institutions'.[5] Moreover, institutions matter profoundly, whatever the whims of academic fashion. For much of the period post-World War II, mainstream political science largely dismissed the centrality of institutions in favour of the explanatory power of individual calculation and self – or group – interest (rational choice and behaviouralist theories).[6] But the nature, structure and quality of institutions, as well as the direction of institutional change, play an independent role in determining the type and nature of a country's political system, as well as the political outcomes it produces. This is hardly a controversial claim today, but a generation ago it would have sounded strange to many. Not, however, to readers of Archie Brown's work on Soviet politics, which always recognised the crucial importance of institutions, even when such an approach was at its least fashionable.[7]

As an example of how perilous it can be to underestimate the importance of institutions, Russia's failed attempt to build democracy in the 1990s is difficult to match. There was a direct link between the Yeltsin Administration's failure to build adequate democratic institutions and the derailing of Russia's transition to liberal democracy and a genuine market economy, as both Archie Brown and Alex Pravda, to name just two, have demonstrated. In the Yeltsin leadership's 'mistaken belief, which Western free-marketeers helped instil in the minds of susceptible Russian reformers, "that [building] capitalism *inevitably* leads to democracy"', the Kremlin and Russia's external advisors did not focus sufficiently on the need build adequate democratic institutions.[8] Such misconceptions reduced the sense of urgency about setting up state institutions strong enough 'to regulate the market and make both business and political elites legally and democratically accountable'.[9] The result was institutions built around 'diamond quadrangles', as Archie Brown called them – in short, the symbiosis of political structures, banking, industry and the media – that caused the development of a hybrid political system, 'a mixture of kleptocracy, arbitrariness and democracy'.[10] The latter element, democracy, with its weak institutional anchors, was easily washed away by eight years of Vladimir Putin's leadership.

So, institutions are primary. But the questions of *how* to evaluate them and how to identify sources of institutional change pose a serious challenge that has caused debate for decades. The reductionist, rational-choice approach to political science downplays the role of history and culture in understanding contemporary politics.[11] Applied to institutional theory, this functionalist approach tends to assume that new institutions form as the outcomes of a design process that is 'determined by the nature of the incentives and constraints being built into the institutions'.[12] They are the products of 'bargains' made by individual leaders, who calculate that they can best resolve specific problems, obtain greater power for themselves and achieve collective goals, through institutional action.[13] For such theorists, the ideas or beliefs of a given leader are not particularly relevant. Nor is the past history of the institution of real concern.[14] Instead, incentives trump history; changing the incentive structure can easily change institutional behaviour.

However, rational actor models or interests *alone* are not very good at explaining *change* or institutional conversion. Why did post-Soviet Russia's new pluralist institutions steadily evolve in a neo-authoritarian direction, when alternative – and, in many cases, more efficient – solutions were available? Rational choice may be good at providing 'explanations for behaviour within *existing* sets of rules', but it is less good – by itself, at least – at explaining how those rules get created in the first place and what they are meant to do.[15] In response, recent analysts have returned to institutional theory's more classical roots – what is often called the 'new institutionalism'.[16] ('We are all institutionalists now' was a political science battle cry by 2002.[17]) In this view, political life must not be divorced from its cultural and human roots; and political change in post-Soviet Russia over two decades of intensely traumatic 'great state transformation'[18] is most satisfactorily explained when the analyst stands, as mentioned above, at the intersection of multiple, often contingent factors, including institutional structure, leadership, ideas/culture, and interests.

For Archie Brown, standing at analytical intersections is nothing new. His natural interest in these crucial interrelationships allowed him to perceive the undercurrent forces of change at work in Czechoslovakia well before the Prague Spring;[19] it kept him from following misguided academic fashions or indulging in the 'conceptual stretching' that led others to overstate the degree of institutional pluralism in Brezhnev's USSR;[20] it permitted him before others in the West to spot the potentially profound significance of the rise of an 'open-minded, intelligent...anti-Stalinist' to the apex of Soviet power in 1985;[21] it enabled him early in the Gorbachev era to understand the independent importance of *ideas* and their potentially transformative power when combined with the institutional power of the Soviet General Secretary;[22] and it has helped him more recently to offer hard-hitting but highly nuanced accounts of Yeltsin's and Putin's Russia.[23] The point is that throughout this long history, his judgement has been exceptionally good.[24]

Like Archie, the authors in this book also analyse political junctures where complex, causal elements intersect. Though the book's title mentions only three of those elements – 'institutions', 'ideas' and 'leadership', without explicitly mentioning 'culture' or 'interests' – the latter two are important throughout these pages. Culture is discussed within the context of ideas, since the two elements are connected, though clearly distinct. Ideas are not necessarily deeply rooted; they can change quickly. But they need institutional bearers in order to cause political change. This suggests that the Russian leadership's intellectual orientation and its preferences for certain ideas or categories of thinking can be crucial. As for culture, it is deeply rooted and changes slowly, but change it can. It is important in so far as it helps explain political change or continuity – a particularly important point here. This volume begins with Archie's work on political culture, narrowly defined in terms of 'subjective orientations' (beliefs, values, excluding behaviour).[25] Building on that definition, we find it helpful to start with deeply held norms, values and beliefs and then move on to consider the *context* in which those beliefs are held. Our focus is 'culture-as-context', as Charles King describes it – 'a set of social mechanisms that may create and enhance perceptions, beliefs, and values but whose primary power lies in conditioning social action'.[26] This added dimension enables us to widen our focus to 'the ways in which particular actions can be enabled and conditioned by the contexts in which they occur'.[27] Values and deeply held beliefs are also particularly important within the traumatic, transformative times in which Russian institutions and their leaders functioned over the last two decades.

As for interests, the impact of this factor is not analysed *in depth* in this volume due to lack of space. But leadership interests, institutional interests, economic or financial interests or politicians' interests are all considered here, most directly in the chapters by Thomas Remington and William Tompson. To a large extent, this volume considers interests in the context of how agents *perceive* their interests. The way, for example, in which Gorbachev, Yeltsin and Putin assessed their and their country's interests was partly subjective; ideas (especially New Thinking ideas for Gorbachev) and Soviet/Russian political culture (especially traditional normative orientations for Putin) influenced their perception of national interests. What we are concerned with in this volume, therefore, are not just interests in a purely material or exogenous sense, but also *'perceptions* of interests'[28] and their interrelationship with ideas and culture.

Thomas Remington – in his chapter analysing leadership and institution-building from Gorbachev to Putin – points to crucial links between leadership, interests, culture and institutional change. Remington begins by explaining that evolution as the outcome of rational-actor calculations of two innovative leaders (Gorbachev and Yeltsin) who made structural-institutional mistakes. This explanation stresses the leadership's rational solutions to immediate dilemmas, the outcomes of which affected broader political structures, which in turn became a further source of institutional evolution.

As Remington explains, Gorbachev and Yeltsin both needed greater power for themselves to resolve increasingly difficult political dilemmas. In response, they improvised 'grand bargains' which exchanged 'an ever-stronger presidency in return for a system of parties' (Chapter 2). Gorbachev gave away participatory rights to others, including the right to multiparty competition and contested elections, in exchange for the creation of a new presidency – one that, crucially, would be free from party control. By de-linking the presidency in this way, while refusing to carve out from the Communist Party of the Soviet Union (CPSU) a new reformist party over which he could preside, Gorbachev created a presidency that was structurally elevated beyond party reach. As for Yeltsin, he progressively traded off rights to political factions in return for their political support, while he also remained unwilling to make the presidency into a party office or name himself as a party leader. Both leaders' 'bargains' were institutionalised, first in Gorbachev's reforms of 1990, and then in Yeltsin's Constitution of 1993, within a semi-presidential structure.

Such constitutional arrangements posed fundamental problems. Indeed, they masked important structural flaws that would, over time, help undo Russia's democratic transition. The presidency quickly became the only real arena for policy-making. Political parties were largely superfluous, like an actor who comes onto the stage with no lines to speak and no action to perform. As an 'above-parties president',[29] who did not submit himself to popular election, Gorbachev had no base for mustering the broad, representative support necessary to push on with tougher reforms. This situation ultimately undermined the power and authority of Gorbachev himself.[30]

Yeltsin encountered a similar problem, as Remington also shows. The presidency and parliament often operated in fierce competition with each other, or at best, in parallel. Without any base of majority support, Yeltsin was forced to rule by decree – rendering the whole system increasingly *super*-presidential within its semi-presidential framework. Parties became accountable to the president, not society. They floated above society, and developed anaemically during the Yeltsin era, with only weak links to the social interests they were meant to represent. The presidency, meanwhile, risked gaining a 'monopoly over the aggregation of interests' (Remington). Such developments, flowing from the Yeltsin leadership's institutional, constitutional 'bargain', had dark implications for a country emerging from authoritarianism. Indeed, as Alfred Stepan points out in Chapter 9, 'no stable democracy in the world, and certainly no European Union member country, has a constitution that is remotely close to being "super-presidential semi-presidentialism"'. Nor is there any stable democracy that does not link executive power to political parties that contest free and fair elections.

How did this happen? Paradoxes of Gorbachev and Yeltsin eras

The question is: *how* and *why* did this happen? Why did both Gorbachev and Yeltsin make 'bargains' that paradoxically created institutional structures that gradually led to the undoing of their larger goals? After all, institutions are built in part to fulfil *'normative* purposes' and to represent norms.[31] For Gorbachev, those norms were clear by 1989–90 and included democratic accountability, contested elections, political pluralism and social democracy – the 'values, ideas and priorities that Gorbachev embodied'.[32] In Brown's view, Gorbachev deliberately used 'the highest office in the land to undermine the party structures in which he had made his career.' He did this *precisely* to introduce ideas and values of 'political pluralism and a whole range of freedoms into a system whose longevity had depended on its vigilance in combating manifestations of group autonomy...'[33] But what went wrong? Why did Gorbachev and then Yeltsin ultimately make the kinds of institutional-design decisions that helped to undermine their democratic goals? Alternative structural choices certainly existed, even within the exceedingly difficult political context in which they operated. Gorbachev, for example, might have taken the risk of splitting the Communist Party in either 1989 or mid-1990, whereupon he would have taken the helm of a new Social Democratic Party that could have, at that point, attracted 'several million members'.[34] Had he become the new party leader, Gorbachev would have linked the new presidency to a democratic political party – a crucial step in rendering the presidency democratically accountable. But Gorbachev insisted on waiting, believing that a party split was premature and fearing that it might cause him to forfeit key institutions and resources to CPSU conservatives.[35] As for Yeltsin, he also resisted linking the presidency to any new political party. It is likely that both he and Gorbachev were acting on the basis of rough calculations of the balance of political power. But as it turned out, the 'risks of keeping the Party superficially united [for Gorbachev] were even greater'[36] than the risks of splitting it. Similarly, the dangers posed to the democratisation process by Yeltsin's decision *not* to take the helm of a political party throughout the 1990s may have outweighed the dangers of doing so.

To explain such paradoxes, one cannot ignore the role of culture as an underlying force that 'reinforced' the *way* Russian leaders calculated interests and weighed decisions. Indeed, the way that both leaders assessed risk, leading each to reject leadership of a new party, is linked (in part) to the weight of Soviet political culture – bringing us to the interrelationship between leadership, institutional structure and culture – or rather 'culture-as-context', to recall King's phrase.[37] Seventy years of Communist Party monopoly left an extremely negative legacy that deeply tarnished public views of political parties. According to the Levada Centre and the All-Russian Centre for the Study of Public Opinion (VTsIOM) from the early 1990s on, political parties ranked at the *very bottom* of public trust in civic institutions (except for 1998–99 when Yeltsin's presidency ranked even lower).[38] In such an environment, it is hard to imagine that *any* President would stake his authority on a political party, whatever the case for doing so. Furthermore, as Remington points out in his chapter, the 'legacy of a patrimonial form of communism inhibited the formation of social cleavages that could sustain party competition'. Russian society also 'lacked the foundation of social and civic organisations that could pool support for parties'. All this meant, as Cindy Skach (writing elsewhere) put it, the country had *no* 'majoritarian mentality'.[39] Nor did Russia have the institutional and cultural preconditions necessary for such a mentality – unlike France, where the semi-presidential model had a strong enough '*vocation majoritaire*' and democratic culture to overcome 'the real challenges to democracy posed by French semi-presidentialism'.[40] Indeed, this model is a 'source of strain' even for *French* democracy,[41] Skach explains; but for many post-communist countries, importing this model was positively counter-productive to democratic consolidation. In the early 1990s, advocates of the French semi-presidential model neglected the fact that this model's earliest incarnation was *Weimar Germany*, not France. They did not consider that 'many of these newer semi-presidential democracies have institutional and social [as well as political cultural] characteristics that bear a relatively strong resemblance to Weimar [Germany] – not France'.[42]

Not surprisingly then, post-Soviet Russian governance increasingly resembled that of Weimar Germany, rather than France. The combination of Russia's imported semi-presidential *structure*, with its non-majoritarian, non-party, non-civic *culture* produced a 'solid decade of "minority politics"', with the head of state and head of government often battling each other with differing agendas.[43] Though this situation was worsened by the battle of interests during the traumatic post-communist transformation, it was originally the interrelationship between the leaderships' negotiated institutional designs and the Soviet Union's cultural inheritance that undermined the Gorbachev and Yeltsin leaderships' stated democratic goals and made it easy for a traditionally minded leader like Vladimir Putin to bring Russia's political institutions back to their familiar, reassuring authoritarian profiles.

How did this happen? The Putin era

Mainwaring writes of Brazil's political development that, 'It is not only *personalities* and *political culture*, but also *political structures* that explain why presidents have acted against parties' and democratic institutions generally. While agreeing, Russia-watchers could also make a slightly different statement.[44] It is not only leadership (*'personalities'*) and institutions (*'political structures'*) that matter, but the interaction between them might either emphasise or alter pre-existing *political culture*. The interactive influence flows in *both* directions, down from leadership and structure as well as up from culture. The Putin era contains particularly vivid examples of such two-way interaction.

These three factors merge in Vladimir Putin himself. Alfred Stepan once commented that whenever he thought of the Putin era, he was struck by the close relationship between leadership, institutions and [institutional] culture. Putin brings these factors together more clearly than the others, he noted.[45] This is in great contrast to Gorbachev. In the era of *Perestroika*, these three factors were in conflict with each other: leadership affected Soviet institutions in ways that deeply challenged pre-existing institutional culture. Gorbachev's democratic ideas were alien to pre-existing institutional norms. And though the Gorbachev leadership had made progress in instilling ordinary Soviet citizens with new democratic values, habits and beliefs between 1989 and 1991, that progress – overt, at least – proved relatively short-lived.[46] If 'democratic values become strongly internalised through successful *experience* of democratic political systems',[47] such values did not become deeply internalised in Russia because Russia's *post*-Soviet experience with democracy was anything but successful or genuine. Part of the explanation for this failure has to do with the structural/institutional problems, which Gorbachev and, to a far greater extent, Yeltsin inadvertently caused. This structural situation made it harder to overturn *pre-existing* political values, and lessened chances for consolidating democratic institutions. As B. Guy Peters argues, formal institutional reforms can be relatively easy to revise and replace: 'If [reformed] institutions do not [yet] have values to constrain the behaviour of individuals, and if the initial choices of those [new] institutions do not tend to persist, then there can be little sense of equilibrium of institutions...'[48]

During the Yeltsin era, the three factors combined to create an ever more extreme disequilibrium: weak leadership combined with incoherent ideas (especially about democracy) and unbroken cultural patterns to drive institutional change in unintended directions. All this was further buffeted by powerful sectarian and financial interests. The result was an unstable system of hybrid institutions.

This situation changed during the Putin presidency. Then, leadership, culture and institutions intertwined in more organic and coherent ways. Putin's strong leadership was characterised largely by 'traditional' ideas and methods.[49] This traditional leadership – together with the institutional-design problems posed by super-presidential semi-presidentialism – recalled Russia's authoritarian institutional culture. The stronger, more coherent combination of these factors consolidated the institutional trends that had begun under Yeltsin (and Gorbachev) and pushed the country in more distinctly authoritarian directions, all of which was underpinned by strong economic growth and the tremendous resources made available to the Putin leadership by the commodities boom of the early 2000s. Making matters worse was the country's political, social and economic exhaustion by the late 1990s. Indeed, the intense trauma of 'the great state transformation' that began in the late 1980s helps explain why President Putin was so popular, despite *taking* power, even excessive power, and reversing many of the democratic reforms that millions of Soviet citizens had joyfully embraced in 1989–1990.

Leadership specialist Barbara Kellerman explains why people anywhere might follow excessive leadership in traumatic conditions. Though she refers to America after 11 September 2001, her comments could equally apply to Russia at the end of the Yeltsin era: 'In our eagerness to quell our anxiety, we are more willing than we would be otherwise to go along with leaders who give the appearance of being strong and certain.'[50] We follow leaders because of our need for 'safety, simplicity, and certainty, but also because of the needs of the group. Groups go along with bad leaders because even bad leaders often provide important benefits. In particular, leaders maintain order, provide cohesion and identity, and do the collective work.'[51] Indeed, Putin did exactly that, and the authors of this book demonstrate how.

As a result of this close coherence between leadership, culture, institutions and interests during his presidency, Putin enjoyed increasing political authority that flowed from two sources: Russian society *and* Russia's political and economic elites. This was a luxury of leadership that neither Gorbachev nor Yeltsin ever knew. Putin thus had enormous power to affect far-reaching change in traditionalist directions against an opposition that was either acquiescent or ineffectual. Paul Goode makes this point in Chapter 3, which explores why and how Putin managed to roll back gubernatorial elections in 2004 with barely a whimper from Russian governors or ordinary citizens. However shocked the West was by Putin's action, abolishing gubernatorial elections involved an implicit *agreement* between all groups and hardly represented a 'crime'. As Goode explains, nearly all concerned parties were compliant. The governors themselves did not complain about the elimination of their own chance for re-election, since elections had meant term-limits – an unfamiliar and undesirable notion – and governors found elections to be so destabilising and costly to rig that they were of little real interest to them. For ordinary citizens, the fact that many elected governors had egregiously rigged their elections meant that voters never had the chance to understand the benefits of elections as a means of holding their governors accountable. Abolishing elections, therefore, seemed more like a positive anti-corruption measure than an infringement of civil rights. Furthermore, a dubiously elected governor had less authority in public eyes than a popular Putin appointee and people found comfort and security in historically familiar approaches to federal arrangements, especially during the horrific Beslan hostage crisis. That crisis – or rather, the Kremlin and society's reactions to it – revealed the strong coherence between Vladimir Putin's preference for vertical power and Russia's cultural comfort zone in tradition. More broadly, extreme periods of national trauma like Beslan are often highly revealing, shedding bright light on the ways that multiple factors can interact and tip the political situation towards important change. Beslan combined factors of President Putin's political orientation, Russia's political-culture heritage, the powerful interests of its political/economic elites, and its inherited institutional structures (an excessively strong executive surrounded by excessively weak institutions) to prompt meaningful political changes – such as, the consensual eradication of gubernatorial elections. To be sure, such institutional changes were part of a broader Kremlin solution for post-Soviet Russia that sought to strengthen the state, which was widely seen as a desirable goal in itself. But the *way* in which the Putin leadership pursued that solution not only eradicated hopes for building genuinely democratic institutions, but undermined efforts to build a well functioning market economy – contributing, *inter alia*, to more corruption and rent-seeking, as well as less accountability and efficiency in some of Russia's most important economic sectors. This statist turn in the economic sphere, moreover, brought few real benefits to ordinary Russians.

Nowhere have these problems become more apparent than in the political economy that Vladimir Putin shaped. In Chapter 4, William Tompson describes the remarkable expansion of the scale and scope of state ownership in Russia, beginning in the Putin era and probably, he suggests, enduring for the foreseeable future. He also explains why and how this dramatic expansion of state ownership happened over four short years (2003 to 2007). While most accounts focus on factional politics, ideology or the nature of Putin's leadership, Tompson widens the lens to focus as well on 'the interaction between Russia's economic structure and its political institutions'. 'Here, as elsewhere, the strength and weakness of [political] institutions matter – specifically, the weakness of state institutions outside the executive branch and the executive's own combination of highly developed coercive capacities and administrative weakness.' These institutional strengths and weaknesses interacted with economic structure in ways that *predisposed* Russia's policy-makers towards re-nationalisation as the solution for Russia. But, while that interaction shaped the incentives facing the Kremlin – by providing the motive, capacity and opportunity to extend the state's control over Russia's most important industrial and financial assets – it was not determinant. Leadership choices still made the critical difference. The Putin leadership, in a hurry for immediate solutions, rejected the alternatives in favour of re-nationalisation and re-centralisation, since that route seemed to present the easiest and shortest path to recovery and modernity.

It is in this context of shortcut solutions that Chapter 5 moves on from political economy to Putin's foreign policy. Putin's end-goal – or Russia's strategic ambition during the Putin Presidency – was to re-establish Russia's great power status *fast*. The immediate return to great powerdom became this leadership's preferred solution, first, to overcome the distress of Russia's 'time of troubles' following the Soviet collapse and, second, to resolve the internal problems and external threats facing Russia in the late 1990s. Putin used three inter-connected and mutually reinforcing means to achieve these ends: an increasingly authoritarian domestic political agenda; next, a state-capitalist economic policy oriented towards the state's capture of resource rents; and last, an independent, multipolar foreign policy. That Putin himself preferred this kind of traditional, statist path is a large part of the reason Russia embarked on it, but again, leadership preference does not explain its intense popularity among ordinary Russians. Obviously, that popularity was first a function of Russia's impressive economic and national recovery during the Putin era. But Putin's path was also popular because of the way that Putin's political ideas and preferences assuaged Russia's national identity crisis. During Russia's 15-year trauma of 'great state transformation', ambiguity and alienation strengthened their hold over Russian identity in a 'tortured way', rendering the unresolved state of Russia's national identity politically significant.[52] By restoring Russia's 'great power' identity from the past, Putin offered solace to his shattered nation. Putin then added clarity and substance to that identity by conceiving it in *statist*, not ethno-nationalist, terms, as Peter Rutland clarifies in Chapter 6. While reuniting his nation around familiar and, to many, comforting state symbols – such as a Soviet national anthem and holidays from pre-Soviet history – Putin took care to avoid the potentially colossal dangers of a Great Russian *ethnic* nationalism. Instead, as a state nationalist or *gosudarstvennik*, he manipulated Russian national identity in pursuit of *state* goals, including consolidating vertical power at home and projecting great power abroad.

In this way, Kremlin leadership converged organically with Russian national identity to direct domestic and foreign policies towards the immediate restoration of great power, conceived by *this* leadership as greatness of the state – known as *derzhavnost'*. This historically familiar path covered huge distances in eight short years to re-establish Russian *derzhavnost'*, as its advocates hailed. But as a consequence, the leadership's authoritarian, or *neo*-authoritarian, inclinations increasingly shaped Russia's institutional architecture.[53]

Exploring those authoritarian consequences further, Kenneth Wilson provides an account in Chapter 7 of what happened – and why – to the crucial institution of political parties during the Putin presidency. While a strong political party system is important to democracy, and while Putin even introduced helpful legislative measures to consolidate Russia's 'floating' party system, his reforms did not further democracy. The contrary was true. As Wilson shows, Russia went from a 'floating party system' in the 1990s to one of 'executive capture' of political parties in the 2000s, 'which from the perspective of democratisation is arguably worse than what went before'. The final cause of this body blow to democratisation, he argues, was the Putin factor. Conditions for democracy 'have far less to do with the condition of the party system than with the attitude of the presidential administration' – an administration that both reflected and encouraged popular disdain for political parties.[54] The problem is that this two-directional and mutually reinforcing inter-relationship between leadership and culture (as well as interests and existing institutions) could allow United Russia's dominance, achieved unfairly, to 'persist for decades, as in the case of Mexico..., in a system where other parties serve to legitimate (not challenge) its grip on power'.

The same dynamic holds true for the rule of law. In Chapter 8, Jeffrey Kahn agrees that the Putin leadership regularly used the law arbitrarily, as an instrument to further its political and economic goals for national regeneration. Wielding law in this fashion turned the declared commitment to the rule of law into yet another institutional support for the increasingly authoritarian regime. But Kahn's analysis shows *how* this happened, despite serious efforts to strengthen the legal system in Russia in nominal ways – the addition of new laws, rules, judges, etc. Again, it happened, to a great extent, at the conjuncture between this particular Russian leadership, Russia's current institutional architecture (with weak checks on a particularly strong executive endowed with excessively powerful coercive capacities), the political and economic interests of elites, and the reinforcing weight of Russian political culture. In particular, it is the dynamic between leadership and culture that most interests Kahn here. Throughout Russian history, the law was conceived in instrumental terms that produced a zero-sum relationship between the state and the individual. Kahn cites an old Russian proverb that compares the law to a wagon shaft: it goes wherever you turn it. This conceptual culture could not be more different from that in the West which views law as a 'causeway' – a raised highway over a bog on which everyone, independent of rank or stature, walks freely, albeit in different directions and for various purposes, but with equal protection from the bog. A causeway cannot be manipulated or turned at the driver's whim like a wagon shaft; a road is just *there* for anyone to use, anyone who has already understood the rules of the road, which apply to all. Russian leaders did not build a legal 'causeway' in the service of democracy, Kahn writes. Instead, the Putin leadership encouraged and extended traditional Russian conceptions of law as an *instrument* in the service of the president's statist political and economic agenda. In short, Putin's predilections dovetailed with conceptual patterns in Russian legal culture, with consequences for the institution of law – not to mention the entire political and economic system – in Russia.

What kinds of 'consequences' do we mean, besides institutional evolution towards authoritarian norms? And is this latter consequence even entirely true? Despite the compelling evidence detailed in these pages about strengthening authoritarian trends during Putin's presidency, were there not important developments running counter to those trends that raise questions for the future? Finally, what was the condition of Russian institutions? To take the last question first, it would be rash to call all Russian institutions other than the executive un- or de-institutionalised.[55] The chapters presented here suggest the picture is more complex. On the one hand, it is true that gubernatorial elections disappeared via 'institutional euthanasia' (Goode, Chapter 3); and other political/electoral institutions (such as presidential and parliamentary elections, the Duma and certain political parties) underwent institutional 'lobotomies'. They underwent normative conversion from institutions *meant* to embody democratic norms back to their traditional functions as institutions *meant* (implicitly) to support executive power. On the other hand, Russia's political-party *system* actually grew stronger during the Putin Presidency, as both Wilson and Remington observe. They show that Putin's party reforms might, in other political circumstances, promote the growth of stronger, more independent parties, capable of challenging the executive. 'It would be highly ironic if Putin, who has striven – at the expense of democracy – to increase the power of the presidency relative to political parties and the Duma – and indeed every other institution in the political system – turns out to have established the institutional framework that helps to strengthen parties, weaken the presidency and foment democracy in the long run' (Remington, Chapter 2).

This suggests that Russia's institutional evolution continues. Russia's 'great state transformation', which began 20 years ago, probably did not end with Putin. Moreover, for the last two decades, Russians have been freer than at any time in their history. Surely, those freedoms, combined with the kinds of institutional 'paradoxes' that Remington and Wilson discuss, could converge to disturb traditional Russian cultural patterns, once again – in the same way that Gorbachev's democratic reforms disturbed such patterns, starting in 1989–1990. As Kahn's chapter reminds us, political culture is not immutable, however slowly it changes. But the degree and durability of that change will depend mostly on the predilections, values and quality of post-Putin leaderships in Russia, where executive power is exceedingly important.

Until then, Russia's interaction with democratic impulses in the outside world could be important. Even troubled Ukraine, 'the only democracy of...twelve CIS states', according to Alfred Stepan in his chapter on a crucial institutional choice by Ukraine, could spread democratic influences to Russia, given the two countries' geographic, cultural and historical interconnectedness (Chapter 9). As Stepan explains, Ukraine's judicious post-independence decision to erect a *state-nation* rather than a *nation-state* peacefully resolved its multinational divide. Moreover, it enhanced Ukraine's prospects for democratic consolidation. The country's ethnic cleavage, which so easily could have become a stumbling block on its path to peace and democracy (as it has been in other countries, such as Sri Lanka), thus served, paradoxically, to facilitate democratic development. The reason, Stepan asserts, is that multinational countries that govern themselves as *state-nations*, rather than *nation-states*, get practice at building common identities around shared civic values.

Russia, though not as manifestly multi-ethnic like Ukraine, also suffered from identity problems in the form of deep ambiguity; nevertheless, unlike Ukraine, it did not manage to turn its identity problem into a democratising asset. As Rutland explains in Chapter 6, post-Soviet Russian leaders did not reformulate Russian national identity in *civic* terms (in the Western sense), despite intriguing, early efforts to do so in the Yeltsin era. Instead, by re-conceiving Russian identity as a tool of the state, the Putin leadership further reduced any chances for democracy in Russia for the short or medium terms.

Ukraine, however, which *did* redefine itself in more civic terms, was able to build inclusive, state-nation political structures – a crucial step that laid foundations for democracy in Ukraine, as Stepan points out in Chapter 9. Those structures created incentives for the kind of 'majority mentality' mentioned earlier. More importantly, state-nations tend to adopt or become parliamentary systems. Over time, it is possible that Ukraine may move towards a more *'parliamentarised* semi-presidential system' – like some of the newest EU-members – and that, writes Stepan, would 'create a greater arena for all-Ukrainian cooperation'. Significantly, it would also strengthen democratic culture among ethnic Russians in eastern Ukraine who are perfectly placed to influence Russians in Russia. Ukrainian Russians already support democracy more strongly than do Russians in Russia (43% versus 19%), in part because Ukraine's state-nation structures rendered the democratic experience of ethnic Russians more rewarding. For all its manifest imperfections, Stepan concludes, Ukraine's democracy has provided for both open public debate and real transfers of power in response to electoral outcomes. If Ukrainian democracy continues to grow stronger, Ukraine's steady transmission of transnational democratic influences to its Russian brother could become very important indeed.

Farther afield, the EU could also be (and is) an important source of transnational democratic influence in Russia, especially in certain

Russian regions, as Tomila Lankina suggests in her chapter on patterns of EU aid to Post-Soviet Russian regions (Chapter 10). EU aid to Russia's regions was a virtuous circle: the EU gave money and advice only to those regions that already had democratic cultures strong enough to advance EU efforts to strengthen democratic institutions there. The aid paid off, as Lankina demonstrates here and elsewhere through abundant data. Regions enjoying EU interest over the past two decades have become the 'high democratic achievers' of Russia. 'The European Union, a major agent of democratic diffusion, served as a counterweight to the spread of authoritarian tendencies. It [along with the Council of Europe] exerted its normative influence through regional aid and the fostering of network connections and exchanges that come with it.'[56] Surely this suggests the outside world can, at least to some degree, affect the direction of ongoing change in Russia, so long as it pays close attention to the dynamic interrelationship between crucial political factors – such as, that between institutions, ideas and leadership.

Notes

1 Vladimir Putin, '50 years of European Integration and Russia' (25 March 2007), http://www.kremlin.ru/eng/speeches/2007/03/25/1133_type104017_120738.shtml. His exclamation was in context of Russia-EU relations, but generally illustrates his attitude towards institutional pluralism.
2 Dmitri Trenin, 'Legacy of Vladimir Putin', Carnegie Moscow Centre (October 2007), www.http:carnegie.ru/en/print/76874-print, 3.
3 Archie Brown, 'Ideas, Interests and Institutions in the Soviet and Russian Transition', presented to the AAASS (Toronto, 20–23 November 2003), p. 26.
4 For a bibliography of Archie Brown's work from 1969 to 2004, annotated by Julie Newton, see Alex Pravda, ed., *Leading Russia* (Oxford: Oxford University Press, 2005), pp. 275–94.
5 B. Guy Peters, *Institutional Theory in Political Science: The 'New Institutionalism'* (London: Continuum Press, 2005), p. 4.
6 Influential rational choice theorists continued to question the exogenous importance of institutions well into the mid-1990s and 2000s. As one theorist wrote in 1995, 'There is, strictly speaking, no separate animal that we can identify as an institution. There is only rational behaviour conditioned on the expectations about the behaviour and reactions of others': cited by Kenneth Shepsle, 'Rational Choice Institutionalism', in R. Rhodes, S. Binder, B. Rockman, *The Oxford Handbook of Political Institutions* (Oxford: Oxford University Press, 1996), p. 26; see also Peters, *Institutional Theory in Political Science*, pp. 1–2.
7 Archie Brown, 'Problems of Group Influence and Interest Articulation in the Soviet Union', review article of Skilling and Griffiths, eds, *Interest Groups in Soviet Politics* in *Government and Opposition*, Vol. 7, No. 2 (Spring 1972): 229–43; Archie Brown, *Soviet Politics and Political Science* (London: Macmillan,

1974 and New York: St Martin's Press, 1976); Archie Brown, 'Policy-making in Communist States', review article, *Studies in Comparative Communism*, Vol. XI, No. 4 (Winter 1978): 424–36. In this next article, a review of Jerry Hough's book, Brown praised Hough's unfashionable emphasis on political institutions, but nevertheless criticised him for going too far. Focusing *too* much on the explanatory power of institutions and political process was as unhelpful as neglecting its importance. Lamenting the fashion for single explanatory models, Brown called for *broader* explanatory frameworks to include political culture, as well as institutions: Archie Brown, 'Governing the USSR', review article, *Problems of Communism*, Vol. XXVIII, No. 5–6 (September–December 1979): 103–8. Never losing sight of the importance of institutions and broad-minded frameworks, Brown was well positioned early on to stress the exceptional significance of the institution of Soviet leadership: Archie Brown, 'The Power of the General Secretary of the CPSU', in Archie Brown, T. H. Rigby, Peter Reddaway, eds, *Authority, Power and Policy in the USSR: Essays Dedicated to Leonard Shapiro* (London and New York: Macmillan, 1980), pp. 135–57.

8   Alex Pravda, 'Archie Brown', in Alex Pravda, ed., *Leading Russia: Putin in Perspective* (Oxford: Oxford University Press, 2005), p. 18 (emphasis added).

9   Ibid., p. 19.

10 Archie Brown, 'Russia and Democratization', *Problems of Post-Communism*, Vol. 46, No. 5 (September–October 1999): 3; Pravda, *Leading Russia*, p. 19 and fn 65.

11 Shepsle, 'Rational Choice Institutionalism', 23–38; Peters, *Institutional Theory in Political Science*, pp. 15–17, chapter 1.

12 Peters, *Institutional Theory in Political Science*, p. 51.

13 Ibid., p. 48.

14 Ibid., p. 51; Explained (critically) in: James March, Johan Olsen, 'Elaborating the "New Institutionalism"', in Rhodes, Binder *et al*, *The Oxford Handbook*, pp. 3–22.

15 Peters, *Institutional Theory in Political Science*, p. 59.

16 Though 'new institutionalism' emerged as an intellectual challenge to mainstream rational choice and behavioural theories in the mid-1980s, those mainstream approaches continued to dominate political science even into the late 1990s. Peters, *Institutional Theory in Political Science*, p. 17.

17 March, Olsen, 'Elaborating the "New Institutionalism"', p. 5.

18 Phrase attributed to Robert Legvold, 'Russian Foreign Policy during Periods of Great State Transformation', in Robert Legvold, ed., *Russian Foreign Policy in the Twenty-first Century and the Shadow of the Past* (New York: Columbia University Press, 2007), pp. 77–143.

19 Archie Brown, 'Pluralistic Trends in Czechoslovakia', *Soviet Studies*, Vol. XVII, No. 4 (April 1966): 453–72.

20 'Problems of Group Influence and Interest Articulation in the Soviet Union', review of article of Skilling and Griffiths, eds, *Interest Groups in Soviet Politics*, in *Government and Opposition*, Vol. 7, No. 2 (Spring 1972): 229–43; Pravda, p. 10.

21 Quote from: Archie Brown, 'Introduction', in Mikhail Gorbachev, Zdenek Mlynar, *Conversations with Gorbachev* (New York: Columbia University Press, 2002), p. xiv; Archie Brown, 'New Man in the Kremlin', *Problems of Communism*, Vol. XXXIV, No. 3 (May/June 1985): 1–23.

22 An example of early insight into the power of ideas: 'Political Science', in A. Dallin and B. Patenaude, ed., *Soviet Scholarship under Gorbachev* (Stanford University, 1988), pp. 33–9.

23 Archie Brown, 'Evaluating Russia's Democratization', in Archie Brown, ed., *Contemporary Russian Politics: A Reader* (Oxford: Oxford University Press, 2001); Archie Brown, 'Vladimir Putin and the Reaffirmation of Central State Power', *Post Soviet Affairs*, Vol. 17, Part 1 (2001): 45–55; A. Brown, L. Shevtsova, *Gorbachev, Yeltsin, and Putin: Political Leadership in Russia's Transition* (Washington: Brookings Institution Press, 2001).

24 For agreement on this point: Pravda, *Leading Russia*, p. 8.

25 Archie Brown, ed., *Political Culture and Communist Studies* (Basingstoke: Macmillan, St Antony's Series, 1984), pp. 2–7.

26 Charles King, 'Culture, Context, Violence: Eurasia in Comparative Perspective', in Stephen Whitefield, ed., *Political Culture and Post-Communism* (Basingstoke: Palgrave Macmillan, 2005), pp. 65, 80; Stephen Whitefield, 'Political Culture and Post-Communism', in Ibid., p. 12.

27 King, 'Culture, Context, Violence', p. 65.

28 Regarding the Gorbachev period, Brown focuses on *perceptions* of interests – that is, Gorbachev's assessment of Soviet interests was informed by ideas: Archie Brown, 'Perestroika and the End of the Cold War', *Cold War History*, Vol. 7, No. 1 (February 2007): 7 (emphasis added).

29 Term used in reference to Poland, but equally applicable here: Alfred Stepan, 'Fifth Republic and Semipresidentialism', *Arguing Comparative Politics* (Oxford: Oxford University Press, 2001), p. 284.

30 Archie Brown, *Seven Years that Changed the World: Perestroika in Perspective* (Oxford University Press, 2007), p. 283.

31 Peters, *Institutional Theory in Political Science*, p. 157.

32 Brown, *Seven Years*, p. 270.

33 Ibid., p. 283.

34 Ibid., p. 205.

35 Ibid., pp. 205–6, fn 37.

36 Ibid., p. 206.

37 King, 'Culture, Context, Violence', p. 65.

38 Steven White, 'The Political Parties', in Stephen White, Zvi Gitelman and Richard Sakwa, eds, *Developments in Russian Politics* (Basingstoke: Palgrave Macmillan, 2005), p. 90.

39 Cindy Skach, *Borrowing Constitutional Designs: Constitutional Law in Weimar Germany and the French Fifth Republic* (Princeton: Princeton University Press, 2005), p. 78.

40 Ibid.

41 Ibid., p. 10. As many as 42 countries, including 11 former communist countries, are now semi-presidential, making it a highly popular model (p. 5); but Skach demonstrates that this model is problematic for democratic consolidation.

42 Ibid., p. 9.

43 Ibid., p. 6. This was exactly the experience of Weimar Germany (p. 9), half of whose life span was characterised by 'divided minority government', in which 'legislative immobilism and cabinet instability' combined with 'continuous presidential dominance'(p. 7). Many post-communist countries, not only Russia, experienced this same phenomenon for a decade (p. 6).

44   Quoted in Stepan, 'Fifth Republic and Semipresidentialism', p. 291, fn 25 (emphasis added).

45   Alfred Stepan, conversation with author (May 2006).

46   Survey research from a 1990 case-study showed that Soviet attitudes and beliefs about democracy had begun to resemble those in the West, including the United States: Jeffrey Hahn, 'Yaroslavl' Revisited', in Stephen Whitefield, ed., *Political Culture and Post-Communism*, p. 151.

47   Brown, *Seven Years*, p. 326.

48   Peters, *Institutional Theory in Political Science*, p. 162.

49   'Traditional' refers to many of the authoritarian characteristic and methods are traditional, including diminished political pluralism, arbitrary use of the law as a political weapon, familiar Russian goals of state greatness and 19th century notions of sovereignty. But there are new twists, including state capitalism. Also new are the relative freedoms of travel and expression that Russians have enjoyed since the late 1980s.

50   Barbara Kellerman, *Bad Leadership: What it is, How it Happens, Why it Matters* (Boston: Harvard Business School Press, 2004), p. 23.

51   Ibid., pp. 23–4. What does 'bad' leadership mean, and does Putin qualify as 'bad', according to Kellerman's criteria? Kellerman lists seven categories of 'bad leaders'; and yes, Putin qualifies, she says, in the 'rigid' category – defined as 'unable or unwilling to adapt to new ideas, new information or changing times (p. 75). Pointing to the Kursk submarine disaster as her example. Kellerman suggests that Putin rigidly refused Western help because he was more worried about belittling the Russian army and Russia's reputation as a military great power than he was rescuing the Russians on board (p. 77).

52   'It's not just that Russia's identity as an empire matters, but it's the tortured way that it has mattered', especially during such 'periods of great transformations when upheaval from above...crosses a qualitative threshold and turns society upsidedown': Legvold, 'Russian Foreign Policy during Periods of Great State Transformation', pp. 25–6.

53   '*Neo*-authoritarian' is perhaps more accurate. Without explicitly using the term, Aral Gat describes the Putin model as a new (and, in his view, superior) twist on authoritarianism, not unlike the China model. See: Aral Gat, 'The Return of the Authoritarian Great Powers', *Foreign Affairs* (July–August 2007): 59–69.

54   In the Putin era, Russians continued to have rock-bottom trust in political parties, despite the (partly manipulated) rise of United Russia. 'The number of people who appreciate the right to choose between political parties was close to zero – only 3 percent.' Only 5% of the population trust political parties – the lowest ranking institution: V. Shlapentokh, 'Trust in Public Institutions in Russia: the Lowest in the World', *Communist and Post-Communist Studies*, 39, 2 (2006): 156–8.

55   Michael McFaul, 'Putin's Plan', *Wall Street Journal* (4 December 2007), http://www.hoover.org/pubaffairs/dailyreport/archive/12201461.html; Masha Lipman, 'Putin Cements his Grip', *The Washington Post* (6 October 2007), http://carnegieendowment.org/publications/index.cfm?fa=view&id=19627&prog=zru; Masha Lipman, 'Putin's Power Vacuum', *The Washington Post* (14 July 2007), www.carnegieendowment.org/publications/index.cfm?fa=view&id=19435

& prog=zru–; Stephen Blank, 'The Putin Succession and its Implications for Russian Politics', *Post-Soviet Affairs*, 24, 3 (2008): 233, 238, 259.

56 Vladimir Gel'man and Tomila Lankina, 'Authoritarian versus Democratic Diffusions: Explaining Institutional Choices in Russia's Local Government', *Post-Soviet Affairs*, 24, 1 (2008): 58.

2
Presidents and Parties: Leadership and Institution-Building in Post-Communist Russia

Thomas F. Remington

Leaders and institutions

Theories of political leadership and theories of institutional change are not always complementary. Because there are typically so many varying contextual factors relative to the number of leaders, it is difficult analytically to separate the efforts of particular leaders from the broad array of political forces that influence them. Therefore, generalisation about the strategies of transformational leaders is hazardous. Certainly, institutional change is not always a product of leaders' entrepreneurship. Often it results from deliberation and bargaining among rival political actors. Still, the important role played by leaders in forging new institutions has prompted a number of efforts to analyse the role of leaders as institution-creators. Recent rational-choice institutionalist and historical-institutionalist theories of leaders have given us new methods for distinguishing the efforts of leaders from the contextual conditions in which they operate.[1] Some studies assess the behaviour of leaders as 'agents' of 'principals', where the principals may be understood as voters in a democracy or specific elite 'selectorates'.[2] Others treat leaders as 'agenda-setters' and 'entrepreneurs'. If the analytical problem for explaining the behaviour of leaders as agents is to understand how leaders reconcile the pursuit of their own policy or personal goals with the objective of transmitting the aggregate will of the electorate or selectorate, creating the possibility of agency loss, the analytical task for understanding the behaviour of leaders as institutional entrepreneurs is to generalise about when and why they transform the rules of the game in return for power and other benefits for themselves. In any case, a substantial literature has developed on the role of leaders as agents of policy and institutional change, including studies of US presidents and congressional leaders, and of Soviet and post-Soviet leaders.[3]

In this chapter I am interested in the strategic use of institution-building by three Russian political leaders, Gorbachev, Yeltsin and Putin. By institutions I am referring to those sets of rules and procedures by which collectivities make choices over alternative policies. Constitutions, electoral systems, legislative procedures for setting their agenda, allocating rights, selecting leaders, proposing, developing, amending, passing and rejecting legislation, and so on, are examples of the types of institutions I am concerned with here. They are distinct from the policy decisions that are the *outcomes* of institutions, and from the organisations that *participate* in decision-making processes, such as political parties, lobby groups, firms, mass media, business and professional associations and labour unions. Institutions can arise in a variety of ways, but I am particularly interested in the path of institution-building whereby leaders offer explicit or tacit exchanges with others that expand participatory and representational rights for other real or latent political groups, solving a collective action dilemma for those groups in return for greater power for themselves. This is not simply a matter of a leader creating a new agency to accomplish a specific policy goal, but rather creating collective rights for a class of actors to participate in the political arena. My question is two-fold: when would leaders create efficient institutions expanding the political rights of potential opponents, and what are the consequences over time of doing so?

Efficient representative and participatory institutions are those that solve collective dilemmas for existing or potential collectivities. Such collective dilemmas include coordination problems that arise when individuals would benefit from some collective good but are unable to organise to supply it – the classic problem of public goods. These collective dilemmas are common in political life. Political activists might want to rally followers to join with them in forming a political party, but unless the political system recognises the rights of political parties, they have little to offer them in return for joining the party. As a result, there is little reason for activists to invest in the hard work of party-building, hammering out their differences, formulating agreed programmatic positions and working to form lasting alliances and organisational structures. An electoral law that makes it advantageous for parties to run candidates therefore solves a collective action problem for both the party's leaders and followers.

Likewise a well-functioning *system* of competitive political parties is a public good because once it comes into existence, many political actors are better off than they are without one, but no one actor is willing to create it alone. Voters are better off in a party system that offers them choices and holds elected officials accountable. They are better off in a system with a relatively small number of well-known parties than in one with a large number of small and unknown parties, because they are less likely to throw away their votes on losers. Candidates are better off in a well-operating party system that can offer them calculable chances of winning public office than in a party system where party labels and identities are unstable.[4] Regional leaders, business, labour, and other social interests benefit if a party system provides a channel for checking and monitoring the activity of the central government. Deputies and factions in a highly fragmented system of parliamentary parties prefer cohesive parties that can provide them access to careers and electoral resources. But none of these actors can solve the problem alone. No one has an incentive to pay the full cost of organising a competitive party system, because each is better off individually with a bandwagoning strategy of supporting the 'party of power' in order to be included in the distribution of patronage benefits. And of course the organisers of a state party or party of power have no incentive to create an effective opposition party, although they may find it expedient to create puppet parties that offer the illusion of multi-party competition.

Institutional theory shows that efficient institutions enable actors to benefit from cooperation and exchange – rather than to beggar one another – by lowering the costs of obtaining information about other actors' strategies and reaching, monitoring, and enforcing agreements with them.[5] As we know, many social settings lack such institutions, with the result that social well-being can remain stuck in a low-level equilibrium trap for years or even centuries. Institutional theory helps explain why we do not observe the convergence of underdeveloped societies to the level of developed societies, as we would expect from neo-classical and other functionalist models of social development.

Although we lack a full theory of the supply of efficient institutions, it is often clear after the fact that some leaders devise new institutions that solve collective dilemmas for society. With respect to Gorbachev, Yeltsin and Putin, the question is: why did they create efficient political institutions by trading new representational rights for others for stronger executive powers for themselves? In all three periods, Russia saw an immense amount of institutional improvisation through the establishment of new structures. Most new initiatives fell by the wayside, but a few proved to be effective and durable. Even Putin, although most of his institutional innovations have restricted participation and representation rather than expanding them, has enacted a few reforms that could have longer-term benefits for society.

The model of 'leader as entrepreneur' assumes that leaders devise institutional solutions to collective dilemmas for others in return for greater power for themselves. As Shepsle and Bonchek put it, the entrepreneurial leader is an 'agent who chooses (or creates) a principal' by transforming the structural environment in which other political actors operate.[6] Such new institutions may be efficient, in the sense that they reduce the costs for other actors to organise and act, or they may redistribute power further to the leader by reducing the range of representational and participatory rights. Either way, we can hypothesise that the leader derives some benefits by the increase in power. She may gain greater policy influence, or psychic or material rewards. Even dictatorial leaders who suppress deviance and dissent may enable groups to benefit from collective effort. The Stalin myth illustrates the model in extreme form. Stalin, according to his hard-core admirers, was a harsh ruler, but he built up a great state and 'died without a *kopek* in his pocket'. They justify the repressive nature of his rule on the grounds that it prevented masses and officials alike from engaging in anti-state behaviour, such as shirking, theft, and wrecking. Dictatorship forced everyone to join in collective effort for the common good. How much the myth corresponds to reality is another question. But the widespread view that Stalin's terror was justified because it enforced collective discipline on an unruly society highlights the point that even in an extreme case, leadership can be understood as an exchange in which a leader provides collective goods to followers in return for the privileges of power. Such an understanding is reinforced by popular expectations in a political culture in which broad strata of the population believe that only such leadership can prevent social chaos.[7]

The benevolent entrepreneur devises new sets of rights enabling collectivities to aggregate the preferences of their members. The leader might extend the franchise to new strata, call elections in which new voters participate, create new representative bodies where those elected meet, grant the new representative bodies fixed rights to initiate policy proposals, participate in decision-making, or give (or withhold) consent to a decision. The leader might create new agencies, courts, and advisory bodies, redraw the boundaries of electoral and administrative units, and expand access to education, health care, communications and state service in ways that widen participation in the political community. Entrepreneurial creativity comes into play as the leader devises institutions that can serve as 'common carriers', in Eric Schickler's term, because they benefit multiple groups with differing interests.[8]

Dictatorial leaders narrow participatory rights. They postpone or cancel elections, or impose tight rules of eligibility on running for office or voting; they increase their own powers to make decisions by suspending the constitution or widening rule by decree; they find grounds to dissolve or arrest opposition groups and shut down independent media; they eliminate the independence of courts or regulatory agencies; they restrict the ability of opposition parties to participate in political life. Moderately dictatorial leaders rule the country as if it were a military organisation or state bureaucracy. Predatory leaders defy bureaucratic rules of order so as to profit from the flow of resources to and from the state treasury. Lacking effective public scrutiny or opposition, the administrative-authoritarian state tolerates corruption and even the flourishing of organised crime rackets. The predatory state descends into state breakdown and warlordism.[9]

If predatory leaders deplete social resources of society and leave wreckage behind, effective ones leave behind efficient institutional frameworks that can sustain themselves over time and adapt to new contingencies. We can view the balance of benefits for society and benefits for the leader as a continuum. At one end are leaders who reduce the net capacity of society to solve collective problems through relentless exploitation of its resources; at the other are leaders who expand society's capacity to meet policy challenges. The increase in society's benefits greatly exceeds the increase in the leader's rents in that case. In between are dictators who restrain predation and rent-seeking by others and expand state capacity through economic development or military mobilisation, but deny participatory and representational rights to competing political groups.

Because it was so centralised, the Soviet state depended on individual leaders to serve as its institutional architects, a pattern followed in most of the successor states. For that reason, the regime changes since the late 1980s under Gorbachev, Yeltsin and Putin provide a particularly fruitful opportunity for investigating the effects of leadership on institutional change. Both the Soviet state and the Russian Federation witnessed vast institutional innovation from the late 1980s through the present, much of it produced by the central leadership. In this paper I will compare Gorbachev, Yeltsin and Putin in their capacity as institutional innovators, examining the balance sheet of gain for the leader and gain for the society in the exchanges that they offered over the course of their tenures in power.

Gorbachev's institutional reforms

Archie Brown, in *The Gorbachev Factor*, observed that the Soviet political system vested enormous power in its top leader but made that power contingent on the tacit consent of a potentially powerful coalition of senior figures – heads of major state agencies, regional bosses, the collective consent of the party apparatus – who could block policy reform. The performance of the system depended heavily on the qualities of the leader, but the leader did not have infinitely wide freedom to change policy or reengineer the institutional foundations of the system. The contingent nature of the leader's power in the old system arose from the fact that decision-making institutions were only weakly governed by constitutional rules or established precedents. As we know, the old Soviet system had highly elaborate procedures for decision-making and monitoring of implementation. These included the procedures for clearance or sign-offs to decisions by affected agencies, the institution of personal responsibility (*kuratorstvo*) by superior party and government officials for supervising particular sets of subordinate organisations, the pattern of consultative and collegial leadership in party and government bodies, and the multiple redundant agencies of supervision over state officials.

In the absence of effective mechanisms for monitoring and scrutiny by the public or opposition forces, however, the cumbersome formal mechanisms for obtaining the consent of affected interests to decisions tended to protect the prerogatives of those interests. Institutions for the aggregation of mass preferences, whether market-based or electoral, were largely absent. In their role as conduit for criticism, the mass media operated under a standing rule of 'don't generalise'. There were no markets for capital or commodities that could measure the relative value of investments. Opposition parties were illegal. Elections proceeded without competition among candidates.

As a result, bureaucratic channels were essentially the only means by which the state pooled information and defined new policy alternatives. As we know, although they were relatively ineffective at responding to accumulating policy problems, Soviet bureaucracies were quite good at demanding incremental increases in resources, blocking unfavourable reports about performance, and preserving autonomous control over policy jurisdictions. State agencies and regional establishments grew resistant to oversight, instead hoarding, concealing and distorting information about their performance. Some party staff officials, media figures, and brave souls from academic and intelligentsia bodies did attempt to fight powerful bureaucratic interests, but they were out-gunned on all fronts. For example, environmental interests found it hard to gain access to the media, so that their protests took the form of literary laments for the loss of the organic harmony of pre-industrial society; opposition to the Soviet state's security and foreign policies was suppressed and driven into the dissident movement; sober analysis of the country's declining economic performance by academic specialists was expressed in cautious, coded language and confined to narrow academic circles. More far-reaching critiques of the system were discussed outside the formal channels of communication and research altogether. Certainly in so complexly structured a state there were many sources of impulses for reform, but, as George Breslauer observed, the pressures to stifle those impulses and preserve the status quo were far stronger than those needed to build coalitions in support of reform.[10]

The reform leader who comes to power in such a system needs, therefore, not only to alter policy, but to be an institutional innovator as well, if he or she is to reshape the environment in which policy is developed, proposed, adopted, and carried out. The leader needs to create institutions for participating in decision-making that will induce the formation of coalitions favourable to policy change. Empowering such institutions with the right to make decisions is risky, however. The leader cannot afford to cede his own power of final decision. Gorbachev's early strategy was to open up channels of communication through *glasnost'* in such a way as to mobilise popular pressure in support of the restructuring programme and constrain the enemies of reform, but without tying his own hands as policy leader. As an institutional innovation, *glasnost'* did not reduce the contingency of Gorbachev's power. To the contrary, his power continued to depend on his reputation, the perception on the part of other senior figures that he could remove his foes and promote his friends, mobilise coalitions of support, and solve collective problems. As in Neustadt's portrait of the power of a US president, the Soviet leader could build or deplete political capital by the skill with which he chose to join a coalition or form one. He needed to judge how early or late in the policy process to make a commitment to a position, decide how much attention and energy to devote to an issue, and figure out how to frame a policy stance in order to minimise blame and maximise credit. These are part of the skill set of leaders in well-institutionalised systems. We can suppose that the more open-ended and uncertain the institutional environment, the more the personal relations of the leader with other players matter for building, maintaining, or expending political capital. Gorbachev altered the institutional environment with *glasnost'*, and his subsequent institutional innovations increased still further the number of representational arenas in which supporters and opponents could act collectively to endorse or block his initiatives. As opponents within the party leadership became better organised and more vocal, he sought alternative points of leverage for control over policy-making. At the same time, he looked for means of providing potential supporters with more voice in the political process and ways of neutralising opponents with harmless participatory rights. This political imperative opened up an opportunity for a series of exchanges in which Gorbachev traded off new participatory rights for others in return for increased executive prerogatives for himself.

The grand bargain

Although most treatments of Gorbachev and Yeltsin tend to emphasise the differences between them in leadership goals and styles, I want to compare them in their role as institutional entrepreneurs.[11] The striking fact is that both created new executive presidencies simultaneously with the foundations of competitive party systems. In both cases, these institutional reforms were bundled into a single constitutional package. Under this 'grand bargain', the leader designed a presidency for himself, a presidency being preferred to the position of chair of a collective leadership, Politburo or Supreme Soviet, and in return granted the right to others to form parties that could represent groups of voters, participate in a competitive electoral process, and gain a voice in policy-making. In both the Gorbachev and Yeltsin periods this grand bargain was then extended through a series of related exchanges within parliament in which the powers of the chair of the parliament were expanded vis-à-vis the Presidium while the rights of parliamentary factions were expanded. Constitutionally, the grand bargain under Gorbachev was first embodied in the 1990 constitutional amendments that amended Article 6 of the Soviet constitution and also created a Soviet presidency (rather than chairmanship of the Supreme Soviet), and was repeated in the 1993 constitutional settlement in the Russian Federation that bundled together a powerful presidency with an electoral law mandating proportional representation in the lower house of parliament. In both cases, the new electoral institutions provided a powerful stimulus to the organisation of parties and party-like organisations.

Likewise, both Gorbachev and Yeltsin created channels of representation to regional interests. Gorbachev experimented with bodies such as the Presidential Council, the Federation Council, and the Novo-Ogarevo negotiations, while Yeltsin employed the Federation Treaty of 1992 to give a crude, initial form to a new framework for federal relations. He improvised the constitutional conference in summer 1993 as a broad representative assembly of social and regional interests, and then, in his new constitution, devised a bicameral parliament with an upper chamber expressly designed to give the executive and legislative branches of each federal subject a voice. Both leaders, in short, offered new representational rights to two sets of political agents: social movements that could organise as political parties in a competitive electoral setting, and regional leaders, who had clear spheres of authority in their own jurisdictions plus a recognised voice in decision-making at the federal level. Both sets of representational rights were traded for support for the leader as president. Presidentialism concentrated the executive power of the leader in a single office rather than a collective body. The new representative institutions of partisan elections and federal chambers multiplied the spheres of rights in which autonomous political actors could oppose the president.

This path of institutional reform differs from pacting. It was incremental, and did not result from explicit bargaining. The first fateful step was taken by Gorbachev at a point when he still had a great deal of discretion. He combined two major reforms into a single package, approved by the party Central Committee and then by the Congress of People's Deputies in March 1990, when he proposed the creation of a Soviet presidency and at the same time eliminated Article 6 from the Constitution. This was an implicit deal in which the legitimacy of multi-party competition was offered in return for giving Gorbachev executive powers as president in his own right, not as chairman of the Supreme Soviet. As Gorbachev put it in his memoirs, these two institutional steps were 'organically related': 'The first meant that our state would cease to be a single-party, even in a certain sense a theocratic, state and that one of the main principles of democracy – ideological and political pluralism – would be introduced. The second meant the recognition of a no less important principle of this democracy, namely the separation of powers.'[12] Amending Article 6 meant legalising multiparty competition, whereas creating an executive presidency, separate from the Supreme Soviet, removed executive power from the Communist Party of the Soviet Union (CPSU) and from the Supreme Soviet. This created for the first time a constitutional separation of powers. These institutional reforms also jointly served a common end for Gorbachev in reducing his dependence on the party for his policy-making authority while forcing the party to enter the arena of competitive party politics. He intended to free himself of the obligations of managing the party apparatus while in return giving channels to the newly mobilised political forces in the country to participate in political life. Both reforms, in short, were intended to weaken the monopoly of the CPSU on power.

To be sure, as Archie Brown has pointed out, when Gorbachev created the new office of president, he lacked the 'experience or knowledge of how to secure the structural underpinnings which would endow that office with real executive power'.[13] Gorbachev was unable to place the state machine under his control. His desperate search for ways to make the presidency an effective source of policy direction for the executive branch led to a series of improvisations. Certainly the government itself did not fully accept the reform. As Prime Minister Ryzhkov commented, 'maybe someday we will adopt an American system of government, but it is too early for this'.[14] Moreover, not only were the structural underpinnings for the presidency absent, but the model of a presidency as the institutional organisation of executive power in the Soviet state was irresistibly tempting to the leaders of all the territorial components making up the union, the more so given the utter incapacity of the newly reorganised soviet bodies to manage their policy-making responsibilities. Each union republic sooner or later revised its own constitution to provide for an executive presidency, as did autonomous republics within the Russian republic. Other territorial jurisdictions also strengthened the executive powers of their leaders. As Gorbachev also noted, the cascade of new presidencies in the republics erased at least half the benefit of forming a new presidency.[15]

Gorbachev's creation of the presidency was a radical step, but by itself it was insufficient to alter the deeply entrenched style of leadership that pervaded all state structures. One reason Gorbachev failed to bring under his control the full set of powers that a General Secretary had was that the new presidential office disrupted the equipoise of 'top-down'/centralised and 'bottom-up'/consultative procedures for decision-making that had been customary within the party and the government as well as between them.[16] The centralised state structures had come to rely on a great deal of horizontal and vertical integration and communication. These institutions provided both for centralised goal-setting and deliberation among the heads of subordinate bodies. The president, in contrast, lacked line authority over managers who deliberated on policy decisions before they were made, then were charged with carrying them out. The close tie between the representation of affected interests in ministerial collegia, party committees, interagency commissions, and other consultative bodies that gave legitimacy to the outcomes of deliberations in the old, sluggish, but well-oiled Soviet policy-making machinery was broken.

At the same time, the new representative bodies that Gorbachev created as part of his experiments in democratisation of the old Soviet system lacked the means for reaching majority agreement on decisions about serious policy matters or resolving their own deep internal cleavages. At the union level, power was divided between the Congress and the Supreme Soviet, between both of them and the Presidium, and between the chairman and the other bodies. Power was fragmented. The new bodies were able to block one another, but they were very poorly equipped to reach decisions that could be transmitted and executed faithfully. There were as yet too few means for shaping coalitions and majorities that would support difficult policy options and ensure their implementation. Occasionally both Gorbachev and Yeltsin were able to win majorities for emergency measures, as when the USSR Congress approved Gorbachev's proposal to create a presidency by the requisite two-thirds majority, and later agreed to give Gorbachev emergency decree powers to fight the mounting economic and political crisis in the country.

Gorbachev's insistence on preserving control as General Secretary of the CPSU, and his refusal to break the party into competing wings or to found a competing party, allowed him to keep the presidency free of party control and prevent any party from gaining majority control over the Congress and Supreme Soviet. In a pattern that has continued to the present, the arena for the newly legitimate party politics was kept carefully separate from the arena for policy-making and control over the executive branch. By the same token, this strategy deprived Gorbachev of an organised base of political support for his reforms.

Yeltsin faced exactly the same dilemma with the Russian Congress one year later: he could persuade it to create a presidency and later to endow it with emergency powers, but he could not find a majority to give him the constitution he wanted incorporating these institutional innovations. Like Gorbachev, Yeltsin therefore also proceeded in piecemeal fashion as a result, improvising and dealing, granting representational rights to organised or latent political constituencies in return for their support. Neither Gorbachev nor Yeltsin was able to win majorities for radical economic reform. Gorbachev had to go around parliament when he wanted to construct a new federal framework in the Novo-Ogarevo talks in 1991. Yeltsin did so when he used his decree authority freely in 1992 and 1993 to launch radical economic reform and privatisation.

For neither Gorbachev nor Yeltsin, in other words, was the presidency won on behalf of a wider partisan movement that could shepherd its policies through the policy-making and implementation processes. Both leaders kept the two elements of the grand bargain separate. The presidency was created alongside a system of parties, but the presidency itself would not be a party office nor would either president use his power to organise a party. The consequence for both was that the development of the presidency and the development of parties tended to proceed in parallel and even in competition with one another. A partisan presidency would have stimulated the development of opposition parties, also set on capturing the executive branch. Instead, seeking to keep the presidency free of party obligations, both Gorbachev and Yeltsin ensured that the government was accountable to the president, not a party majority. The party system was divorced from control over the executive branch. The result was that the presidency itself was unable to attain full political control over the government.

This separation of the arena for party competition from the presidency and its effort to control executive power hampered the development of a system of organised competitive political parties from the start. Many other factors also impeded the emergence of parties, of course. Internal dissent within the CPSU, culminating in the formation of the Democratic Platform and then the Republican Party, did not lead to a competitive party system. Gorbachev tried to maintain control over the CPSU as the Russian branch of the party broke off, but he did not counter it with a party movement of his own. Proto-parties formed in the 1989 and 1990 elections at the USSR level and then in Russia, but then promptly splintered into numerous small factions. What did create an impetus for party development, however, was the opportunity for open political participation in law-making on the part of deputies in the new parliaments, following the proto-partisan electoral contests. In both the USSR and Russian legislative arenas, the chairman – Gorbachev and later Lukyanov in the one case, and Yeltsin and later Khasbulatov in the other – progressively traded off organisational rights to political factions in return for support. But, consistent with the pattern at the constitutional level, neither took responsibility for leading one of them.

Intra-parliamentary institutions

The evolution of party organisations within parliament took the form of a series of steps as an evolutionary sequence over the period from 1989 to 1999. Almost from the beginning of the USSR Congress of People's Deputies in 1989, interest-oriented and political groups were given the right to register as groups, and to act collectively to seek recognition in floor debate, to hold meetings using parliamentary facilities, to circulate their documents and so on. The new political groups formed by adapting accepted models of organisation. The process began when the several hundred democratic reformers who were elected to the Soviet Congress in 1989 modified an older Soviet institutional form, the territorial group, and turned it into something completely new, a political faction. Dominated by Moscow deputies, they sought to unite with like-minded deputies from other cities and so formed the 'interregional group of deputies'. This new form was unprecedented because there had never been an opposition political faction in a soviet. Recognition of their status in turn gave the wily deputy chairman, Anatolii Lukyanov, an opportunity to recognise still other political factions and make them dependent on him by allowing them access to the Presidium. Yet these were the nuclei from which proto-parties emerged that competed in the 1990 elections to the Russian Congress. Over time, Lukyanov allowed political factions to enjoy a higher status in the USSR Supreme Soviet than ordinary groups and to begin to take the initiative in political representation and policy development.

An equivalent path of development was evident in the Russian Soviet Federated Socialist Republic (RSFSR) Congress, as first Yeltsin and then Khasbulatov granted political factions, as an institution, ever greater rights to participate in Presidium deliberations, to represent members on the floor, and to negotiate compromises over legislation. For instance, when Yeltsin was elected Chairman of the Supreme Soviet of the RSFSR in June 1990, he encouraged the free formation of political groups, met with the newly formed groups, and promised to consult with them regularly as a bargaining chip for their support. Likewise, at the end of October 1991, when the RSFSR Congress deadlocked over the election of a chairman to replace Yeltsin, informal consultations among faction leaders produced a deal breaking the impasse and enabling Ruslan Khasbulatov to be elected to the chairmanship of the Supreme Soviet. Several developments occurred at the same moment. Yeltsin was granted sweeping emergency powers to make policy by decree, the Congress adopted a rules change which elevated political factions to privileged status, and Khasbulatov formed the Council of Factions. The coincidence of these events makes it reasonable to suppose that a kind of package deal was put together among the faction leaders, Khasbulatov, and Yeltsin, giving each side something that it wanted. The Council of Factions again supported Khasbulatov in late 1992 at a moment when the communist opposition wanted to vote no confidence in the reformist Gaidar government, and the democratic forces wanted to vote out Khasbulatov as chairman of the Supreme Soviet. The Council worked out a package agreement under which parliamentary support for Gaidar was traded off against support for Khasbulatov.

After Yeltsin dissolved the Russian Congress and Supreme Soviet, he put forward his own draft constitution and decreed an electoral law into being that incorporated his own version of the grand bargain: a presidency with the power of decree and a weak parliament in return for a system of proportional representation requiring party list elections from a single federal electoral district for half the seats in the new Duma. Consistent with the Grand Bargain was a smaller bargain concerning governance in the new Duma. The team Yeltsin appointed to work out the governing structures and procedures for the Duma put power in the hands of a council of factions formed on a parity basis. Once the December elections were held, the successful party leaders quickly agreed to adopt as a steering body for the Duma the proposed new Council of Factions, which replaced the old presidium form, and to run the parliament as a collective enterprise of the parliamentary parties. Yeltsin, in short, gave his opponents enough in the way of participatory rights to solve a collective dilemma for them – how to induce followers to join a party? – in return for their consent to a powerful presidency for himself.

Thus the series of intra-parliamentary trades in both the USSR and RSFSR Congress/Supreme Soviet bodies through which the chair granted successively wider rights of representation and participation to political factions in return for greater power to manage parliamentary operations repeats the pattern of exchange seen at the state level: an ever-stronger presidency in return for a system of parties. Gorbachev began this sequence with the reforms of 1990, and Yeltsin repeated it with the 1993 constitution. In each case, the exchange represented an act of institutional innovation by an entrepreneurial leader, rather than the execution of a programme chosen by his followers or a response to social pressure or forces. In each case the institutional innovation was an act of improvisation by leaders seeking to expand their own base of support by creating rights for others that solved collective dilemmas for them. In turn, each step along the path made the next such incremental reform more likely.

Leaders do have the autonomy to devise new institutions, particularly at times of social crisis and disequilibrium. On the other hand, the new institutional forms may fail to achieve their goals. Gorbachev's presidency failed to stem the rising tide of systemic crisis in the Soviet Union, and the effort to bootstrap a system of competitive political parties into being in Russia ran afoul of severely unfavourable conditions. As a result, while the presidency took over many of the powers and prerogatives that the CPSU had exercised, the party system remained underdeveloped. Indeed, parties' ability to aggregate interests, monitor officials, authoritatively transmit demands and support, and generate legitimacy has declined since the mid-1990s. Consequently, the presidency has taken over more and more of the processes that parties would otherwise perform through parliamentary elections and representation. This process began in the mid-1990s, as the Kremlin used its administrative levers to manipulate the party system. So did regional governors. These 'non-party substitutes', as Henry Hale terms them, tended to crowd out the market for political parties from the mid-1990s on.[17] Moreover, particularly in the Putin era, all forms of open political competition grew nominal at best, while the presidency came to occupy a near-monopoly over the aggregation of interests. The presidency's power expanded in tandem with the decline of other political institutions.

Putin as institution builder

Let us briefly consider the most recent phase of political development. The failure of the party system in Russia to consolidate has been well documented.[18] A number of reasons for this have been identified. The legacy of a patrimonial form of communism inhibited the formation of social cleavages that could sustain party competition.[19] Russian society lacked the foundation of social and civic organisations that could pool support for parties.[20] Non-governmental organisations (NGOs) lacked strong indigenous roots.[21] Business and labour groups fragmented and readily attached themselves to the patronage of powerful political officials. Social capital in Russia is extremely weak, by comparison with other societies.[22] Politicians failed to make lasting commitments to parties. Voters failed to form lasting attachments to parties.[23] The mass media fell under oligarchic control, then once again state domination. Regional leaders manipulated civil society, parties, and legislatures in regions, cultivated personalised relations with the president, and formed collusive alliances with regional business interests.[24] Therefore, one explanation for the overdevelopment of the presidency lies in the underdevelopment of the civic, partisan, communications, and interest-based organisations that would make parliament an effective counterweight to the president. Politicians in a system with more secure avenues for attaining power and making careers would not be so dependent on good relations with the presidential administration. As Mathew Shugart has argued in a number of works, systems with fragmented and incohesive party systems tend to be conducive to powerful executive presidencies, because the presidency solves collective dilemmas for politicians that parties cannot solve, such as the provision of benefits to key constituents.[25] Steven Fish argues that, along with the weakness of civil society and the tendency for political competition to centre on the redistribution of rents from natural resources that is characteristic of oil states, the weakness of parliament, itself a reflection of the weakness of other mediating organisations, has facilitated the accumulation of power in the presidency.[26]

This pattern of mutually reinforcing weakness of the party system and the expanding power of the presidency originates in the initial grand bargain struck by Gorbachev and Yeltsin. The grand bargain was an exchange rather than an integrated solution to the problem of democratic reform. The key point is the grand bargain's failure to link party competition with control over the executive. Neither Gorbachev nor Yeltsin was ready to lead a party himself, or to allow the composition of the government to be determined by the partisan balance of parliament. If either had enjoyed an overwhelming majority among organised political forces, he might have been willing to accept a weaker presidency and stronger party system, where the parliamentary majority determined the composition of the government. Yeltsin came close to accepting such a precedent with the short-lived experiment of the Primakov government in 1998, when the conditions were nearly in place for a party government. This is the only time in Russian history when the government more or less reflected a partisan majority in parliament. If the experiment had continued, it is possible that politicians would have had sufficient incentive to overcome their incessant squabbling over the modest perks they gain by being leaders of small factions in parliament in favour of forming partisan teams responsible for governing. But the brief period of quasi-party government ended, giving way to the carousel of prime ministerial appointments prompted by the Yeltsin entourage's desperate search for a successor. Institutionally, there were ever fewer incentives for party development as the political arena concentrated on access to the power of the presidency. Both oligarchs and governors sought to coalesce around a party of power, not form into competing party teams. The Kremlin looked for a means to guarantee a strong showing in the 1999 elections and a smooth, unchallenged presidential succession. All sides would have been better off if there had been a more orderly, predictable, stable process for managing the succession, but none was willing to take the risk of making a major commitment to a political party unless it already enjoyed broad support. As a result, a healthy viable competitive party system was a public good that went unrealised. Short of that, key governors and oligarchs wanted to rally around a recognised 'party of power' that would be run out of the Kremlin.[27]

Both Gorbachev and Yeltsin ensured that the powers of the presidential office were insulated from the claims of any possible party or coalition majority. Party competition was confined to the electoral and parliamentary arena and kept safely away from control over the executive. This reflected the intense struggle between these leaders and their opposition but it had the effect of depriving party leaders of the institutional incentives that would have allowed a party system to consolidate, and built ties to like-minded officials at lower levels.

As president, Vladimir Putin had even less interest in granting rights to parties to influence policy-making than did Gorbachev and Yeltsin. As many observers have noted, Putin's goal was to establish political order through administrative control rather than through open, competitive democratic politics.[28] His institutional innovations restricted participation in policy-making, instead of creating new arenas and expanding political rights. Unlike Gorbachev or Yeltsin, Putin consistently claimed not only that he wants to create a viable competitive party system but even that such a party system ultimately could lead to parliamentary control over government.[29] At the same time, through a series of explicit and tacit steps that diminish effective opposition and make all parties dependent on the Kremlin's favour, Putin made it virtually impossible for any party but the recognised party of power to participate in public life. These include the more restrictive requirements for registration of parties, the intimidation of oligarchs interested in financing parties, the backroom manoeuvres creating short-lived parties to split the leftist and nationalist vote, the progressive expansion of control over the media, the suppression of organised opposition, the creation of the Public Chamber to offset the Duma's role as public forum, and the concerted effort to build a dominant party. Most fundamentally, the subordination of both chambers of parliament to the Kremlin results in the loss of almost all opportunity for opposition parties to use the parliament for public politics.

Institutional engineering in the realm of federal relations has been similar. Just as Gorbachev and Yeltsin expanded collective representational rights for regional leaders by creating second chambers, Putin created the consultative State Council as a replacement for the representational role of the governors in the Federation Council, and limited their access to federal policy-making still further with the system of federal districts and presidential representatives.

There were two exceptions to this pattern of expanding presidential power and shrinking representational rights for partisan and regional interests during the Putin presidency. First was the requirement that regional legislative elections employ party list proportional representation for at least half their seats. The other was the replacement of the mixed electoral system with an all-PR (public relations) system for the

2007 State Duma elections. Both tended to increase the electoral opportunities for parties able to meet the new, more restrictive conditions for party activity (the 50,000 member requirement for parties to register and the 7% threshold to Duma representation). While the immediate beneficiaries of these changes were United Russia and the Communist Party of the Russian Federation (CPRF), and perhaps Just Russia and the Liberal Democratic Party of Russia (LDPR), they also created a powerful inducement to mergers on the part of smaller parties. In many regions, Putin's second-term legislation began to stimulate more active participation in electoral contests on the part of parties. Parties such as the Union of Right Forces, Yabloko, and the Party of Life, which all failed to clear the 5% threshold in the 2003 Duma election, had several successes at the regional level. Given that Putin relinquished power to President Medvedev, United Russia is increasingly forced to find a firmer base of popular support or face the risk of decline in its ability to attract adherents (much as happened with Our Home Is Russia after the 1995 elections). The legislation could therefore have a longer-term effect of stimulating party competition and weakening the presidency.

Through the Gorbachev and Yeltsin eras, the logic of the exchange of the right to form parties and compete for power for greater power for the chief executive generated a sequence of related institutional reforms in which parties gained rights of representation and participation in parliament in a separation of powers system dominated by a president. The flaw in this evolutionary development is the dual accountability of the government. In Russia's 'presidential-parliamentary' system, the government is formed by and answers to the president, but must be confirmed by the parliament and maintain its confidence. If parliament were to become the arena where parties competed for the right to control government, party leaders would have more effective incentives for maintaining unity and attracting popular support. The government would be partisan, accountable to its partisan backers and scrutinised by its partisan opposition. The logic of this sequence of development would be for Russia to move in the direction of a premier-presidential system, where the chief executive becomes accountable to a parliamentary majority. Future leaders would need to win power and govern through political parties and a parliamentary majority, rather than by exercising the autocratic and personalistic powers of the presidency. It would certainly be ironic if Putin, the one leader of these three who sought to diminish participatory and representational rights for parties, ended up as the one who strengthened the party system by tying the power of chief executive to party government.

Notes

1   Kenneth A. Shepsle and Mark S. Bonchek, *Analyzing Politics: Rationality, Behaviour, and Institutions* (New York: W. W. Norton & Co, 1997), pp. 380–404; Gary W. Cox and Mathew D. McCubbins, *Legislative Leviathan: Party Government in the House* (Berkeley: University of California Press, 1993).
2   On leaders as agents of selectorates, see Bruce Bueno de Mesquita, James D. Morrow, Randolph M. Siverson and Alastair Smith, 'Testing Novel Implications from the Selectorate Theory of War', *World Politics* 56:3 (April 2004): 363–88.
3   Richard Neustadt, *Presidential Power and the Modern Presidents: The Politics of Leadership from Roosevelt to Reagan* (New York: Free Press, 1990); Eric Schickler, *Disjointed Pluralism: Institutional Innovation and the Development of the U.S. Congress* (Princeton: Princeton University Press, 2001); Randall Strahan, 'Leadership and Institutional Change in the Nineteenth-Century House', in David W. Brady and Mathew D. McCubbins, eds, *Party, Process, and Political Change in Congress: New Perspectives on the History of Congress* (Stanford, CA: Stanford University Press, 2002), pp. 237–69; Stephen Skowronek, *The Politics Presidents Make: Leadership from John Adams to George Bush* (Cambridge: Harvard University Press, 1993); George W. Breslauer, *Khrushchev and Brezhnev as Leaders: Building Authority in Soviet Politics* (London: Allen & Unwin, 1982); George W. Breslauer, 'Evaluating Gorbachev as Leader', *Soviet Economy* 5, 4 (1989); George W. Breslauer, 'Personalism Versus Proceduralism: Boris Yeltsin and the Institutional Fragility of the Russian System', in Victoria E. Bonnell and George W. Breslauer, eds, *Russia in the New Century: Stability or Disorder?* (Boulder, CO: Westview, 2001), pp. 35–58; George W. Breslauer, *Gorbachev and Yeltsin as Leaders* (Cambridge: Cambridge University Press, 2002); Archie Brown and Lilia Shevtsova, eds, *Gorbachev, Yeltsin, and Putin: Political Leadership in Russia's Transition* (Washington, DC: Carnegie Endowment for International Peace, 2001); William J. Tompson, 'Khrushchev and Gorbachev as Reformers: A Comparison', *British Journal of Political Science* 23 (1993): 77–105.
4   John H. Aldrich, *Why Parties? The Origin and Transformation of Political Parties in America* (Chicago: University of Chicago Press, 1995).
5   Douglass C. North, *Institutions, Institutional Change and Economic Performance* (Cambridge, Cambridge University Press, 1990).
6   Shepsle and Bonchek, *Analyzing Politics*, p. 393.
7   The problem is analogous to the distinction between 'vertical' and 'horizontal' institutions made by Robert Putnam in the context of his study of social capital in Italy. The atomised, suspicious pattern of social relations in the south encourages people to turn to paternalistic and coercive leaders to solve collective action dilemmas. Northern regions, where trust and cooperation are grounded in social capital, are able to sustain cooperative institutions based on reciprocal trust. Robert D. Putnam, Putnam, with Robert Leonardi and Raffaella Y. Nanetti, *Making Democracy Work: Civic Traditions in Modern Italy* (Princeton: Princeton University Press, 1993).
8   Schickler, *Disjointed Pluralism*, p. 13.
9   Mark R. Beissinger and Crawford Young, eds, *Beyond State Crisis: Postcolonial Africa and Post-Soviet Eurasia in Comparative Perspective* (Washington, DC: Woodrow Wilson Centre Press, 2002).

10 Breslauer, *Khrushchev and Brezhnev as Leaders*; Thane Gustafson, *Reform in Soviet Politics: Lessons of Recent Policies on Land and Water* (Cambridge: Cambridge University Press, 1981).

11 George W. Breslauer, *Gorbachev and Yeltsin as Leaders*; Archie Brown and Lilia Shevtsova, eds, *Gorbachev, Yeltsin, and Putin: Political Leadership in Russia's Transition*.

12 Mikhail Gorbachev, *Memoirs* (New York: Doubleday, 1995), p. 318.

13 Archie Brown, *The Gorbachev Factor* (Oxford: Oxford University Press, 1996), pp. 316–17.

14 Yulia Shevchenko, *The Central Government of Russia: From Gorbachev to Putin* (Aldershot, UK: Ashgate, 2004), p. 24.

15 Gorbachev, *Memoirs*, p. 320.

16 Paul Lawrence and Charalambos A. Vlachoutsicos, *Behind the Factory Walls: Decision Making in Soviet and US Enterprises* (Boston: Harvard Business School Press, 1990).

17 Henry Hale, *Why Not Parties in Russia? Democracy, Federalism, and the State* (Cambridge: Cambridge University Press, 2006).

18 Richard Rose and Neil Munro, *Elections without Order: Russia's Challenge to Vladimir Putin* (Cambridge, Cambridge University Press, 2002); Richard Rose, Neil Munro and Stephen White, *The 1999 Duma Vote: A Floating Party System* (Glasgow: Centre for the Study of Public Policy, University of Strathclyde, 2000); Michael McFaul, *Russia's Unfinished Revolution: Political Change from Gorbachev to Putin* (Ithaca, NY: Cornell University Press, 2001); Michael McFaul, 'The Fourth Wave of Democracy and Dictatorship: Non-cooperative Transitions in the Postcommunist World', *World Politics* 54, 2 (2002): 212–44; Michael McFaul, Nikolai Petrov and Andrei Ryabov, 'Post-script: The 2003 Parliamentary Elections and the Future of Russian Democracy', in Michael McFaul, Nikolai Petrov and Andrei Ryabov, *Between Dictatorship and Democracy: Russian Post-Communist Political Reform* (Washington, DC: Carnegie Endowment for International Peace, 2004); Regina Smyth, 'Building State Capacity from the Inside Out: Parties of Power and the Success of the President's Reform Agenda in Russia', *Politics and Society* 30, 4 (2002): 555–78; M. Steven Fish, 'The Executive Deception: Superpresidentialism and the Degradation of Russian Politics', in Valerie Sperling, ed., *Building the Russian State: Institutional Crisis and the Quest for Democratic Governance* (Boulder, CO: Westview, 2000): 177–92; M. Steven Fish, 'When More Is Less: Superexecutive Power and Political Underdevelopment in Russia', in Victoria E. Bonnell and George W. Breslauer, eds, *Russia in the New Century: Stability or Disorder?* (Boulder, CO: Westview, 2001): 15–34; M. Steven Fish, 'The Impact of the 1999–2000 Parliamentary and Presidential Elections on Political Party Development', in Vicki L. Hesli and William M. Reisinger, eds, *The 1999–2000 Elections in Russia* (Cambridge: Cambridge University Press, 2003): 186–212.

19 Herbert Kitschelt et al, *Post-Communist Party Systems: Competition, Represent-ation, and Inter-Party Cooperation* (Cambridge: Cambridge University Press, 1999); Herbert Kitschelt and Regina Smyth, 'Programmatic Party Cohesion in Emerging Postcommunist Democracies: Russia in Comparative Context', *Comparative Political Studies* 35, 10 (2002): 1228–56.

20 Laura Belin, 'The Russian Media in the 1990s', *Journal of Communist Studies and Transition Politics* 18, 1 (2002): 139–60; Sarah Oates, 'Television, Voters,

and the Development of the "Broadcast Party"', in Vicki L. Hesli and William M. Reisinger, eds, *The 1999–2000 Elections in Russia: Their Impact and Legacy* (Cambridge, Cambridge University Press, 2003), pp. 29–50.

21 Sarah L. Henderson, *Building Democracy in Contemporary Russia: Western Support for Grassroots Organisations* (Ithaca, NY: Cornell University Press, 2003); Sarah E. Mendelson and John K. Glenn, eds, *The Power and Limits of NGOs: A Critical Look at Building Democracy in Eastern Europe and Eurasia* (New York: Columbia University Press, 2002).

22 Marc Morje Howard, *The Weakness of Civil Society in Post-Communist Europe* (Cambridge: Cambridge University Press, 2003).

23 Timothy J. Colton, *Transitional Citizens: Voters and What Influences Them in the New Russia* (Cambridge, MA: Harvard University Press, 2000); Stephen White, Richard Rose and Ian McAllister, *How Russia Votes* (Chatham, NJ: Chatham House Publishers, 1997).

24 Kathryn Stoner-Weiss, 'The Limited Reach of Russia's Party System: Under-institutionalisation in Dual Transitions', *Politics and Society* 29, 3 (2001): 385–414.

25 Matthew S. Shugart and John M. Carey, *Presidents and Assemblies: Constitutional Design and Electoral Dynamics* (Cambridge: Cambridge University Press, 1998); Matthew Soberg Shugart, 'The Inverse Relationship Between Party Strength and Executive Strength: A Theory of Politicians' Constitutional Choices', *British Journal of Political Science* 28 (1998): 1–29; Matthew Soberg Shugart, 'Presidentialism, Parliamentarism, and the Provision of Collective Goods in Less-Developed Countries', *Constitutional Political Economy* 10, 1 (1999): 53–88.

26 M. Steven Fish, *Democracy Derailed in Russia: The Failure of Open Politics* (Cambridge: Cambridge University Press, 2005).

27 Olga Shvetsova, 'Resolving the Problem of Preelection Coordination: The 1999 Parliamentary Election as an Elite Presidential "Primary"', in Vicki L. Hesli and William M. Reisinger, eds, *The 1999–2000 Elections in Russia: Their Impact and Legacy* (Cambridge: Cambridge University Press, 2003), pp. 213–31.

28 Dale R. Herspring, 'Putin and Military Reform', in Dale R. Herspring, ed., *Putin's Russia: Past Imperfect, Future Uncertain*, 2nd edition (Lanham, MD: Rowman & Littlefield, 2003), pp. 185–204; Richard Sakwa. *Putin: Russia's Choice*. (London: Rutledge, 2004); Lilia Shevtsova, *Putin's Russia* (Washington, DC: Carnegie Endowment for International Peace, 2003); Mark Urnov, 'Federal'naya vlast' v Rossii v period prezidentstva V. Putina: Tochka zreniya liberala', in M. Urnov and V. Kasamara, *Sovremennaia Rossiya: Vyzovy i otvety* (Moscow: Ekspertiza, 2005), pp. 25–44.

29 Putin's 2005 message to parliament suggested that the president would appoint as governors individuals supported by party majorities in the regional legislatures. In his 2003 message he suggested that in the future, the prime minister would be chosen as the representative of a party majority in the Duma: 'I have already said that I support a course for strengthening the role of parties in public life. And taking into account the results of the coming elections to Duma, I think it would be possible to form a professional, effective government relying on a parliamentary majority.' 2005 text taken from Polit.ru, April 25, 2005; 2003 text taken from presidential website: www.kremlin.ru/text/appears/2003/05/44623.shtml.

3
Russia's Gubernatorial Elections: A Postmortem

J. Paul Goode[1]

The demise of Russia's gubernatorial elections bore all the makings of a great murder mystery, with many possible explanations and much disputed evidence. The Kremlin argued that the institution of gubernatorial elections was so corrupt and disorderly that it was terminally ill. From this perspective, the elimination of gubernatorial elections was a form of euthanasia designed to spare the country from further suffering (largely owing to self-inflicted wounds). Critics of Vladimir Putin's regime cried foul play, arguing that the institution's untimely demise was no mercy killing. As the story goes, the Kremlin increasingly lost control over the governors since Putin came to power, often failing to get its own candidates elected or even to maintain control over those it did. Hence, the elimination of electoral institutions was nothing more than a desperate bid to restore central authority in the regions, implemented by a regime that knew little about democracy and a great deal about coercion.

This chapter presents something of a forensic investigation into the demise of Russia's decade-long experiment with gubernatorial elections. As with any postmortem, the first and most important question concerns the cause of death. Assuming we can rule out accidental death and spontaneous combustion, is there any clear evidence of foul play? If so, was it a crime of passion or an act of mercy? Did the Kremlin act alone? Was it an inside job with accomplices in the regions? After all, the lack of any clear defensive wounds on the victim suggests the involvement of those closest to the victim.

The chapter begins with a brief history of the deceased – the establishment of gubernatorial elections in the 1990s and the governors' relationship with the Kremlin.[2] The next section turns to the question of motive: who stood to gain (or lose) from the transformation of

Russia's governors into presidential appointees? After considering central debates over Putin's proposed changes in the State Duma, the following section examines the questions of motive and complicity among regional actors: was the decision to eliminate gubernatorial elections a defensive move by the Kremlin, or was it a successful and aggressive intervention? And if the decision was imposed from above, why was there little in the way of resistance?

Gubernatorial elections and the Kremlin

The evolution of the elected governorship was bound up with Russia's emergence from Soviet rule. Following Mikhail Gorbachev's proposal at the 19th Party Conference in 1988 to transfer power from regional party committees to the soviets, the executive committees of regional soviets (*ispolkomy*) were strengthened in 1990. Boris Yeltsin later proposed that executive power in the regions be transferred from the *ispolkomy* to the new post of 'head of administration' (*glava adminis-tratsii*) during the Russian Soviet Federated Socialist Republic (RSFSR) presidential campaign in spring 1991. This new post was supposed to be subject to multi-candidate elections and the Russian Congress of People's Deputies adopted corresponding legislation for the election of heads of administration in October 1991. When Yeltsin was granted emergency decree powers in November 1991, however, he was handed the power to appoint regional governors. Gubernatorial elections were postponed three times, until December 1996.[3]

In the few regions where Yeltsin permitted gubernatorial elections (by decree), the results were disastrous for the Kremlin's appointees. In December 1992, the legislative assemblies in eight regions voted no confidence in the governor.[4] When gubernatorial elections were held in April 1993, incumbents lost to Communist-supported candidates in all but one region (Krasnoyarsk).[5] Only one election was allowed in 1994, while 13 elections took place in 1995.[6] Nevertheless, 45 out of 49 *oblast'* governors were appointed by Yeltsin (39 in the months following the August 1991 coup attempt) through to December 1995.[7] The first large round of gubernatorial elections occurred from June 1996 to March 1997, during which elections took place in 55 regions. In 48 of these regions, Yeltsin's appointees faced election for the first time.[8] Incumbents suffered significantly throughout Russia's regions during the 1996–97 election cycle: of the 52 elections held in 1996, incumbents were defeated in 36 regions (69%), and in 1997 incumbents were defeated in nine regions out of 17 (53%).

The gubernatorial elections in 1996–97 yielded a number of important lessons for the Kremlin and for local political elites. The widespread rejection of Yeltsin's appointed governors reflected popular dissatisfaction with the centre's lack of a regional policy. Governors who were appointed in 1991–93 fared the worst, with few exceptions. The most successful of Yeltsin's appointees were those who came to power later, in 1994–96, and ran on platforms that there had been insufficient time for them to implement their goals. The sweeping defeat of incumbents also reflected the Kremlin's lack of a consistent strategy for supporting Yeltsin's appointees. The Presidential Administration often split over whom to support, tacitly supported challengers, or failed to provide adequate resources to incumbents.[9] In the absence of a coherent central strategy for contesting regional elections, the governors' ability to dominate the regional elite and their effective use of regionalism emerged as the common denominators of electoral success.[10]

Regionalism combined with electoral legitimacy was a potent combination, reflected in the immediate rise in the durability of incumbent governors. The difference between Yeltsin's appointed governors and the elected representatives of the regional elite was vividly illustrated by the next large round of gubernatorial elections, in 1999–2000, in which incumbents lost in just 20 out of 59 contests (34%). Incentives for elected governors to cooperate with the Kremlin further diminished and separatism ceased to be the exclusive purview of the republics. Slider points out that deviations from federal laws and presidential decrees previously were more characteristic of the republics, but that gubernatorial elections changed this by providing a 'shield of democratic legitimacy' for provincial leaders.[11] Though Russia's governors grew stronger within their own domains throughout the 1990s, the same could not be said of their commitment to regional democracy. Incumbent governors were known to employ a variety of dirty tricks to preserve power, including the notorious use of 'administrative resources', the deployment of bogus opposition candidates (*dublery* or *dvoiniki*), the monopolisation or intimidation of regional media, and various manipulations of regional electoral law.[12]

Under Putin, governors had to contend with a resurgent federal government, as the Kremlin increasingly contested their control and authority on their own territories.[13] The Kremlin played a more active role in regional elections, often seeking to prevent undesirable or 'accidental' (*sluchainye*) candidates from participating. Additionally, the federal centre could alter the balance of power between the centre and the regions at election time by manipulating key appointments and by the payment (or non-payment) of federal officials in the regions. Informal channels for influencing the outcomes of regional elections were equally significant: earning Putin's support – whether moral or material – was a crucial advantage, as it also served as an implied threat to those backing the 'wrong' candidate. The rising importance of laying successful claim to Putin's endorsement posed a novel problem for the Kremlin of singling out genuine loyalists among contenders.[14]

This renewed activism on the part of the Kremlin during the Putin presidency came on the heels of a broad-based assault on regional autonomy and the status of Russia's governors, including: the removal of the governors from the upper house of parliament, the Federation Council; the creation of the seven Federal Districts and reform of the system of Presidential Representatives to oversee the regions; the campaign to bring regional laws and charters into conformity with federal law; the revision of the Tax Code in the centre's favour, rendering even 'donor' regions dependent upon federal transfers; the Kozak Commission's re-allocation of the more lucrative joint constitutional powers (those listed in Article 72 of the Russian Constitution) to the federal centre; the elimination of regional parties that often served as electoral vehicles for the governors; and the campaign to merge regions.[15]

Putin remained committed to maintaining the institution of gubernatorial elections throughout his first term.[16] Yet on 13 September 2004, he announced sweeping changes at an enlarged session of his government which included all of Russia's governors. The essence of his address was that the Beslan hostage crisis had exposed the ongoing weakness of the state and, particularly, the executive branch on the regional level. Putin concluded that the time for half-measures was past, contending that, 'The system of executive power should not simply be adapted, but fundamentally reconstructed.'[17] The centrepiece of Putin's address was the proposal to eliminate gubernatorial elections and implement a system of presidential appointments.[18] Within three months, the institution of gubernatorial elections became a casualty of Russian politics.

For the budding forensic investigator, Putin's post-Beslan address may be found wanting as an accurate account of motive. First and foremost, there is no *a priori* connection between the elimination of electoral institutions and success in fighting domestic terror or insurgency. Second, the rationale of strengthening the executive chain of command became something of a boilerplate justification for state centralisation under Putin. Lastly, the speed with which the Kremlin drafted and submitted legislation to the State Duma suggests that plans to eliminate gubernatorial elections were already in the works, while all that remained to be decided was timing and opportunity.[19]

If the President's public statements do not provide a sufficient guide to motive, the manner in which his proposals were presented and defended helps to flesh out their meaning and significance – not just for the Presidential Administration, but for the broader array of political forces in Moscow supportive of the ongoing centralisation of power. The next section begins with the question of motive by examining the debates in the State Duma over approval of Putin's move to eliminate gubernatorial elections. While the debates reveal a pair of motives that provided support 'from above', they do not account for the relative lack of resistance among the regional political elite. The following section considers the governors' possible motives for accepting their transformation into presidential appointees, as well as the surprising quiescence of regional parliaments.

Debating the demise of gubernatorial elections

The draft legislation introduced by Putin proposed that governors would no longer be directly elected, but would be nominated by the President and 'elected' (confirmed) by regional assemblies. Putin would also gain the power to fire governors under ambiguous criteria, expressed as 'loss of the President's confidence'. In addition to the governors being transformed into appointed officials, regional assemblies were faced with the prospect of dissolution if they twice rejected the proposed candidate.[20] Governors who were elected prior to the passage of the law would be allowed to serve out their term of office. At the first reading of the legislation in the State Duma on 29 October 2004, presidential representative Aleksandr Kosopkin emphasised that the justification for the dissolution of regional assemblies was to prevent them from depriving the region of a 'normally functioning system of executive power', though they would still have some recourse to the courts. The Chairman of the Duma's Committee for Federal Affairs and Regional Policy, Viktor Grishin, added support to Kosopkin by stressing that the constitution allowed the regional executive branch to be formed either through direct election or other means by representative institutions.[21] The ensuing debate revealed two broadly acceptable motives for the elimination of gubernatorial elections: the first concerned the constitutionality of eliminating gubernatorial elections and what it entailed for the powers of the presidency, and the second stemmed from a general dissatisfaction with Russia's federal system.

Constitutionality

In his address on 13 September 2004, Putin staked his claim to Article 77 of the Russian Constitution, which grants regions the right to determine their own system of government 'independently and according to the principles of the constitutional system of the Russian Federation and the general principles of the organization of representative and executive bodies of state authority fixed by federal law'.[22] Putin further leaned on the constitutional provision that federal and regional governments make up a 'single system of executive power', taking this to mean that regional governments should be formed upon the same principle as the federal government.[23] Immediately following Putin's address, former Constitutional Court Chairman Vladimir Tumanov indicated that the interests of national security made it possible to sacrifice 'the full realization of certain constitutional principles', including the principle of the separation of powers.[24] Putin received additional support from Aleksandr Veshnyakov, Chairman of the Central Electoral Commission, who held that the proposed changes only affected the areas of joint competency between the centre and the regions and not (presumably) the inalienable rights of Russian citizens.[25]

In the debate on the draft law, several deputies suggested that regional assemblies should be bypassed altogether and governors appointed directly by presidential decree. Others expressed concern that the law concentrated too much power in the president's hands and that the provision that governors could be sacked for 'loss of confidence' was too ambiguous and easily abused. Opposition to the proposal drew attention to the Constitutional Court's decision of 18 January 1996, which ruled that Altai *Krai*'s assembly could not choose the region's governor and required direct elections.[26] In the Duma debates, the president's representative side-stepped the Constitutional Court's 1996 decision as well as the issue of citizens' rights in observing that the federal law required by Article 77 simply did not exist at the time of the Court's ruling.[27] This stance was supported by Grishin's interpretation of Article 32, which holds that Russian citizens have 'the right to participate in managing state affairs both directly and through their representatives', as meaning that regional executive branches could be formed either by direct election or by 'representative institutions'.[28] In this manner, the Presidential Administration protected the maximum degree of autonomy and manoeuvrability for the president, while the issue of whether regional assemblies would actually 'elect' or merely 'confirm' the candidate proposed by the president was circumvented.

In the event, attempts to obtain a ruling by the Constitutional Court fell on deaf ears. An opposition letter signed by several independent State Duma deputies (Vladimir Ryzhkov, Oksana Dmitrieva, Mikhail Zadornov, Svetlana Goryacheva and others), as well as members of Motherland (Sergei Glaz'ev and Oleg Shein) and 'Committee-2008' (including Gary Kasparov, Boris Nemtsov, and Irina Khakamada), called upon the Chairman of the Constitutional Court to 'defend the Constitution'.[29] The Court responded – through its press service – that it could only act on complaints regarding *existing* laws.[30] In November, the Communist Party failed to get enough votes in the Duma to request an official opinion from the Constitutional Court on the applicability of Article 11 regarding the degree of independence possessed by the regions in determining their own form of government, as well as the right of citizens to exercise power through direct elections or through the state.[31] Various attempts by the Union of Right Forces to bypass the State Duma and obtain a request for a ruling through regional parliaments proved equally ineffective. The lone successful attempt to obtain a hearing from the Constitutional Court was brought by a citizen of Tyumen *Oblast'*, Vladimir Grishkevich, who disputed the appointment of Sergei Sobyanin in February 2005. In its ruling, the Court merely confirmed expectations that it would make use of the opportunity to renounce its 1996 ruling.[32] In effect, Putin remained the sole and ultimate arbiter of the governors' fate, while regional assemblies were reduced to the role of petitioners.

Regarding constitutionality, the Kremlin demonstrated its motives through the ebb and flow of debate. Rather than engage the substantial issue of citizens' entitlement to directly elected executive bodies, the Presidential Administration turned the debate into an assertion of the presidency's maximum latitude for action, with all other issues coming a distant second. From this perspective, there ought to be no difference – legal or practical – between elected governors and presidential appointees in terms of subordination to the Kremlin. And since Putin largely achieved the practical subordination of the governors during his first term, formalising their legal subordination was simply the next logical next step.

Federalism

Closely related to the legal subordination of the governors to the presidency was the broader issue of centre-regional relations. Upon the announcement of Putin's proposals, Lyudmila Alekseeva of the Moscow Helsinki Group worried that they effectively killed off the very idea of federalism.[33] This was an accurate assessment of the aims pursued by major parties, based on the debates in the State Duma.[34] In presenting United Russia's case for the reform, Andrei Klimov justified the move by reference to Russia's history – Tsarist and Soviet – of maintaining a strong 'ruling vertical' for 600 years, only to suffer total disintegration just two years after allowing elections during the Gorbachev era. In Klimov's estimation, it would be much easier to correct 'personnel mistakes' (*kadrovie oshibki*) with a proper ruling vertical than by using 'electoral technology'. The Liberal Democratic Party of Russia (LDPR) and Motherland (*Rodina*) argued that the law did not go far enough. Vladimir Zhirinovskii argued that federalism was the same thing as separatism, that governors were too bound by local interests ('mafia, bureaucrats, political parties, and voters'), and that the governors should be given a freer hand in their own domains. He further claimed (not entirely coherently) that all 89 governors should be fired and *arrested*, closing with the observation that Russia could learn much from China's version of the 'ruling vertical'. Dmitrii Rogozin added that the ultimate goal of such a reform would be to do away with '*matreshka* federalism' and the cycle of 'conflict along national borders' every 25–30 years. He added that the process of appointments should begin at once rather than waiting for the terms of sitting governors to end. In this way, the process of regional enlargement (*ukrupnenie regionov*) could proceed apace to create a form of 'unitary federalism'. At the other end of the spectrum, Deputy Ivan Mel'nikov of the Communist Party argued that the proposed changes not only represented an egregious violation of the principle of separation of powers, but that it strengthened the mechanisms for pressuring regional assemblies.

At the law's second reading on 1 December 2004, Grishin opened debate by observing that the Committee for Federal Affairs and Regional Policy had received more than 400 proposed amendments to Putin's draft law, mostly from State Duma deputies but also fourteen regions.[35] The amendments approved by the committee would require the president to engage in conciliation procedures for 30 days if his proposed candidate was rejected twice by the regional assembly. If nothing resulted from the negotiations, or if the president's candidate was rejected a third time, the president would still have the right to dissolve the regional assembly. Importantly, the amendments did not specify with whom the president should conduct negotiations. The changes further specified that the governor would coordinate activities of regional government agencies and organise their cooperation with federal structures. Finally, provision was made for current governors to appeal directly to the president for appointment before expiry of their term of office. The committee pointedly rejected amendments, which imposed qualifications or credentials for Putin's nominees, or otherwise limited 'the legal capabilities of the president' (*pravovoe pole prezidenta*). On the question of dissolving regional assemblies, Grishin emphasised that the measure was not a punishment, but a means for resolving intractable conflict.

The handful of dissenters pointed out that the public was being cut out of the process, with no means to initiate the process of removing governors once appointed. Some called attention to the fact that the president did not require the approval of regional assemblies to fire his governors, suggesting that their approval in the first place was, in fact, a mere formality. As during the first reading, deputies took issue with the law's use of the term 'election' for a process which was anything but. Others hoped to specify that candidates would be drawn from regional party lists, or to specify that the president must consult or negotiate with regional assemblies over gubernatorial candidates. Over the course of five hours of deliberation, however, not a single amendment (of more than 400 proposed) was passed, aside from those initially approved by the Duma's committee. Two days later, Putin's proposals sailed through the third reading in the Duma.[36] They were approved by the Federation Council in due course[37] and signed into law.[38] Only *after* the law was passed did Putin issue a decree that specified the procedure for appointments.[39] The Presidential Representatives (*polpredy*) in the Federal Districts would prepare a short list of candidates for the head of the Presidential Administration, who in turn would narrow the list to two candidates for the President to consider. Suggestions were to be made no later than 90 days before the end of governor's term (or ten days in the event that a governor resigned early). Proposals for candidates were required to include a summary of the results of preliminary consultations, 'other informational materials', and statements by the candidates agreeing to consideration for the post. These last requirements did not initially apply to governors appealing directly to the president, though Putin changed this by decree in late June 2005.[40]

As with the issue of constitutionality, the debate over the future of Russia's federal system ultimately asserted the right of the presidency to define the extent of its own powers vis-à-vis the regions. The debates further revealed a general dissatisfaction with the shape of Russian federalism, but little consensus regarding the appropriate remedy. In this sense, the proposal to eliminate gubernatorial elections was converted – whether by design or by accident – into a divisive debate over the

substance of federal structure that closely resembles a collective action problem. This left the Presidential Administration in a privileged position to structure the debate, uniquely positioned to resolve the deadlock through the dispensation of selective (and non-binding) benefits. In the end, the Kremlin actually ceded very little ground from its original proposals, despite giving the appearance of compromise.

Governors and regional assemblies

The heads of Russia's regions fell over themselves to approve the President's mechanism for gubernatorial appointments – even prior to its formal adoption – despite the apparent assault on their autonomy. Moscow's Mayor Yurii Luzhkov noted approvingly that a governor should be concerned with the regional economy first and foremost, acting as 'a manager first, and, to a lesser degree, a politician'.[41] Many governors even argued that the system of appointments needed to be taken *further* such that governors would have the right to appoint mayors in order to complete the 'ruling vertical'. As Krasnoyarsk's Governor Aleksandr Khloponin lamented, governors already *de facto* appointed mayors, but they had virtually no means to remove them 'except to wait for the next elections'.[42] The few governors who openly opposed the elimination of gubernatorial elections had already fallen from the Kremlin's good graces, including Nenets Autonomous Okrug's Vladimir Butov, Ivanovo oblast's Vladimir Tikhonov, and Murmansk oblast's Yurii Evdokimov.[43] More typical, however, was Yaroslavl's Governor Anatolii Lisitsyn, who enthusiastically suggested that all governors should be appointed by spring 2005, hastening to add that he'd suggested appointing governors as early as 1998.[44]

What incentives could Russia's governors possibly have to cooperate with this latest attempt by the Kremlin to diminish their standing? After all, being a governor was quickly losing its material appeal as the centralising measures undertaken during Putin's first term hit squarely at their status and resources. In light of these changes, the governors' greatest remaining resource by the start of Putin's second term was their elected status. Indeed, it has been argued that this was one area where the Kremlin had lost ground, often failing to get its own agents elected to displace incumbent governors.[45] If this were the case, then Putin's move to eliminate gubernatorial elections would show the Kremlin on the defensive (if not desperate). Yet this view would be difficult to reconcile with the governors' enthusiastic support for their own political defeat.

Table 3.1   Kremlin Support in Gubernatorial Elections, 2001–2004*

Year	Total Elections	Incumbent supported	Challenger supported	Wins	Losses	Success rate
2001	22	12	3	9	6	60%
2002	17	10	5	11	4	73.3%
2003	30	17	8	22	3	88%
2004	23	18	7	14	10	58.3%

* For all tables, the January 2005 election in Nenets *Autonomous Okrug* is included in the total for 2004.

Note: Data were drawn from an analysis of central press reports prior to each election, accessed through the Eastview database, as well as English-language reports by *Radio Free Europe/Radio Liberty* and regional correspondents of the *Russian Regional Report*. First and second rounds of elections are treated separately as this allows for an increase in the number of observations while reflecting tactical repositioning between rounds. Cases where incumbent and challenger were both supported by the Presidential Administration were coded as support for each.

In order to assess these competing accounts, it is useful to review the Kremlin's record in influencing the outcomes of gubernatorial elections under Putin. The number of campaigns in which the Presidential Administration expressed clear support for incumbents or challengers from 2001 to 2004 is presented in Table 3.1. The Kremlin's 'success rate', or cases where candidates favoured by the Presidential Administration were elected or re-elected, increased dramatically from 60% in 2001 to 88% in 2003. Though the Kremlin's success rate dropped in the first half of 2004 to 33%, it recovered dramatically in the second half of the year for an overall success rate of 60.9%.[46]

Still, one might question whether the Kremlin did not merely back the candidates that already stood a good chance of winning. Indeed, the Presidential Administration remained neutral in the lion's share of gubernatorial elections in 2000, as it initially focused on regaining control over federal agencies in the provinces.[47] While it is difficult to assess the relative weight of Kremlin support in the electoral success of incumbent governors, an examination of the Kremlin's role in supporting challengers is more meaningful. As shown in Table 3.2, the Kremlin's ability to turn an election appears more prominently when one examines just those cases in which it backed a single challenger to the incumbent.[48] This table is further suggestive of the active role the Kremlin often took in advance of elections, to which one could add the striking of candidates from the ballot (the most notorious case being Aleksandr Rutskoi in Kursk *Oblast'*) or even keeping candidates on the

Table 3.2   Kremlin Support for Challengers in Gubernatorial Elections, 2001–2004

Year	Win	Loss	Success rate
2001	Tyumen Oblast', Evenk *AO**, Komi	Primorskii *Krai****	75%
2002	Sakha-Yakutiya**, Adygei, Ingushetiya*, Smolensk *Oblast'*	Kalmykiya	80%
2003	Magadan *Oblast'* (1st round) St. Petersburg* Kirov *Oblast'*** Tver *Oblast'* Bashkortostan	Magadan *Oblast'* (2nd round)	67%
2004	Ryazan *Oblast'* Briansk *Oblast'*** Ul'yanovsk *Oblast'***** Kamchatka *Oblast'*****	Nenets *AO***	80%

Notes:
*   Incumbent withdrew in advance of election.
**   Incumbent denied chance to run for third term.
*** Incumbent displaced (sacked or promoted) by Kremlin.

ballot against their will to ensure that elections were not declared invalid.[49] Another telling indicator of the influence of the Presidential Administration is found in elections where the main challenger was an outsider – that is, a candidate who was not a native of the region. This is a particularly salient indicator given the pressure placed on regional assemblies during Putin's first term to remove the restrictions on candidacy for the governorship to residents of the region. From 2001 to 2004 the Kremlin supported the winning candidate in nine out of 12 cases, and only lost one race in which it supported an outsider against the incumbent (see Table 3.3).

Contrary to the conventional wisdom that the Presidential Administration was losing control, these data suggest that the Kremlin was surprisingly successful in fighting gubernatorial elections despite a handful of high-profile defeats. In this light, the decision to end gubernatorial elections no longer appears defensive and reactionary. Rather, it fits a broader pattern by which the Presidential Administration clawed back the sources of gubernatorial prestige and autonomy. Under such circumstances, the governors' willingness to abandon their electoral mandates for the presidential team starts to make sense.

As it transpired, the potential advantages of presidential appointment may have provided sufficient motive for the governors to forego the

Table 3.3   Kremlin Support and Outsider Candidates, 2001–2004

Year	Region	Incumbent supported	Outsider supported	Winner	Result for Kremlin
2001	Tyumen *Oblast'*	Yes	Yes	Outsider	Win
2001	Evenk *AO*	No	Yes	Outsider	Win
2002	Penza *Oblast'*	Yes	No	Incumbent	Win
2002	Ingushetiya	No	Yes	Outsider	Win
2002	Kalmykiya	No	Yes	Incumbent	Loss
2003	St. Petersburg	No	Yes	Outsider	Win
2003	Chechnya	Yes	No	Incumbent	Win
2003	Bashkortostan	Yes (2nd round)	Yes (1st round)	Incumbent	Win
2003	Tver *Oblast'*	No	Yes	Outsider	Win
2004	Altai *Krai*	Yes	No	Outsider	Loss
2004	Kurgan *Oblast'*	Yes	No	Incumbent	Win
2005	Nenets *AO*	No	No	Outsider	Loss

benefits of direct election. In the first place, the shift from elections to appointments removed the niggling legal issue of term limits from the agenda (thereby depriving regional assemblies, procurators, and electoral commissions of a common tool for frustrating governors' attempts to retain power).[50] For those less fortunate, many governors took advantage of Putin's campaign to bring regional charters and constitutions into accordance with federal law to rename their office and, as a result, roll back the odometer for term limits. Yet these episodes clearly were disruptive enough that the governors were happy to be relieved of the issue once and for all. Indeed, the prevailing opinion among the governors appears to have been that elections themselves were more destabilising than they were worth.

Second, securing presidential appointment for many governors would mean exchanging dubious mandates earned through (often scandalous) regional elections for a direct mandate that derived from the most popular and respected figure in Russian politics. The endemic confrontations that characterised relations between governors and regional assemblies would no longer be a concern – not just because the assemblies would be complicit in confirming Putin's choice for governor, but also because opposing the governor would now be tantamount to opposing Putin (and therefore the nation that elected him). In this sense, the governors' power within their own territory may actually have *increased* vis-à-vis local forces despite the loss of autonomy in relations with the Kremlin.

If one examines Putin's first gubernatorial appointments (see Table 3.4), the extent to which governors benefited from the new system starts to

Table 3.4 Gubernatorial Appointments, January 2005–March 2006

	Region	Incumbent	Date	Appeal/Nominate?	New Governor?
1.	Primorskii *Krai*	Sergei Dar'kin	Feb 2005	Appeal	No
2.	Tyumen *Oblast'*	Sergei Sobyanin	Feb 2005	Appeal	No
3.	Vladimir *Oblast'*	Nikolai Vinogradov	Feb 2005	Nominate	No
4.	Kursk *Oblast'*	Aleksandr Mikhailov	Feb 2005	Appeal	No
5.	Khanty-Mansiisk *AO*	Aleksandr Filipenko	Feb 2005	Nominate	No
6.	Amur *Oblast'*	Leonid Korotkov	Feb 2005	Appeal	No
7.	Evrei *AO*	Nikolai Volkov	Feb 2005	Nominate	No
8.	Saratov *Oblast'*	Dmitrii Ayatskov	Mar 2005	Nominate	Yes
9.	Evenk *AO*	Boris Zolotarev	Mar 2005	Appeal	No
10.	Yamalo-Nenets *AO*	Yurii Neelov	Mar 2005	Nominate	No
11.	Tatarstan	Mintimer Shaimiev	Mar 2005	Appeal	No
12.	Tula *Oblast'*	Vasilii Starodubtsev	Mar 2005	Nominate	Yes
13.	Chelyabinsk *Oblast'*	Petr Sumin	Apr 2005	Appeal	No
14.	Koryak *AO*	Oleg Kozhemyako	Apr 2005	Nominate	Yes[a]
15.	Orel *Oblast'*	Egor Stroev	Apr 2005	Appeal	No
16.	Kostroma *Oblast'*	Viktor Shershunov	Apr 2005	Appeal	No
17.	Kemerovo *Oblast'*	Aman Tuleev	Apr 2006	Nominate	No
18.	Samara *Oblast'*	Konstantin Titov	Apr 2005	Appeal	No
19.	Penza *Oblast'*	Vasilii Bochkarev	May 2005	Appeal	No
20.	Lipetsk *Oblast'*	Oleg Korolev	May 2005	Appeal	No
21.	North Ossetiya	Aleksandr Dzasokhov	Jun 2005	Nominate	Yes
22.	Rostov *Oblast'*	Vladimir Chub	Jun 2005	Appeal	No
23.	Orenburg *Oblast'*	Aleksei Chernyshev	Jun 2005	Appeal	No
24.	Ingushetiya	Murat Zyazikov	Jun 2005	Appeal	No
25.	Smolensk *Oblast'*	Viktor Maslov	Jun 2005	Appeal	No
26.	Tambov *Oblast'*	Oleg Betin	Jul 2005	Appeal	No

Table 3.4 Gubernatorial Appointments, January 2005–March 2006 – *continued*

	Region	Incumbent	Date	Appeal/Nominate?	New Governor?
27.	Kaluga *Oblast'*	Anatolii Artamonov	Jul 2005	Appeal	No
28.	Nizhegorod *Oblast'*	Gennadii Khodyrev	Aug 2005	Nominate	Yes
29.	Altai *Krai*	Mikhail Evdokimov	Aug 2005	Nominate	Yes[b]
30.	Chavash republic	Nikolai Fedorov	Aug 2005	Appeal	No
31.	Irkutsk *Oblast'*	Boris Govorin	Sep 2005	Nominate	Yes
32.	Kaliningrad *Oblast'*	Vladimir Egorov	Sep 2005	Nominate	Yes
33.	Agin-Buriat *AO*	Bair Zhamsuev	Sep 2005	Nominate	No
34.	Kabardino-Balkariya	Valerii Kokov	Oct 2005	Nominate	Yes[c]
35.	Chukotka *AO*	Roman Abramovich	Oct 2005	Nominate	No
36.	Stravropol *Krai*	Aleksandr Chernogorov	Oct 2005	Appeal	No
37.	Perm *Krai*	Oleg Chirkunov	Oct 2005	Nominate	No
38.	Kalmykiya	Kirsan Ilyumzhinov	Oct 2005	Appeal	No
39.	Mordoviya	Nikolai Merkushin	Oct 2005	Appeal	No
40.	Sverdlovsk *Oblast'*	Eduard Rossel'	Nov 2005	Appeal	No
41.	Ivanovo *Oblast'*	Vladimir Tikhonov	Nov 2005	Nominate	Yes
42.	Tyumen *Oblast'*	Sergei Sobyanin	Nov 2005	Nominate	Yes[d]
43.	Komi republic	Vladimir Torlopov	Dec 2005	Nominate	No
44.	Altai republic	Mikhail Lapshin	Dec 2005	Nominate	Yes
45.	Dagestan republic	Magomedali Magomedov	Feb 2006	Nominate	Yes
46.	Kareliya republic	Sergei Katanandov	Mar 2006	Nominate	No
47.	Ul'yanov *Oblast'*	Sergei Morozov	Mar 2006	Appeal	No

Notes:
[a] Incumbent was sacked so no appeal was possible.
[b] Incumbent died in office.
[c] Incumbent resigned due to ill health.
[d] Incumbent promoted to Presidential Chief of Staff.

become clear. Despite the legal provision allowing sitting governors to finish their terms, just over half (24 out of 47) appealed for Putin's decision in advance of their term's expiry. In most cases, these appeals were made during or immediately following individual meetings with Putin under the rubric of discussing the 'socio-economic conditions in the region'. As if to underscore the importance of personal loyalty in assessing a governor's claim to office, the only governors to lose office were those who failed to appeal directly to Putin and instead followed the standard nomination procedure.[51] Moreover, the appointment process did not rigorously adhere to the requirement that consultations in the region be conducted prior to nominations. The decision to replace Tula *Oblast'* Governor Vasilii Starodubtsev with Vyacheslav Dudka was made known even before consultations with social organisations were conducted.[52] On occasion, members of regional assemblies have complained that consultations were conducted with unknown people and may even have taken place outside of the region. And until July 2005, the requirement could be altogether bypassed when a governor appealed directly to Putin.

From January to July 2005, Putin did not make active use of the new power to replace incumbents at will: out of 27 appointments, only four were new governors. This is not to say, however, that the appointment of incumbents was automatic, or that the governors were any less exposed to Kremlin intervention. The replacement of four governors over six months may not seem like much of a bloodbath, but it is worth recalling that the governors were virtually unsackable under Yeltsin, and that Putin's ability to 'persuade' Primorskii *Krai* Governor Evgenii Nazdratenko to quit his job in early 2001 was considered a significant achievement.[53] The fact that Putin chose not to sack notorious regional leaders such as Tatarstan's Shaimiev and Samara's Konstantin Titov tended to overshadow the extent to which governors became vulnerable to replacement. This was much more evident in the second half of 2005, when eight new governors were appointed out of 17. The appointment of Yurii Luzhkov's Deputy Mayor Valerii Shantsev to replace Gennadii Khodyrev was a national sensation, weakening Luzhkov's team while removing a troublesome governor in one fell blow.[54] Putin appointed another of Luzhkov's deputies, Mikhail Men', to replace Vladimir Tikhonov in Ivanovo *Oblast'*.[55] In Irkutsk, Boris Govorin was replaced with a political outsider, Aleksandr Tishanin, after Govorin resisted the Kremlin's design to merge the region with Ust'-Orda Buriat Autonomous *Okrug*.[56] The most populist use of the appointments system fell upon Stavropol *Krai*'s Aleksandr Chernogorov. On national television,

Putin read a complaint from a pensioner who had no water in her county (*raion*), and then announced that he would not sign the papers for Chernogorov's appointment until the governor repaired the area's water pipes. The bulldozers and tractors rolled out the next morning and Chernogorov got to keep his post.[57]

In an ironic twist, those who were most vulnerable to Kremlin interference may have been the most likely to benefit individually from the elimination of gubernatorial elections. It is important to bear in mind that subordinating the governors to presidential authority is not the same as decapitating the regional elite. Governors were more vulnerable to central intervention, but they actually became *stronger* within their own regions. To understand why, it is worth considering the sources of the governors' power during the brief period of direct elections. Henry Hale argues convincingly that gubernatorial power was related to the combination of Soviet institutional legacies and transitional dynamics, which 'left in place concentrations of power and resources that were *fungible* vis-à-vis elections'.[58] In centre-regional and centre-local relations, the elected governor represented the whole range of interests based on the region's territory, and was therefore capable of bargaining and negotiating to a greater extent than any other political actor.

In eliminating gubernatorial elections, the governors' position at the apex of the regional political establishment was not diminished – only the source and extent of their autonomy vis-à-vis the Kremlin. As the president's point men in the regions, they remained uniquely capable of representing their region's variety of interests, and enjoyed privileged access to the Presidential Administration. Indeed, their room for manoeuvre was potentially even greater since they were no longer held directly accountable by regional voters and regional assemblies had no direct means of replacing them. Putin refrained from creating transparent mechanisms for determining gubernatorial appointments or issuing unambiguous criteria for evaluating governors' performance.[59] He even suggested that appointed governors would regain many of the powers taken from their elected predecessors, including influence over appointments to federal agencies in the regions.[60]

Confronting regional assemblies

Even if one can identify governors' motives to comply with Putin's initiative, one might reasonably expect to find defensive wounds among regional assemblies. Prior to the law's adoption by the Duma, much debate in regional assemblies focused on the clause granting Putin the right to dissolve regional parliaments should they reject his candidate. The opposition was led by Tatarstan's State Council, which labelled Putin's initiatives to be nothing less than a *coup d'état*.[61] Other regional assemblies hoped to limit or remove the clause concerning the dissolution of regional parliaments, to increase the role of regional assemblies in selecting candidates for the president, to clarify foggy concepts such as 'loss of confidence', or to extend the procedure to include appointing mayors.[62] With few exceptions, however, regional assemblies put up little resistance.

A major factor in this appears to have been the overwhelming satisfaction at the apparent increased status of regional assembly speakers.[63] While regional parliamentarians were concerned by the possibility of dissolution should they repeatedly reject the president's nominee, they also perceived an opportunity to exercise joint *kontrol'* over the governors with the president (particularly regional parliamentarians belonging to United Russia).[64] Regional assemblies became more assertive in their relations with Putin's appointed governors, overturning gubernatorial legislative initiatives and challenging appointments to regional administrations in Irkutsk, Yaroslavl' and Nizhnii Novgorod.[65] As with the governors, then, regional assemblies enjoyed increased *status* on the regional level, but this did not translate into greater *power* on the federal level. Regional assemblies did not have a strikingly successful record in opposing the centre. During Putin's first year in office, regional parliaments moved quickly under threat of dissolution to revise charters and constitutions to bring them into accordance with federal law. In many cases these revisions worked to the governors' advantage. If regional assemblies were expected to show more backbone after 2004, there was little evidence to support it. With the passage of the new federal legislation for appointing governors, regional assemblies once more faced the threat of dissolution if corresponding changes were not made to regional charters and constitutions. Some assemblies emphasised the significance of regional parliamentary institutions on the national level in response.[66] Despite the common concern about granting the president the power to dissolve regional parliaments, however, protest dwindled as the deadline approached.

The new system of gubernatorial appointments provided, at first glance, an opportunity for regional assemblies to dislodge unpopular governors. Rather than wait for the next election and hope for the best, the new system permitted regional assemblies to lobby the Presidential Administration for a change of administration. In March 2005, Altai *Krai's* legislative assembly voted no confidence in Governor Mikhail Evdokimov and requested that Putin fire him. Instead, Putin asked Evdokimov to find a resolution to the conflict without discussing the assembly's vote. The assembly responded with a second vote of no confidence.[67] Siberian *polpred* Anatolii Kvashnin insisted that the governor and assembly find a solution to the conflict, after which Evdokimov fired his entire administration. The regional parliament remained divided, however, and continued to seek Putin's direct intervention.[68] Following the Altai example, Nizhegorod *Oblast''*s regional assembly demanded that Governor Gennadii Khodyrev put a question of confidence before Putin early.[69] Deputies in Ivanovo *Oblast'* asked the assembly speaker to request that the Presidential Administration exclude current Governor Vladimir Tikhonov as candidate for appointment. A similar letter was prepared in the Ivanovo City Duma.[70] Though the regional assemblies received a change in governor, it was not the one they were expecting. In Altai *Krai*, it came as a result of Evdokimov's untimely death, leading to the appointment of an outsider – Aleksandr Karlin, formerly director of Presidential Administration's department for civil service.[71] In the latter two cases, Putin appointed complete outsiders to the region – Shantsev in Nizhnii Novgorod, Men' in Ivanovo – and bypassed the assemblies altogether. In other words, the assemblies did not get their way because of their new status in law. Perhaps a more salient point is that the right of regional assemblies to 'elect' – or rather, exercise joint *kontrol'* over – the region's governor was not matched by the power to fire the governor without the president's intervention.

The approval of additional legislation granting majority parties in regional assemblies the power to nominate gubernatorial candidates had the potential to enhance the standing and autonomy of those assemblies.[72] Since over half of regional assemblies were controlled by United Russia, this new provision did not generate challenges to Putin's presidency. To date, not a single regional assembly has openly challenged a presidential nomination for governor.

Conclusion

It is now possible to assemble a brief picture of the factors contributing to the demise of Russia's gubernatorial elections. While the timing of Putin's initiative was a matter of chance and opportunity afforded by national tragedy, the move capitalised on the momentum of earlier steps towards centralisation. The debates in the State Duma made virtually no mention of the purported link between gubernatorial elections and the incidence of domestic terrorism. Instead, the key issue emerging in the Duma was the imperative to preserve the President's legal room for manoeuvre. The few dissenters in the State Duma and limited opposition among regional assemblies were overwhelmed by the shared dissatisfaction among central politicians with Russia's federal structure, which generated additional support for abolishing gubernatorial elections even in the absence of a clear consensus regarding the proper shape of Russian federalism.

In order to account for the relative ease with which Putin did away with gubernatorial elections, however, one needs to take into account the motives of regional actors. Russia's governors were largely complicit in their own transformation from elected public servants to presidential appointees. Though this gives the appearance of an inside job, one could not term this a full-blown partnership between the Kremlin and regional elites. Rather, there was a sense of inevitability and resigned acceptance to the elimination of gubernatorial elections, as governors were increasingly vulnerable to central interference, while the material rewards and prestige of elected office were on the decline. If one strains to find defensive wounds on regional assemblies, it is largely because they were made an offer they couldn't refuse. Taken at face value, Putin's proposal would elevate the status of regional assemblies – and particularly the post of regional speakers – and grant a more efficient means to resolve endemic disputes between regional assemblies and troublesome governors. Yet this apparent gain was offset by the provision that assemblies could be dissolved for refusing Putin's appointees, as well as the lack of provision for assemblies to compel the dismissal of an appointed governor. To this end, regional assemblies made half-hearted attempts to steer Putin's legislation in a less punitive direction but they lacked coordination and, ultimately, influence over the votes cast in the Federal Assembly.

In the end, the mystery surrounding Putin's sudden decision to end Russia's gubernatorial elections is less concerned with identifying a culprit than with establishing whether a crime was committed in the first place. It is noteworthy that the opposition to Putin's plan focused on the defence of the institution of gubernatorial elections but did not rush to the defence of individual governors. Likewise, the Kremlin's decision to put an end to gubernatorial elections met with public ambivalence and even found support among its apparent victims. In the end, the presentation of Putin's decision as a form of institutional euthanasia proved a successful gambit. The question of whether Russia's system of gubernatorial elections is deserving of a eulogy should be left to its closest relatives. As for the possibility of its resurrection, a brief public debate early in the tenure of Putin's successor, Dmitrii Medvedev, concluded with the reaffirmation of the Kremlin's commitment to gubernatorial appointments.[73] It appears that the institution of gubernatorial elections – along with democracy and federalism – must await the passing of Putinism.

Notes

1 Parts of this article, which is otherwise new, appear in a piece by the same author: J. Paul Goode, 'The Puzzle of Putin's Gubernatorial Appointments', *Europe-Asia Studies*, Vol. 59, 3 (May 2007): 365–99. The editors thank Taylor & Francis Ltd (http://www.informaworld.com) for their permission to use this copyrighted material.

2 The term 'governors' is used here to refer to the heads of regional executive branches, including the various titles of regional president, head of government, government chairman, head of administration, and so forth.

3 V. Tolz and I. Busygina, 'Regional Governors and the Kremlin: the Ongoing Battle for Power', *Communist and Post-Communist Studies*, 30, No. 4 (1998): 402, 410–11.

4 The regions were Amur, Briansk, Chelyabinsk, Lipetsk, Orel, Penza, and Smolensk *oblasty*, and Krasnoyarsk *krai*.

5 S. L. Solnick, 'Gubernatorial Elections in Russia, 1996–97', *Post-Soviet Affairs*, 14, 1 (1998): 50. Republican elections were also held in Ingushetiya, Kalmykiya, Bashkortostan, and Chuvashiya.

6 Among the 1995 elections, the most significant was the April 1995 election in Sverdlovsk oblast. In this case, Yeltsin's former appointee, Eduard Rossel', contested the moratorium on gubernatorial elections in the Constitutional Court and forced a compromise in which the complaint was withdrawn in exchange for a decree allowing the election to take place. G. M. Easter, 'Redefining Centre-Regional Relations in the Russian Federation: Sverdlovsk Oblast'', *Europe-Asia Studies*, 49, No. 4 (1997): 617–36.

7 J. W. Hahn, 'Democratization and Political Participation in Russia's Regions', in *Democratic Changes and Authoritarian Reactions in Russia, Ukraine, Belarus, and Moldova*, ed., K. Dawisha and B. Parrott (Cambridge: Cambridge University Press, 1997), p. 157.

8 Solnick, 'Gubernatorial Elections in Russia, 1996–97', p. 48.

9 Ibid., pp. 62–4. Among the opposition candidates, the most successful were those who had previously served as chairs of regional assemblies. A. Shatilov and V. Nechaev, 'Regional'nye vybory: osobennosti tekhnologii i kharakter predpochtenii', *Svobodnaya Mysl'*, No. 6 (1997): 60.

10 E. V. Popova, 'Problemnye izmereniya elektoral'noi politiki v Rossii: gubernatorskie vybory v sravnitel'noi perspektive', *Polis*, No. 3 (2001): 47–62; S. Barzilov and A. Chernyshov, 'Manevry mestnoi elity: politika informatsii i manipuliatsii v regionakh', *Svobodnaya Mysl'*, No. 3 (2001): 35.

11 D. Slider, 'Pskov Under the LDPR: Elections and Dysfunctional Federalism in One Region', *Europe-Asia Studies*, 51, No. 5 (1999): 765–6.

12 C. Ross, *Federalism and Democratisation in Russia* (Manchester: Manchester University Press, 2002): 158–64.

13 Robert Orttung and Peter Reddaway, 'What Do the Okrug Reforms Add Up To? Some Conclusions', in *The Dynamics of Russian Politics: Putin's Reform of Federal-Regional Relations*, ed., R. Orttung and P. Reddaway (Boulder: Rowman & Littlefield, 2004), pp. 285–6.

14 J. C. Moses, 'Political-Economic Elites and Russian Regional Elections 1999–2000: Democratic Tendencies in Kaliningrad, Perm and Volgograd', *Europe-Asia Studies*, 54, No. 6 (2002): 912.

15 J. P. Goode, 'The Push for Regional Enlargement in Putin's Russia', *Post-Soviet Affairs*, 20, No. 3 (2004): 219–57; E. Huskey, 'Political Leadership and the Centre-Periphery Struggle: Putin's Administrative Reforms', in A. Brown and L. Shevtsova, ed., *Gorbachev, Yeltsin , and Putin: Political Leadership in Russia's Transition* (Washington, DC: Carnegie Endowment for International Peace, 2001), pp. 113–41; M. Hyde, 'Putin's Federal Reforms and their Implications for Presidential Power in Russia', *Europe-Asia Studies*, 53, No. 5 (2001): 719–43; P. Reddaway and R. W. Orttung, eds, *The Dynamics of Russian Politics: Putin's Reform of Federal-Regional Relations*, vol. 1 (Boulder: Rowman & Littlefield, 2003); R. Turovskii, 'Federal'nye okruga: politiko-geograficheskii podkhod v teorii i na praktike', *Federalizm*, No. 1 (2003): 217–50.

16 *Kommersant* (14 September 2004).

17 *Izvestiya* (13 September 2004); *Rossiiskaya Gazeta* (14 September 2004).

18 Putin's other proposals were not insignificant, particularly the elimination of single member district voting for the State Duma, though a full discussion of these additional changes would go well beyond the boundaries of the present analysis.

19 While such extensive changes normally would require about two months of work to produce a draft law, Putin's team produced a bill within two weeks. *Izvestiya* (28 September 2004).

20 *Izvestiya* (29 September 2004).

21 *Stenogramma zasedanii Gosdumy* (29 October 2004): 56–8.

22 N. Gul'ko, 'Rus' vertikal'naya', *Kommersant-Vlast'* (20 September 2004): 16.

23 In other words, that governors should be appointed in the same manner that the president appoints the prime minister.

24 *Kommersant-Vlast'* (20 September 2004).

25 *Rossiiskaya Gazeta* (15 September 2004).

26 *Kommersant* (14 September 2004); *Vremya Novostei* (14 September 2004).

27 *Stenogramma zasedanii Gosdumy* (29 October 2004): 61.

28 Ibid., p. 57.

29 *Kommersant* (30 September 2005).

30 A. Konitzer, *Voting for Russia's Governors: Regional Elections and Accountability under Yeltsin and Putin* (Washington, DC: Woodrow Wilson Centre Press, 2005), p. 6.

31 *Kommersant* (18 November 2004).

32 *Gazeta* (15 June 2005); *Kommersant* (16 June 2005); *Rossiiskaya Gazeta* (22 December 2005).

33 *Vremya Novostei* (14 September 2004).

34 The following summarises speeches in: *Stenogramma zasedanii Gosdumy* (29 October 2004): 65–75.

35 *Stenogramma zasedanii Gosdumy* (1 December 2004): 34–6.

36 The vote was 358–62 with 2 abstentions: *Stenogramma zasedanii Gosdumy* (3 December 2004): 19–21.

37 *Rossiiskaya Gazeta* (9 December 2004).

38 Federal'nyi zakon Rossiiskoi Federatsii ot 11 dekabrya 2004 g. N 159-FZ 'O vnesenii izmenenii v Federal'nyi zakon "Ob obshchikh printsipakh

organizatsii zakonodatel'nykh (predstavitel'nykh) i ispolnitel'nykh organov gosudarstvennoi vlasti sub'ektov Rossiiskoi Federatsii" i v Federal'nyi zakon "Ob osnovnykh garantiyakh izbiratel'nykh prav i prava na uchastie v referendume grazhdan Rossiiskoi Federatsii"', Published in *Rossiiskaya Gazeta* (15 December 2004).

39 Ukaz Prezidenta Rossiiskoi Federatsii ot 27 dekabrya 2004 g. N 1603: 'O poriadke rassmotreniya kandidatur na dolzhnost' vysshego dolzhnostnogo litsa (rukovoditelya vysshego ispolnitel'nogo organa gosudarstvennoi vlasti) sub'ekta Rossiiskoi Federatsii'. Published in *Rossiiskaya Gazeta*, (29 December 2004).

40 Ukaz Prezidenta Rossiiskoi Federatsii ot 29 iyunya 2005 g. N 756: 'O vnesenii izmenenii v Polozhenie o poryadke rassmotreniya kandidatur na dolzhnost' vysshego dolzhnostnogo litsa (rukovoditelya vysshego ispolnitel'nogo organa gosudarstvennoi vlasti) sub'ekta Rossiiskoi Federatsii, utverzhdennoe Ukazom Prezidenta Rossiiskoi Federatsii ot 27 dekabrya 2004 g.' N 1603. Published in *Rossiiskaya Gazeta* (2 July 2004).

41 *Izvestiya* (14 September 2004). For samples of other governors' reactions see: *Strana.ru* (14 September 2004); *Nezavisimaya Gazeta* (20 September 2004).

42 *Izvestiya* (23 September 2004).

43 For their statements regarding Putin's proposals, see: *Kommersant* (26 October 2004).

44 *Nezavisimaya Gazeta* (12 November 2004).

45 E. A. Chebankova, 'The Limitations of Central Authority in the Regions and the Implications for the Evolution of Russia's Federal System', *Europe-Asia Studies*, 57, No. 7 (2005): 941–2.

46 For a discussion of explanations for this lapse in 2004, see: D. Kamyshev, 'Altai-boltai i drugie', *Kommersant-Vlast'* (12 April 2004): 14–16.

47 A. Brown, 'Vladimir Putin and the Reaffirmation of Central State Power', *Post-Soviet Affairs*, 17, No. 1 (2001): 45–55.

48 For discussion of the Kremlin's apparent losses, see: *Vedomosti* (23 December 2003); I. Bulavinov, 'Bez Kremlya v golove', *Kommersant-Vlast'* (24 February 2003): 20–1, Y. Shabaev, 'Nenets Race Heads Into Runoff', *Russian Regional Report* (2 February 2005), V. Ulyadurov, Elista, and A. Barakhova, 'Vybory. Respublika Kalmykiya', *Kommersant-Vlast'* (14 October 2002): 24.

49 Bulavinov, 'Bez Kremlya v golove', p. 21.

50 This is not to say that term limits were strictly imposed – on the contrary, the Kremlin made special exception for regional leaders deemed necessary for maintaining local order. *Kommersant* (25 January 2001).

51 The one exception was Koriak AO Governor Vladimir Loginov, who became the first governor to be sacked owing to the 'loss of the President's confidence'. *Kommersant* (10 March 2005); *Kommersant* (8 April 2005). Governors are lodging appeals increasingly in advance of the expiry of their term in office, rather than waiting until the last moment to avoid the nomination process.

52 *Izvestiya* (24 March 2005).

53 *Segodnya* (15 February 2001); *Kommersant* (15 February 2001).

54 *Kommersant* (3 August 2005); *Nezavisimaya Gazeta* (3 August 2005).

55 *Gazeta* (18 November 2005).

56 *Kommersant* (21 September 2005).

57 *Gazeta* (24 October 2005).

58 H. E. Hale, 'Explaining Machine Politics in Russia's Regions: Economy, Ethnicity, and Legacy', *Post-Soviet Affairs*, 19, No. 3 (2003): 240.

59 In 2006, the Regional Development Ministry proposed a list of 134 criteria that would be used to evaluate governors' performance. *Novye Izvestiya* (12 October 2006). After Dmitrii Kozak was named Minister for Regional Development in September 2007, he began working on new proposals to decentralise economic control while strengthening performance-based accountability to the Kremlin. D. Slider, 'Russian Federalism: Can It Be Rebuilt from the Ruins?', *Russian Analytical Digest*, No. 43 (2008): 2–4.

60 *Izvestiya* (4 July 2005).

61 *Kommersant* (26 October 2004); *Nezavisimaya Gazeta* (27 October 2004).

62 *Rossiiskaya Gazeta* (28 October 2004); *Parlamentskaya Gazeta* (29 October 2004).

63 *Rossiiskaya Gazeta* (4 November 2004).

64 For a sampling of comments by regional parliamentary deputies, see: *Altaiskaya Pravda* (16 November 2004); *Kaliningradskaya Pravda* (15 September 2004); *Saratovskie Vesti* (28 October 2004).

65 E. Chebankova, 'The Unintended Consequences of Gubernatorial Appointments in Russia, 2005–6', *Journal of Communist Studies and Transition Politics*, 22, No. 4 (2006): 457–84.

66 Ibid., p. 476.

67 *Kommersant* (21 March 2005); *Izvestyia* (1 April 2005); *Gazeta* (5 April 2005); *Nezavisimaya Gazeta* (29 April 2005).

68 *Regnum.ru* (11 May 2005).

69 *Izvestiya* (6 May 2005).

70 D. Guseva, 'Dobrovol'no-prinuditel'naya otstavka', *Politcom.ru* (8 June 2005).

71 Though Karlin had previous career experience in Altai *Krai*, he had not worked in the region since the late 1980s. *Kommersant* (18 August 2005); *Izvestiya* (12 September 2005).

72 Federal'nyi zakon Rossiiskoi Federatsii ot 31 dekabria 2005 g. N 202-FZ 'O vnesenii izmenenii v stat'yu 18 Federal'nogo zakona "Ob obshchikh printsipakh organizatsii zakonodatel'nykh (predstavitel'nykh) i ispolnitel'nykh organov gosudarstvennoi vlasti sub'ektov Rossiiskoi Federatsii" i v Federal'nyi zakon "O politicheskikh partiyakh"'.

73 *Vedomosti* (17 June 2008); *Nezavisimaya Gazeta* (23 June 2008).

4
Back to the Future? Thoughts on the Political Economy of Expanding State Ownership in Russia

William Tompson[1]

The period since early 2004 has seen a significant expansion of the direct role of the Russian state in owning and managing industrial assets, particularly in 'strategic sectors' of the economy, such as power-generation machines, aviation, oil and finance. Policy seems to have been focused less on market reforms than on tightening the state's grip on the 'commanding heights' of the economy. Many factors have contributed to this shift – factional, ideological, geopolitical and conjunctural – and, as will be argued below, there is not one single process at work, but several. This chapter seeks to understand what has been driving the expansion of state ownership in Russia over the recent past and what that expansion might imply for the future. Its central conclusion is that a great deal of the explanation for this trend is in fact structural. While press coverage and public discussion, particularly ahead of the Putin succession in 2008, focused largely on factional rivalries among Kremlin 'clans' and on the political conjuncture between the Kremlin and big business, a deeper understanding of the growth of the state requires an examination of the interaction between state capacities and Russia's industrial structure. Here, as elsewhere, the strength and weakness of institutions matter – specifically, the weakness of state institutions outside the executive branch and the executive's own combination of highly developed coercive capacities and administrative weakness.[2]

The chapter begins with a look at the scale and scope of the expansion of state ownership. This is followed by an analysis of the interaction between Russia's economic structure and its political institutions, which highlights the role that the characteristics of specific branches of industry may play in Russia's political economy. The oil industry receives particular attention in this context. Finally, the chapter looks briefly at the implications of recent trends for Russia's future and at the potential impact of the economic contraction of 2008–09 on those trends.

The scope of expanding state ownership

The trend towards state expansion after 2003 was unmistakable. To be sure, the Russian government has continued throughout the recent past to stress its commitment to further privatisation and to economic development based on private entrepreneurship and competitive markets; individual acquisitions have consistently been explained as 'one-off' events dictated by the specific circumstances of particular companies or sectors. Each is in some way exceptional. Yet the scale and scope of the expansion have been remarkable (Table 4.1). The state-owned share of Russia's equity market capitalisation rose from just 20% in mid-2003 to an estimated 35% in early 2007.[3] To some extent, of course, this reflects the fact that the state's shareholdings are concentrated in oil and other minerals sectors, and the values of those companies have out-performed the market as a whole. However, that is far from the whole story: at the end of 2003, the state held about 11% of the voting shares in Russia's 20 largest companies by market capital-isation. Three years later, the figure was 40% and rising. Since the com-position of the top 20 changed very little, this increase reflected state acquisitions rather than changes in relative stock prices.[4] Indeed, between September 2004, when ConocoPhillips acquired 7.6% of Lukoil from the government, and October 2006, when a $30bn merger between aluminium giants RUSAL and SUAL was announced, no major industrial or financial asset in Russia passed into the hands of a new *private* owner: all major changes of ownership involved acquisitions by the state or by state-owned companies.

After 2007, the trend waned somewhat: there were no major acquisi-tions from the autumn of 2007 until the onset of the financial crisis, at which point a number of state-owned banks did acquire control of troubled financial institutions like Globex, Kit Finance, Sobinbank and Svyaz. Perhaps surprisingly, the Kremlin did not – as some had feared – take advantage of the crisis to take over further large industrial hold-ings in 'strategic' resource sectors, despite much speculation about the possible nationalisation of metals giants like Norilsk Nickel and RUSAL.[5]

The growth of the state has, of course, been most pronounced in the energy sector. In 2003, state-controlled companies accounted for about

Table 4.1 Major State Acquisitions, 2004–07

Company	Sector	Date	Mechanism
Guta Bank	Banking	August 2004	State-owned bank Vneshtorgbank purchases 85.8% stake with central bank support.
Mosenergo	Electric power	Summer–Autumn 2004	Gazprom raises its stake above "blocking" (25%+1) level.
Promstroibank St Petersburg	Banking	September 2004	Vneshtorgbank purchases a blocking (25%+1 share) stake.
Atomstroieksport	Nuclear construction	October 2004	Gazprom-controlled Gazprombank purchases 54% stake.
RAO UES	Electric power	Autumn 2004	Gazprom raises its stake to 10.5%.
Tuapse of oil refinery	Oil refining	December 2004	Rosneft purchases 40% from minority shareholders to take full control of the refinery.
Yuganskneftegaz	Oil and gas	December 2004	Rosneft purchases 76.8% stake from the firm OOO "Baikalfinansgrupp", the winner of a state-organised auction of Yuganskneftegaz shares to settle tax debts.
Tambeyneftegaz	Oil and gas	May 2005	Gazprombank purchases a 25% stake from Novatek.
Northgas	Oil and gas	June 2005	Gazprom regains control of independent gas producer Northgas, taking over a 51% stake following litigation.
Izvestiya (daily newspaper), Chas pik (weekly newspaper)	Media	June–September 2005	Gazprom-Media purchases control.

Table 4.1 Major State Acquisitions, 2004–07 – *continued*

Company	Sector	Date	Mechanism
Gazprom	Oil and gas	July 2005	State-owned Rosneftegaz purchases 10.7% of Gazprom to raise state's direct stake in Gazprom above 50%.
Selkupneftegaz	Oil and gas	July 2005	Rosneft purchases 34% stake from independent gas producer Novatek.
Sibneft	Oil and gas	October 2005	State-owned gas monopoly OAO Gazprom buys 69.66% stake for $13.1bn.
Verkhnechonskneftegaz	Oil and gas	October 2005	Rosneft purchases 25.9% stake from Interros Holding.
AvtoVAZ	Autos	October 2005	State arms export concern Rosoboroneksport takes control over 62% and installs new management.
OMZ	Machine-building	November 2005	Gazprom-controlled Gazprombank purchases a 75% stake.
Ulan Ude Aviation Plant, Moscow Helicopter Plant, Kazan Helicopter Plant, Kamov Holding, Rosvertol, Moscow Machine-building Plant "Vpered", OAO "SMPP"	Aviation	2005	State-owned defence company Oboronprom takes control of these enterprises in the course of forming a single, state-controlled helicopter holding via the consolidation of shares already held by the state, purchase of additional shares and share swaps.
Power Machines (*Silovye mashiny*)	Machine-building	December 2005	Electricity monopoly RAO UES purchases 22.4% stake, raising its stake above 25%, and acquires voting rights to another 30.4% until end-2007.

Table 4.1 Major State Acquisitions, 2004–07 – *continued*

Company	Sector	Date	Mechanism
Udmurtneft	Oil	June 2006	Rosneft acquires a 51% stake from Sinopec after the latter buys 96.7% from TNK-BP for an estimated $3.5bn.
Sibneftegaz	Gas	June 2006	Gazprombank purchases a 51% stake from Itera.
Novatek	Gas	June–July 2006	Gazprom purchases a 19.9% stake for a sum reportedly exceeding $2bn.
VSMPO-Avisma	Titanium	September 2006	State arms export concern Rosoboroneksport purchases 41% stake for an undisclosed sum.
Komsomol'skaya pravda	Media	November 2006	Gazprom-Media buys the popular daily.
Yamal SPG	Gas	November 2006	Gazprombank-invest and Gazprominvestkholding buy 25.1% and 74.9% respectively, securing Gazprom's control over the Yuzhno-Tambey gas condensate deposit.
Sakhalin-2 PSA	Oil and gas	December 2006–April 2007	Under December 2006 agreement, Gazprom in April pays $7.45bn to Shell, Mitsui and Mitsubishi for 50% plus one share of the project.
Yukos legacy assets	Oil and others	March–July 2007	Rosneft and Gazprom win bankruptcy auctions for stakes in Tomskneft, VSNK, Samaraneftegaz, Yukos Ladoga, Belgorodnefteprodukt, Bryansknefteprodukt, Voronezhnefteprodukt, Lipetsknefteprodukt, Oryolnefteprodukt, Penzanefteprodukt, Tambovnefteprodukt, Ulyanovsknefteprodukt, U-Tver, Yukos Petroleum, Aviaterminal, Yukos Aviation and Unitex.

Table 4.1 Major State Acquisitions, 2004–07 – *continued*

Company	Sector	Date	Mechanism
Rusia Petroleum	Gas	June 2007	Gazprom buys 62.9% from TNK-BP for a reported $800m.
ZIO Podolsk	Machine-building	September 2007	78.6% stake acquired by EMAl'yans-Atom, in which the state-owned Atomenergomash holds a majority stake.
Northern Taiga Neftegaz	Oil and gas	October 2007	Gazprom Neft raises stake in joint venture with Chevron from 30% to 75%.
Ural'skoe zoloto	Gold and molybdenum	October 2007	VSMPO Avisma buys 33% stake from UGMK, with the express intent of eventually acquiring majority control.

Note: The table excludes acquisition of foreign assets by state-owned companies.
Source: OECD from various sources.

16.0% of crude production. By early 2007, that figure had exceeded 40% and was still rising.[6] However, as Table 4.1, above, and Figure 4.1, below, make clear, the expansion of the state encompassed a wide range of sectors, many of which it would be hard to call 'strategic', even on the most elastic understanding of that concept. From a domestic political perspective, the expansion in media is perhaps most disturbing, reinforcing, as it does, concerns about the further erosion of democratic freedoms in Russia. There has also been a wide variation in the circumstances that have prompted the state or state-owned companies to expand their holdings: the state has intervened in response to perceived market failures (such as the troubles at AvtoVAZ and in the military aviation sector) and also in response to apparent market success (Yukos). In the banking sector, the criteria sometimes appear political rather than economic: after the onset of the financial crisis, institutions were rescued, and taken into state ownership, that could not in any sense be regarded as systemically important. This has prompted concerns that the criterion applied was not so much 'too big to fail' as 'too (politically) connected to fail'. And while the government has initiated or supported some of the acquisitions as part of its industrial policies, cash-rich state companies have been behind much of the activity – sometimes over the vociferous objections of leading ministers but apparently with the implicit backing of officials in the Presidential Administration.

The legal and political onslaught launched against the oil company Yukos in the summer of 2003 has, of course, been the most visible and controversial sign of the shift towards greater state control. The

Figure 4.1 The State-owned Share of Listed Companies by Sector, 2008

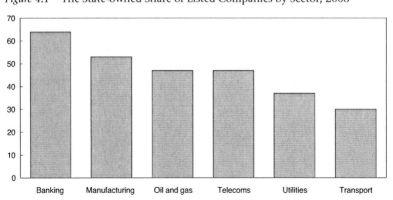

Source: OECD (2009).

expropriation of Yukos' assets in a series of auctions to settle tax debts and bankruptcy claims has represented the largest and most crudely engineered instance of re-nationalisation to date.[7] Nevertheless, the Yukos case remains unique as an instance of straightforward, judicially administered expropriation: no other company has found itself under the kind of pressure brought to bear on Yukos, and most other state acquisitions have involved at least the appearance of orderly commercial transactions. Appearances notwithstanding, however, the fact is that the state has certainly not been paying fair market value for its new acquisitions: many of the businesses listed in Table 4.1 changed hands after their previous owners came under mounting regulatory, legal and political pressure. Various members of the Sakhalin oil and gas consortia came under such pressure prior to selling stakes to Gazprom and Rosneft, and so did the owners of Tambeyneftegaz, Nortgaz, Novatek and Rusia Petroleum, to name but four. In the case of AvtoVAZ, the takeover in late 2005 was executed without any formal purchase being necessary. Thus, while the methods used to bring assets back into state ownership have generally been somewhat more civilised than the heavy-handed tactics used against Yukos, they have often involved a degree of coercion that would be hard to reconcile with any genuine respect for property rights. The *methods* by which the state has been making acquisitions are thus as much a source of concern as is the *fact* of increasing state ownership.

It would be a mistake to see this expansion of the state as proceeding according to some well-defined plan – different groups appear to be pursuing different agendas, often in competition with one another. However, the process is neither random nor chaotic: there is clearly a coherent *approach* towards resource sectors, which merit special consideration, and the general context has been favourable towards state expansion in general. The once bankrupt Russian state found by 2003 that it had both the cash and the coercive capacity to acquire what it wanted, and private owners were unpopular and widely regarded by the public as illegitimate, which made them particularly vulnerable to official pressure.[8] Moreover, the authorities in Russia, anxious to pursue ambitious development goals very rapidly, appear increasingly impatient of indirect methods of economic governance, such as regulation, and wary of the uncertainties involved in reliance on market-based solutions. For politicians in a hurry, direct intervention offers a degree of (apparent) control and certainty about outcomes that reliance on markets cannot. All this, then, makes for an environment in which a large number of state actors have the means, the motive and the opportunity to extend the state's control over important industrial and financial assets.

Russian industrial structure and state control

Underlying all of the above considerations is the industrial structure that Russia inherited from the Soviet Union. When a state's production/ export structure is highly concentrated – as Russia's undoubtedly is – the character of its leading sector(s) can shape its political economy, especially if state institutions are relatively weak.[9] The politics of state ownership are thus influenced by the sectoral characteristics not only of Russia's mineral sectors but also of much of its heavy manufacturing.

The problem may be summarised as follows. An unusually large share of Russian industrial production is generated by sectors that are capital intensive and characterised both by a high degree of asset specificity[10] and significant economies of scale. Such sectors tend to be subject to very high barriers to entry and exit, and are generally dominated by a small number of large companies. This presents two political problems, which can be particularly acute in situations of state weakness. First, as Pekka Sutela has observed, someone must own these companies.[11] Secondly, regardless of who owns them, such companies tend to be very demanding vis-à-vis the state: their size means that they are likely to be very politically powerful and their asset specificity is likely to make them relatively inflexible – that is, faced with changing economic circumstances, they find it difficult to adapt and instead lobby the government to adapt its policies in order to support or protect them. Faced with such companies, weak states, in particular, often find state ownership appealing, as they feel threatened by the power of private owners, whether foreign or domestic. Where the state's administrative, extractive and regulatory capacities are weak, state leaders may fear exploitation by private owners, whom they will find difficult to govern. They may also fear 'state capture'.[12] Moreover, if the polity is insufficiently robust, conflicts among domestic private owners could prove difficult to contain and might even be destabilising: one need only recall some of the '*kompromat* wars' in Russia's recent past to see the relevance of this concern for Russia's rulers. Finally, foreign domination of leading sectors may be seen as politically unacceptable to sovereignty-conscious elites, particularly where natural resources are concerned. Clearly, if foreign ownership is rejected and domestic private ownership is regarded as dangerous, then state ownership remains the only feasible solution.[13]

That, to put the matter very briefly, is what seems to have happened in Russia. Given its industrial structure, Russia would probably have a fairly high concentration of ownership of industrial assets in any circumstances, but this concentration was even greater in the early 2000s as a result of the flawed privatisation processes of the 1990s, which were largely geared to excluding foreigners and ensuring that the country's most valuable industrial assets passed into the hands of a few very well connected businessmen. The state thus found itself faced with the need to govern an economy dominated by a small number of relatively large private companies – companies, moreover, whose owners had demonstrated their willingness to meddle extensively in electoral and policy-making processes in order to advance their interests. Both the legal order in Russia and the state's administrative and regulatory capacities were and are weak.[14] There was thus an obvious temptation to rely on direct control rather than on contract, regulation and taxation. In the Russian case, this temptation was probably all the greater precisely because, whatever its other weaknesses, the Russian state possesses very substantial coercive capacities, capacities that are arguably out of all proportion to any of its other capabilities.[15] This combination of state strengths and weaknesses also explains the tendency of the Russian state to resort to nationalisation in all circumstances: whether faced with an oil price-fuelled consumption boom or an economy in the throes of a severe contraction, successive governments have stepped in and taken direct control over enterprises, in part because other, less direct instruments of policy are non-existent, perceived as too weak or simply too slow and indirect.

Re-nationalising the oil sector: the return of the 'obsolescing bargain'?

The foregoing arguments apply with particular force to minerals sectors, particularly oil. Most major oil-producing countries have state-dominated industries, and this is also true, albeit to a lesser extent, of many other mineral sectors. Indeed, Russia prior to 2003 was the only major oil exporter in the world with a predominantly private oil industry. The leading role of the private sector was an anomaly, and it might thus be argued that Russia has merely moved towards the international norm.[16]

If we ask *why* major mineral sectors tend to be state-dominated worldwide, at least two factors, in addition to those discussed above, would seem to merit attention. First, state ownership of the subsoil is almost universal; if private companies are to be involved in resource extraction, then they will act as the state's agents rather than as resource owners in their own right. The contracts involved will therefore need to be very well designed and very carefully monitored in order to ensure that agency losses are kept to a minimum and that the state's property rights are not violated. The more technically complex the conditions of extraction, the more difficult this will be.[17] Secondly, politicians are likely to want to dispose of resource rents as freely as possible, particularly in societies where democratic accountability is in any case low. Capturing resource rents from private agents via contract and taxation may be more efficient than reliance on direct control, but it is also more transparent than reliance on a state-owned company, whose cash flows and investment plans can be manipulated for political or personal gain. This is particularly true in Russia, given the degree to which the budget reforms of the past decade and the creation of a functioning treasury have reduced the scope for hidden manipulation of the federal budget on the kind of scale that was previously possible. If politicians wish to maximise their freedom to appropriate the rents for themselves or to allocate them to favoured constituencies, they will prefer opacity.

In such circumstances, nationalisation may appear a simple solution. Greater direct control makes it easier for state elites to appropriate and allocate resource rents; and managing a state-owned company may be – or may *appear* to be – easier than trying to govern powerful private players. In short, weak institutions tempt rulers to opt for feasible, if sub-optimal, solutions – in this case, a reliance on direct control and coercion rather than contract, regulation and taxation. The solutions adopted, in turn, create obstacles to institutional improvements, as second-best solutions often help to entrench the very weaknesses that gave them birth. Ironically, the same institutional weaknesses that generate incentives to rely on direct control also undermine the state's ability to manage state-owned companies well. Where institutions like the rule of law and the administrative capacities of the state are weak, the creation of large state companies is likely to be associated with high levels of opacity, corruption and rent-seeking by insiders, who will be tempted to run the companies for their own benefit and will face strong incentives to resist increased transparency and accountability.

These considerations suggest that it is not the re-nationalisations of the mid-2000s that need explaining but the privatisation policies of the 1990s. The real puzzle may be the emergence of a private oil industry in Russia in the first place. The story is in fact fairly well known[18] and may be summarised very roughly as follows. A politically fragile regime succumbed to pressure from powerful regional, industrial and financial interests to break up and privatise the oil industry. In return, it gained badly needed domestic political support. Brief as it is, this two-sentence account points to some of the reasons for the reversal of course in the early 2000s.

To understand what has happened, it may be helpful to look first at the histories of an earlier generation of oil-producing states. Until the 1960s, a handful of international oil companies dominated the market, and oil-producing states had little option but to accept a substantial degree of foreign ownership and control over their reserves. Oil-producing states' need to attract large-scale investment gave the oil companies tremendous leverage over taxation, regulatory policies and questions of institutional design. Over time, however, the original bargains between the oil companies and host governments 'obsolesced',[19] as local elites' leverage increased. This resulted from a combination of learning within the state administration and the emergence of smaller competitors to the international majors, competitors who were willing to cede more revenue and greater managerial control to host governments in order to capture market share from their larger rivals. Governments also profited from the rise of western oil services companies, which provided yet another way to access the kind of technology and expertise that the majors provided. In these circumstances, developing countries were able to conclude more favourable contracts with foreign investors, and in many cases, to nationalise their respective oil sectors outright. The capital-intensive nature of oil extraction helped, of course, since it imposed high barriers to exit when states began to revise the original bargains.[20]

It is not difficult to see elements of the obsolescing bargain at work in Russia today. In the 1990s, a very weak regime made concessions to investors that it probably would not have made in other circumstances. These concessions became less palatable as oil prices rose, and the state's extractive and coercive capacities recovered. The role of the oil boom should not be overlooked here: a host government's assessment of the cost–benefit ratio of its original bargain with investors is more likely to deteriorate if the investment is more profitable than anticipated. Dramatic oil price increases thus put that bargain under strain – and would have done so even in the absence of the kind of political conflicts that led to the state's confrontation with Yukos in 2003. The state's new assertiveness is hardly a surprise. David Woodruff points to a more general problem of which this is but one example: when institutions are still relatively weak and in a state of flux, sharp jumps in the value of assets can make it harder to stabilise/secure property rights.[21] The greater the incentives for predators to try to seize assets, the stronger a property rights regime needs to be. Dramatic jumps in asset values increase those incentives, prompting agents to work all the harder to circumvent or simply overcome whatever legal or institutional protections are in place.

Asset allocation and the emerging political order

These arguments about economic structure and obsolescing bargains should not by any means be taken to imply that factors such as ideology, 'clan' politics, geopolitical calculations or rent-seeking do not matter. On the contrary, they clearly form an important part of the story. As Thomas Remington observes, the expansion of state ownership and control during Vladimir Putin's second term occurred against the backdrop of a process whereby the Kremlin used an ever expanding array of commercial and fiscal activities of the state to reward its supporters.[22] The shifts in economic policy in evidence since 2003 seem to be closely linked to the construction of a dominant-party regime around United Russia. Thus, Remington argues that

> ... although much of the legislation the Duma passed consisted of measures centralising power... the Duma also, at the president's behest, created a number of new state corporations, social spending programs, and state investment funds. These initiatives generate substantial opportunities to provide jobs and income streams for state officials, Duma deputies, and party functionaries. In effect, parliament entered into a grand bargain with the president, delegating wide autocratic power to Putin in return for a plethora of patronage opportunities for the elite.[23]

It is here, of course, that one sees the political links between the growth of state ownership and the larger process of redefining the state's economic role described in the 2006 OECD Survey.[24] Whatever their other merits, the creation of a large number of new state-owned companies and other 'development institutions', the so-called 'priority national projects' and a host of other distributive policies pursued during Putin's second term all served to extend still further the potential patronage resources that could be used to solidify United Russia's hegemony. In short, recent trends in economic policy dovetailed nicely with the evolution of the regime itself.

It is important to emphasise that political leadership *does* matter. Institutional weaknesses do not predetermine policy choices, in Russia or elsewhere, but they *do* structure the choices political leaders face: the opportunities for pursuing private/factional interests, geopolitical ambitions or ideological visions via (*de facto* or *de jure*) nationalisation are largely defined by the structural features of the situation. This suggests, in turn, that the recent expansion of state control in Russia's 'strategic' sectors will not soon be reversed. While the political conjuncture could quickly change, the underlying structure of the Russian economy will evolve more slowly. It would therefore be unwise to expect a sharp reversal in the coming years; those who believe that the Medvedev era will see a new wave of large-scale privatisation, as the incumbent elite tries to 'cash out', are likely to be disappointed. Indeed, the months leading up to Dmitrii Medvedev's accession to the presidency witnessed an acceleration of efforts to consolidate state control over assets in some quarters – most notably in the exceptionally ambitious expansion drive of the newly formed state company 'Russian Technologies'. In principle, Russian Technologies was created to help attract investment to Russia's troubled high-tech sector. However, its mission grew ever more blurred as its ambitions expanded, and by early 2008 the company had acquired, or was in the process of pursuing, assets in everything from passenger airlines to the production of railway wagons to copper mining. In December 2007, the company reportedly submitted to the government a list of no fewer than 250 state assets that it wished to consolidate under its aegis – a move widely seen as part of the elite scramble for assets ahead of the Putin succession.

It is striking, therefore, that the expansion of the state seemed to slow markedly after Medvedev's accession: even the economic and financial crisis of 2008–09 did not trigger the kind of aggressive renationalisation of troubled industrial companies that many had predicted. This represents one of the few pieces of evidence in support of the view that Medvedev and his circle are somewhat more 'liberal' than the Putin team. Neither, however, has the Medvedev presidency yet led to a renewed wave of privatisation. While privatisation returned to a prominent place on the political agenda in 2009, as the authorities struggled to cope with the fall-out from the financial and economic crisis, there were still few signs of plans for a reversal of the state's take-over of the 'commanding heights' of the economy. If insiders wish to profit from privatisation, they are likely to prefer the sale of minority stakes, which would enable them to profit from the process, while leaving the bulk of the companies involved in state hands.

The implications of state expansion for economic performance

The likelihood that the recent expansion of state control will persist makes it all the more important to understand what these shifts imply for the performance of the sectors affected. Economically speaking, the expansion of state ownership in Russia since 2004 must be regarded as bad news. A large and growing body of research confirms that privately owned companies generally perform better than state-owned firms or those in mixed ownership, especially in sectors characterised by robust competition.[25] There is little reason to think that Russia will prove an exception to this rule. On the contrary, the Russian state's poor track record when it comes to owning and operating businesses would suggest the opposite: it has proved to be an exceptionally ineffective owner. At issue, then, is not merely the general question of state versus private ownership but the capacity of the Russian state, in particular, to manage large companies in technically complex sectors, given the country's institutional weaknesses.

A number of problems are already becoming apparent. First, policy-making in sectors where the state is particularly active tends to be characterised by long delays, frequent reversals of course and the prevalence of non-commercial considerations. Nowhere is this more evident than in the oil sector: the authorities have delayed reform of the subsoil legislation for years on end, while continuing to use the defects of the current licensing regime to pressure companies. Even apparently clear decisions, such as the much-discussed Gazprom–Rosneft merger, can be reversed almost without warning. Not surprisingly, the contradictions and delays that afflict government decision-making in most spheres of policy also affect the corporate decision-making of the companies it controls. This not only undermines the performance of state companies, it also creates problems for the remaining private companies in those sectors. The performance of private oil and gas companies like Lukoil and TNK-BP, in particular, has been affected by the state's expansion, which has raised questions about whether and to what extent they can expect a more or less level competitive playing field in future. Similar concerns have recently been raised about the distorting impact of large-scale state ownership on product markets in other sectors.[26] Part of the problem is that many of the new state-owned conglomerates that have been formed to manage recently acquired state assets are officially non-commercial and are neither limited liability companies nor state agencies. The legislative framework governing them is weak and is often *sui generis*, based on individual federal laws that specify in detail the aims, governance and structure of each. They can, and do, take ownership of state assets and budget funds without being subject either to the possibility of bankruptcy proceedings or budgetary scrutiny.

Secondly, the country's existing large state-owned companies are hardly models of good corporate governance,[27] and their recent histories suggest that expanded state ownership will result in poorer performance by the companies affected. In general, Russian state-owned companies are run for the benefit of corporate insiders and their patrons in the state administration. They also tend to be remarkable for their financial opacity, even in an economy as notoriously opaque as Russia's. Many observers have commented on their poor reporting practices. This lack of transparency makes them attractive sources of funding for informal political or policy initiatives that, for various reasons, the authorities wish to keep off-budget.

Yet rent-seeking and abuse of position are only part of the problem. Even if all the agents involved were honest, well qualified and competent, the system of corporate governance devised for the major Russian state-owned companies would ensure that they could not operate efficiently. The 'directive' system for agreeing the positions to be adopted by state representatives at board meetings is cumbersome and frequently ensures that decisions simply have to be put off – the state institutions involved are unable to agree common positions quickly enough. Moreover, the boards of state companies are dominated by state appointees, many of whom really do not understand either the board's role or the business itself and do not have incentives to invest time and effort into mastering these issues. While President Medvedev insisted that this should change and that private-sector executives should be recruited to the boards of state companies, there has been little evidence of any move in this direction, even in the case of Gazprom, which Medvedev himself once chaired. In any case, the whole notion of state representatives in mixed-ownership companies contradicts Russian companies law, which insists that board directors do not represent specific shareholder interests. *All* directors are jointly and severally responsible to *all* shareholders. The directive system clearly violates that principle.

A third, and related, problem stems from the tendency to appoint representatives of 'line ministries' to the boards of companies in the very sectors those ministries regulate; this leads to a conflation of regulatory and commercial functions. Far from effecting a clear separation of sectoral policy and ownership, the Russian government frequently combines the two. The direct involvement of line ministries in the governance of

state companies is only part of the problem: sometimes the state effectively vests regulatory functions in state companies like Gazprom and
Russian Railways. The major firm on a market may thus find itself regulating its rivals, with all the conflicts of interest that such an arrangement
entails.[28]

Unfortunately, it is not clear that the players involved have any incentive to correct these deficiencies. Too many of them have good reasons
not to want good corporate governance in state-owned companies. One
of the clearest indications of this is the continued existence of thousands
of state unitary enterprises (GUPs). These are state concerns that are not
even organised as corporations. The GUP was only ever intended to be a
transitional form of ownership – GUPs were either to be corporatised
(usually as a prelude to privatisation) or converted into treasury enterprises, operating as state bodies subject to tight financial controls. Because
GUPs were meant to be a temporary phenomenon, the legislative framework governing their activities was never fully elaborated. While amendments to Russian law in 2002 went some way to correcting this, the
legislation remains problematic: property rights are poorly regulated and
monitoring is weak. This has made the GUP a popular organisational
form for state enterprise managers and the bureaucrats who oversee them;
GUP managers and the state institutions that oversee particular GUPs
have often put up fierce resistance when attempts were made to corpor-
atise them. Even if no privatisation is envisaged, corporatisation involves
a degree of transparency and accountability that GUP insiders and their
patrons in the bureaucracy often wish to avoid.[29]

The overly complex structures of state-owned corporations similarly
reflect a desire to reduce transparency and accountability, by ensuring
that valuable assets are held in subsidiaries, or subsidiaries of subsidiaries,
of state-owned firms. Rosneftegaz, for example, was created solely in
order to serve as a vehicle for holding state shares in Rosneft that were
used as collateral for the financing of the state's purchase of Gazprom
shares held by Gazprom subsidiaries. When the credits used to finance
the purchase were paid off, Rosneftegaz was to be liquidated, and the
shares it held in Rosneft and Gazprom were to be transferred back onto
state's balance sheet. In fact, this did not happen, and the explanation
given for Rosneftegaz's continued existence was that it allowed for greater
'flexibility' in the management of the assets in question.[30] Keeping the
shares in question off the state's balance sheet ensured that they would
not fall under the provisions of privatisation legislation and thus could
be managed or even disposed of with far less scrutiny than otherwise.
Income generated by the management or sale of the shares would also

fall safely outside the norms of budgetary and privatisation legislation that would otherwise apply. Moreover, senior managers of large state companies often supplement their incomes by drawing large salaries for sitting on the boards of subsidiaries.[31] It takes little cynicism and less imagination to see insiders' interest at work here. Critics of Russian Technologies were quick to note that its breakneck expansion in early 2008 was proceeding on similar lines: by structuring the state corporation as a giant holding company, those in control of the concern preserved its right to dispose fairly freely of its subsidiaries and limited the scope for real government oversight.

Those who seek to defend the recent trend towards state control in Russia often point to the chaotic and often spectacularly corrupt privatisation processes of the 1990s and argue that a backlash was more or less inevitable. What has happened since 2003 might yet be seen as part of a broader process of correcting past abuses and creating a more orderly, stable set of property relations in Russia. However, in view of the often overt manipulation of political, legal and regulatory processes seen since 2003, one could not easily argue that the re-nationalisation of 'strategic enterprises' in Russia is being executed in any more transparent or honest a fashion than were the most notorious privatisations of the previous decade. Moreover, as unpopular as many of the privatisations of the 1990s and early 2000s proved to be, they undoubtedly brought real economic benefits in their wake, in terms of improved performance.[32] It would be difficult to argue that the re-nationalisation wave of 2004–07 has brought any benefits whatsoever to ordinary Russians, nor is it likely to do so in future. It likely rather to generate more rent-seeking, less efficiency and slower growth in some of Russia's most important economic sectors.

Notes

1   The author is a Senior Economist in the Economics Department of the Organisation for Economic Cooperation and Development (OECD). The views expressed in this chapter are his own and do not necessarily reflect the position of the OECD or its member states.
2   On weakness of the judiciary, the parliament and the regions, see the chapters by Kahn, Remington and Goode in this volume.
3   C. Weafer and E. DePoy, 'Rossiiskie aktsii: Gosudarstvo kak benefitsiyar', Alfa-bank Research Note, 20 February 2006; *Vedomosti* (13 February 2007).
4   J. Bushueva, 'Market May Be Underplaying Election Risks', Aton Capital Strategy Research, Moscow (12 December 2006).
5   On those two companies, see *Vedomosti* (15 January 2009) and (23 March 2009).

6　These comparisons are based on 2003 production data; obviously, differences in the rate of production growth in 2004–05 have altered somewhat the relative shares of different companies in total output.

7　For a close look at the affair, see W. Tompson, 'Putting Yukos in Perspective', *Post-Soviet Affairs* 21: 2 (April–June 2005).

8　This is partly the authorities' doing. Russia's new private owners have never been popular, owing to memories of the chaotic and often criminal privatisation processes of the 1990s; however, the authorities have in recent years acted so as to undermine, rather than reinforce, the legitimacy of past privatisations and thus to keep these questions alive on the political agenda.

9　See, in particular, D. M. Shafer, *Winners and Losers: How Sectors Shape the Developmental Prospects of States* (Ithaca, NY: Cornell University Press, 1994).

10　In other words, assets to support particular purposes would have far lower value if they were redeployed for any other purpose and might, indeed, prove extremely expensive or even impossible to redeploy in any case.

11　P. Sutela, 'The Political Economy of Putin's Russia', *BOFIT Russia Review* 3 (March 2005), available at http://www.bof.fi/NR/rdonlyres/319EB069-3EDC-4E9C-A244-639A6ED697F7/0/BRR2005.pdf.

12　On the concept of 'state capture', with particular reference to transition countries, see J. Hellman, G. Jones and D. Kaufmann, '"Seize the State, Seize the Day": State Capture, Corruption and Influence in Transition', *World Bank Policy Research Working Paper*, 2444 (September 2000), www.worldbank.org/wbi/governance/pdf/seize_synth.pdf.

13　Cf. K. Chaudhry, 'The Myths of the Market and the Common History of Late Developers', *Politics & Society* 21: 3 (1993).

14　See, in this connection, Chapter 8 by Kahn in this volume.

15　Nor is nationalisation the only purpose for which they are used: it is often a matter of private companies 'voluntarily' undertaking social projects or infrastructure investment at the behest of the authorities. This is 'corporate social responsibility' *with attitude*.

16　As I have argued elsewhere, private domination of the oil sector was an anomaly, but it was a *positive* anomaly in economic terms; see R. Ahrend and W. Tompson, 'Realising the Oil Supply Potential of the CIS: The Impact of Institutions and Policies', *OECD Economics Department Working Papers*, No. 484, OECD, Paris (2006). The politics of the state's re-nationalisation of a large part of the oil industry are relatively easy to understand, but this development is unfortunate all the same.

17　For a discussion of this issue, see ibid.

18　For an overview, see D. Lane, *The Political Economy of Russian Oil* (New York: Rowman & Littlefield, 1999); A. Barnes, *Owning Russia: The Struggle over Factories, Farms and Power* (Ithaca: Cornell University Press, 2006); or S. Fortescue, *Russia's Oil Barons and Metal Magnates: Oligarchs and the State in Transition* (Basingstoke: Palgrave Macmillan, 2007).

19　For the original model of the 'obsolescing bargain', see: R. Vernon, *Sovereignty at Bay: The Multinational Spread of US Enterprise* (New York: Basic Books, 1971). See also P. Jones Luong, 'Rethinking the Resource Curse: Ownership Structure and Institutional Capacity', Paper prepared for the Conference on Globalization and Self-Determination, Yale University (14–15 May 2004); T. H. Moran, *Multinational Corporations and the Politics of Dependence: Copper in*

Chile (Princeton: Princeton University Press, 1974); and F. Tugwell, *The Politics of Oil in Venezuela* (Stanford, California: Stanford University Press, 1975).

20   Some argue that bargains between states and multinationals in manufacturing sectors are far less likely to obsolesce, in large part because their investments tend to be smaller, more mobile and more closely tied to knowledge-based, firm-specific advantages. See L. Eden, S. Lenway and D. A. Schuler, 'From the Obsolescing Bargain to the Political Bargaining Model', *Bush School Working Paper No. 403*, Texas A&M University (January, 2004): 6, available at http://bush.tamu.edu/research/working_papers/leden/Eden-Lenway-Schuler-FINAL-GBS.pdf.

21   D. Woodruff, 'Kogda nel'zya no ochen' khochetsya: korni nestabil'nosti sobstvennosti v Rossii', mimeo, Harvard University (21 June 2005), available at http://personal.lse.ac.uk/woodruff/_private/materials/kogdanelzia.pdf.

22   T. F. Remington, 'Patronage and the Party of Power: President-Parliament Relations under Vladimir Putin', *Europe–Asia Studies*, 60, No. 6 (August 2008): 959–87.

23   Ibid.: 975.

24   OECD, *OECD Economic Surveys: Russian Federation*, Organisation for Economic Cooperation and Development, Paris (2006): 33–40.

25   For an overview of international experience, see A. E. Boardman and A. R. Vining, 'Ownership and Performance in Competitive Environments: A Comparison of the Performance of Private, Mixed and State-Owned Enterprises', in E. E. Bailey and J. Rothenberg Pack (eds), *The Political Economy of Privatization and Deregulation* (Cheltenham, UK: Edward Elgar Publishing Ltd, 1995); on the Russian case, see W. Tompson, 'Privatisation in Russia: Scope, Methods and Impact' (University of London, October, 2002), available at http://www.bbk.ac.uk/polsoc/download/bill_tompson/. See also W. Megginson and J. Netter, 'From State to Market: A Survey of Empirical Studies on Privatization', *Journal of Economic Literature* 39: 2 (June 2001), available at http://faculty-staff.ou.edu/M/William.L.Megginson-1/prvsvpapJLE.pdf; S. Commander, M. Dutz and N. Stern, 'Restructuring in Transition Economies: Ownership, Competition and Regulation', Paper prepared for the Annual World Bank Conference on Development Economics, Washington, DC (28–30 April 1999), available at http://siteresources.worldbank.org/INTABCDEWASHINGTON1999/Resources/stern.pdf; and the work surveyed in J. Nellis, 'Time to Rethink Privatization in Transition Economies?' International Finance Corporation Discussion Paper No. 38 (1998), available at http://ifcln1.ifc.org/ifcext/economics.nsf/Attachments ByTitle/dp38/$FILE/dp38.pdf.

26   OECD, *OECD Economic Surveys: Russian Federation*, Organisation for Economic Cooperation and Development, Paris (2009).

27   See ibid., and OECD, 'Russian Corporate Governance Roundtable: Enforcement of Corporate Governance Rules and Corporate Governance of State-Owned Enterprises: Synthesis Note' (2–3 June 2005).

28   On these issues, see *OECD Economic Surveys* (2006 and 2009).

29   Ironically, managers have an incentive to resist, regardless of their motivations, since the benefits of corporatisation accrue to the owners, not management. For an honest, efficient and competent manager, corporatisation involves significant costs and no obvious benefits for him/her. Additional oversight and reporting will simply be a hassle. For any other manager, it

represents a threat, as his/her dishonesty, inefficiency or incompetence risk being exposed.

30 *Vedomosti* (24 and 27 July 2006) and (28 December 2006).
31 For details on the cases of Gazprom and Russian Railways, see *Vedomosti* (11 July 2007).
32 See Tompson, 'Privatisation in Russia'; and *OECD Economic Surveys* (2004, 2006, 2009).

5
Shortcut to Great Power: Russia in Pursuit of Multipolarity[1]

Julie Newton

No major power embraces the concept of a multipolar world order as fully as Russia does. Nor does any go as far in its rhetorical efforts to revise the unipolar global structure. Since the mid-1990s, Russia has declared an abiding ambition to replace the US-dominated international order with a multipolar one, in which emerging powers – with Russia in the vanguard – would join the highest ranks of the global system. Increasingly, multipolarity has informed the intellectual foundations of Russian thinking about international relations and, in turn, influenced the shape and content of foreign policy. It has served as Moscow's measuring stick for gauging Russian power relative to that of its competitors, not unlike the Soviet Union's notion of the 'correlation of East-West forces'. And it is viewed in Moscow as the best, if not the only, hedge against the emergence of narrow US-Chinese bipolarity, which could challenge and greatly circumscribe Russia.[2]

All this became particularly evident during Vladimir Putin's second presidential term, when, in the Kremlin's view, progress towards a multipolar international structure lurched forward due to America's mistakes, China's rise, Russia's luck and Putin's skill.[3] Russia's unexpectedly strong economic performance and favourable geopolitical situation after 2004 injected fresh confidence and added new muscle to Moscow's multipolar pursuits, prompting Russia to shift definitively from the integrated European power that it had striven to become from the late 1980s to the independent, Eurasian and rhetorically revisionist power that it finally became by 2004–05.

But the fact that Moscow embraced multipolarity with such unwavering conviction for so long is somewhat surprising. Multipolarity in international relations has a bad historical reputation. It is associated with war, instability and fragility, as ambitious poles of power compete in

Hobbesian anarchy.[4] Aware of these inherent dangers, Putin's Russia rhetorically stressed the importance of multilateral global governance. But multilateralism requires countries to surrender some sovereignty to international institutions in exchange for greater security and benefit for all, which contradicted an age-old Russian leitmotif upholding the inviolable sovereignty and independence of Russia in world affairs. In addition, multipolar diplomacy, with its emphasis on independence without integration, complicated Russia's chances for ongoing reform and formal integration into the global economy, both of which were necessary for Russia to take full advantage of globalisation.[5] Russia chose the opposite foreign policy path from China, a country that, despite its rhetorical support for multipolarity, refused in practice to try and unravel the US-led trade and economic system into which it is formally integrated and which has benefited it so well.[6] Furthermore, Russia's multipolar doctrine helped alienate the West. It encouraged the rise of other centres of power, such as Iran, whose ambition for great-power status via the acquisition of nuclear weapons was hardly universally welcomed in Moscow. And it was probably not the only, or even best, hedge to protect Russian interests in a US-Chinese bipolar world. Finally, while it is true that Putin confidently espoused multilateral multipolarity as part of a coherent, revisionist strategy (rhetorically, at least), Russian policies were often incoherent, contradictory and reactive. In practice, they were more about consolidating aspects of the status quo, including strengthening backward-looking tendencies towards extreme state-centrism in international relations, than about revising the international system towards multipolarity. As a result, Moscow's multipolarity policy was either unrealistic, or Moscow was vague or divided about its goals.

Given these problems and contradictions, why did Putin's Russia actively embrace multipolarity? This question, which goes to the heart of Russia's deepest goals, national identity and historical legacy, is the subject of this chapter. The answer boils down to the fact that multipolarity – or rather, 'multipolar diplomacy', to use Foreign Minister Sergei Lavrov's terminology[7] – was less important for itself than as an instrument to be used in pursuit of a higher goal: it served as a tool in Putin's quick-fix toolbox to ensure Russia's rapid return to great power. And *that* was the Kremlin's 'Holy Grail', the central foreign and domestic policy quest of the Putin Presidency. The emphasis here was on speed: multipolar diplomacy was employed to achieve that quest *quickly*.

Throughout history, great speed was deemed essential in all Russian modernisation campaigns because, in Russia's view, of the persistent and pernicious nature of external and internal threats to its very existence.

Given that Russia has been invaded by the West, and resisted those invasions, more than any other power in modern history, Russia has traditionally sought great power fast whenever it felt weak or perceived renewed threats to its external security or territorial integrity. By the dawn of the 21st century, Russia appeared at critical risk on both fronts, and was even fighting a war to keep itself together.

In response, Putin put Russia on a fast-track strategy to great power using three tools. As this chapter will argue, multipolar diplomacy became the *third* such tool to achieve quick economic and political renewal, rapid modernisation, great-power parity, and, wherever possible, global advantage. The other two included a domestic policy of authoritarianism and an economic policy of state capitalism. Together, these three instruments (authoritarianism, state capitalism and multipolar foreign policy) promoted Moscow's current 'shortcut' strategy to restore Russian grandeur in the eyes of the world in order to keep external and internal threats at bay.

Moscow's strategic 'shortcut' unfolded thus: though Russia in the 1990s was materially less powerful than in the recent past, it continued to view itself as a *velikaya derzhava* (great power) with distinct, indeed superior, qualities. Determined to regain international power quickly to protect its interests vis-à-vis the United States, Europe and a rising China, consolidate its influence within the former Soviet space, and retrieve a global role commensurate with its self-image as a 'great power', Russia adopted 'multipolar' foreign policies from 1996. Historically, this amounted to a variation on an old theme.[8] Russia's post-Soviet variation on this theme meant working for the long term to erect poles of power, starting with the EU and Russia, China, India and Brazil, whose combined economic clout could offset America and, in turn, increase the power of a temporarily enfeebled Russia.[9] The aim was to 'leverage' Russian power on the world stage through multi-vectored foreign policies, following the examples of Prince Gorchakov, the architect of Alexander II's diplomacy after Russia's Crimean War defeat, and President Charles de Gaulle, who sought to augment France's exhausted political power by similar means. Stating his particular admiration for de Gaulle, Putin pursued a Russian version of '*à tous azimuths*', though he softened, diluted and revised it during his first term to attenuate its implicit challenge to America and to encourage Washington's support for Russian membership in global economic institutions, such as the WTO. Officials of the Russian Ministry of Foreign Affairs (MID) thus replaced the word 'multipolarity' with 'multi-directionalism'.[10] In this view, a 'multidirectional' policy addressed

Russian interests in a world that was objectively becoming multipolar, but that policy was not pointedly aimed at undoing American dominance. From 2000 to 2003, Putin's Moscow eschewed the anti-American bravado of multipolarity and focused pragmatically on integrating Russia into Western economies. MID's 2000 Foreign Policy Concept stressed good relations with economic and political partners abroad before even mentioning Russia's aspiration for multipolarity.[11] Integrating Russia into the global economy drove Putin first to lean heavily in the European direction (2000–2001), then towards America, as he sought to capitalise on American gratitude for Russian support after the 11 September terrorist attacks, and then back to Europe, namely France and Germany, to block America's invasion of Iraq in 2003. But none of these westward tactical orientations paid off.

By late 2003, Putin was returning to a more multipolar and independent foreign policy, abandoning the softer multidirectional language of the preceding years in order to generate greater leverage, 'punch higher' and re-establish Russian greatness. But Putin understood that highly leveraged political power would be ineffective on its own – a message amplified by the failure of the Paris-Berlin-Moscow triumvirate to block America's invasion of Iraq. He had long understood that Russia's only solution was economic leverage, so he set out to build a global economic powerhouse in record time by riding the crest of globalisation while avoiding its dangers. To do that, he no longer showed any hesitation about embracing two other expedient – and historically recognisable – instruments for achieving greatness: state-dominated economic modernisation and a centralised, vertically structured polity. Taking advantage of turning-point events, such as the September 2004 Beslan hostage crisis and the January 2005 Orange Revolution in Ukraine, Putin accelerated Russia's progress towards state-capitalism and authoritarianism. In addition, he charted a more assertive multipolar foreign policy that shunned value-based, permanent alliances abroad and encouraged nationalism and anti-Westernism at home. These three instruments allowed Putin to take Russia, yet again, down a new variation of the same 'shortcut to greatness' that previous Russian rulers had taken – this time towards an energy-driven 'supercorporation' with global reach.[12]

Such a fast modernisation strategy raises huge questions and problems for Moscow and the world. First, where will this shortcut eventually take Russia? One possibility is that Putin's administration represented the beginning-of-the-end of Russia's 'great state transformation', which began over two decades ago.[13] If so, it raises the possibility that this shortcut might simply perpetuate the centuries-old pattern, whereby Russia falls behind the West, prompting state-led modernising campaigns to catch up, succeeded by falling behind the West again. Some suggest that Putin did not, and could not, break this old pattern, given the weight of Russia's authoritarian history,[14] as well as its institutional, economic and demographic weaknesses.[15] There was also a real risk that multipolar policies would exacerbate Russia's isolation from international institutions.

A more optimistic – and plausible – view is that the Putin era represents yet another transitional stage in the transformative process begun by Mikhail Gorbachev.[16] Putin's strategy, however historically familiar, could lead Russia to a freer and more prosperous place. After all, this most recent shortcut does differ from the past: it tolerates freedom of some printed media, travel and private property; and it heralds the slow rise of a property-holding middle class, necessary for political pluralism and democracy over the long run,[17] even if that class remains overly tied to the Kremlin for now.

In fact, however, there is nothing certain about the outcome of this shortcut. Whether or not it will lead Russia towards greater liberalism over the long term will depend on the nature of future leaderships in Russia, the kinds of political institutions they build, the kinds of ideas they hold, and the way they react to fast-changing events buffeting the country from inside and outside. It will rest on how Russia copes with its weighty absolutist tradition and its ambiguous identity, which, in times of turmoil, foment Russia's sense of insecurity. It will also depend on whether it can overcome its '*gosudar*' [master/owner] mentality', in which the social order is organised around a master and his dependents. This mentality, implicit in the Russian word for 'state', *gosudarstvo*, has historically made it difficult for generations of Russians to perceive society as anything other than a dependent or function of the state, which has complicated the rise of civil society.[18] It will depend, too, on the way Russian political and economic institutions evolve over the medium term, and on the quality of relations between Russia and the West. All these contingencies, to which we will return below, will require luck, wisdom and courage on the part of those inside *and* outside Russia.

The rest of this chapter will analyse one aspect of this important 'shortcut to greatness': Moscow's pursuit of a multipolar world order. Three parts follow. The first explores *causality*: why has Moscow historically pursued greatness with such urgency? And what are the sources of Putin's fast-track shortcut that predisposed Russian foreign policymakers towards multipolar pursuits? Three causes stand out: external threats, internal weakness and ideational factors, including ideas and identity. In the second part, there follows an *analysis* of Putin's multi-polar strategy itself, including the ultimate goals and underlying contradictions of this strategy during his second term. Finally, while avoiding judgement about the pros and cons of multipolarity, the last part looks at the *consequences* of Russia's multipolar 'shortcut to greatness' thus far, for both Russia and the world.

Throughout this story, history helps to highlight relevant patterns and dilemmas in the Russian experience that shed light on Putin's strategic choices. But history is in no way determinate, since the present and the future are shaped as much by contingency as history, if not more so.

Part I   Reasons for urgency in Russia's quest for greatness

It is commonplace to claim that Russia has a great power mentality and has sought great power status throughout much of its history.[19] Few eyebrows are raised anymore when Vladimir Putin asserts that 'Russia was and will remain a great power. It is preconditioned by the inseparable characteristics of its geopolitical, economic and cultural existence. They determined the mentality of Russians and the policy of the government throughout our history and they cannot help but do so now.'[20] To say that 'the Russian mentality is a great power mentality' hardly counts as news.[21]

The more interesting question is why. Why has greatness become Russia's 'Holy Grail', its ultimate strategic goal, especially when the quest for it has encouraged Russian leaders to choose variations on the same shortcut that historically have led to relative backwardness, persistent authoritarianism and poverty? The explanation lies in the three factors that caused Russia to seek greatness urgently.

1st cause: External threats

The first cause is external, geopolitical and over 500 years old. The rise of European power during the Renaissance compelled Russia – backwards and poorly endowed in natural defences – to find immediate ways to resist imperial Western might. During that time, as Marshall Poe points out, the outside world repeatedly marched into Russia. Since the 17th century, the Poles, Ottomans (twice), Swedes (twice), Prussians, French and Germans (twice) all invaded Russia.[22] And yet, despite its porous borders and open expanses, its relative poverty and weak society, Russia always succeeded in resisting the West. In fact, as Poe reminds us, Russia is the only modern non-European polity to have maintained its independence from European hegemony, and it has done so for five centuries.[23] This is because Russia staved off domination as well as internal dissolution by rapidly transforming itself via the *shortest and fastest* path possible into a modern power as great or greater than the West, even if the kind of greatness that Russia achieved (benefiting the state primarily) differed substantially from its European counterpart (benefiting the nation as a whole). While Western expansion or Western-led globalisation over the centuries may have encouraged Russia to cope with such challenges by seeking greatness,[24] Russia's own vested interests and historical habits, including those of authoritarianism, also played their part in tilting the choice between competing *forms* of greatness in favour of *derzhavnost'* [power for the Russian state]. In combination, all these factors encouraged Russia to choose *derzhavnost'* to ensure cohesion of internal forces and guarantee sovereignty from outside challenges that came historically from the West, but that today emanate from the East as well.

To President Putin in his second term, these external challenges appeared extensive and wide-ranging, and included economic, political and security threats from Western-led 'thick globalization' and expansion.[25] The greatest manifestation of these threats was NATO's ongoing assertive expansion deeper and deeper into former Soviet space, despite impassioned Russian protests, and US 'schemes' to inject flows of cash in the Commonwealth of Independent States (CIS) 'to meddle in our domestic affairs'.[26] In fact, said Putin, threats from the West to Russia were not diminishing. 'They were only transforming, changing their appearance', he argued. 'In these new threats, as during the time of the Third Reich, are the same contempt for human life and the same claims of exceptionality and diktat in the world.'[27] America and others want to 'pursue their own aims within our country, soften our position on important international aims and force us to make decisions that are in our partners' advantage'.[28] Later, he compared the threat to Russia from America's Ballistic Missile Defence Programme (BMD) to that to America during the Cuban Missile Crisis, 'when the Soviet Union put rockets in Cuba', and then suggested that BMD was worse, since 'such threats for our country are today being created [literally] on our own borders'.[29] In this same vein, President Putin also railed against the West for 'interfering in the internal affairs of other countries' by transforming the Organisation for Security and Co-operation in Europe (OSCE) and NGOs into 'vulgar instruments to promote foreign policy interests of one or a group of countries'.[30]

Worse, argued the Kremlin, Western campaigns to continue NATO expansion deeper into former Soviet states represented Western reactions to Russia's growing strength. The West hoped to eat into Russia's natural spheres of influence in order to undermine Russian authority and reverse the rising tide of change from unipolarity to multipolarity.[31] The West was pursuing a 'consciously provocative plan to transform the North Atlantic Alliance…into a global "union of democracies"' that deliberately excludes and *encircles* Russia and appears all the more threatening to Russia due to the US-led 'remilitarisation of international affairs' via initiatives such as NATO expansion and BMD.[32] Foreign Minister Lavrov argued that BMD was like the 'missing piece of the jigsaw puzzle' that revealed Washington's scheme to encircle Russia with anti-missile defence deliberately placed around its perimeter.[33] This was not a matter of Russian misunderstanding, Putin said, since Western intentions had become clear in the mid-1990s when the West broke its guarantee to Russia *not* to expand NATO beyond Germany and then excluded Russia at the most structural, essential levels of European security.[34] '…We have the right to ask: against whom is this expansion intended?… It is obvious that NATO expansion does not have any relation with…ensuring security in Europe. On the contrary, it represents a serious provocation…'.[35] Such Russian perceptions of deliberate Western provocation were sincere and, in turn, contributed to the pool of factors influencing the evolution of Russian foreign policy towards increasingly tougher lines against the West.

In response, Lavrov warned the US to go no further: do not cross 'red lines' inside the CIS.[36] Defending those 'red lines' and ensuring Russian sovereignty over its spheres of interest go to the heart of Russia's existentialist priorities, according to this Kremlin. 'Russia will either be independent and sovereign or will most likely *not exist at all*…'.[37] It will 'not exist', the thinking went, because the West's 'inculcated desire for a feeble and weak Russia' might succeed if Western encroachment into the CIS and Russia itself were left unchecked.[38] The only way to check the West and maintain the Eurasian status quo was to approximate parity with the United States (and superiority over the EU), and that meant great power *fast* via the most expedient shortcut.

2nd cause: Internal weaknesses

The second reason for Russia's urgent pursuit of great power was internal: great power was required to maintain internal cohesion. Russia's persistently weak society created a 'greatness dilemma', linking greatness of the Russian state to Russia's sovereignty and territorial integrity. 'Russia had to be a great power in order to remain a power at all', wrote Alfred Rieber.[39] Any weakening of power at the centre would intensify centrifugal forces on the periphery, leading to the possible disintegration of the Russian state. In the Yeltsin era, that possibility looked real enough. Russia's federal authority over far-flung Russian territories looked ominously weak after regional leaders extracted special financial privileges, exceptions from federal obligations, and autonomous powers of appointment from the federal centre in a 'parade of [bilateral] treaties'.[40] Consequently, Putin faced colossal problems, echoing excruciating periods in Russia's past and evoking its two most long-standing fears. First came fear of unstoppable internal dissolution due to loss of control by the centre, thereby encouraging external encroachment via continued NATO and EU expansion and democratisation. Second, Russia feared the loss of meaningful economic and political sovereignty, especially its capacity to wield influence in areas of great concern to it. These deep-seated collective anxieties partly explain why, in 2005, Putin lamented the collapse of the Soviet Union as 'the major geopolitical tragedy of the century';[41] why, in 2006, he dubbed the 1990s as Russia's new 'Time of Troubles', when Russia's very survival as a cohesive, sovereign and independent country was in question;[42] why, in 2007, as Russian economic growth continued to soar, the Russian President went further and suggestively praised the *end* of those internally troubled times as 'more than [just] *a victory over foreign invaders*';[43] and why, in 2007, Putin went abroad to Munich to castigate Western expansion (via NATO, the EU, OSCE and NGOs) as invasive encroachments into Russia's historic lands, or its spheres of interest.[44] Ordinary Russians applauded Putin every time.[45]

From the start, Putin acted to 're-gather' Russia's lands across the Federation, re-establish Russian authority throughout the CIS, and safeguard the CIS's territorial status quo through a defensive combination of administrative and legal changes, new institutional arrangements and, in places, peace-keeping alibis.[46] In the eyes of this Kremlin, Moscow's authority in the Russian Federation and its influence across the CIS were interdependent. The Kremlin thus seized opportunities to gain control over Russian energy and other natural resources, beginning with the arrest of Mikhail Khodorkovsky in October 2003. It set out to regain control over transit pipelines crisscrossing the CIS, and it secured privileged access to CIS energy sources. By 2005, these efforts had hardened into a strategy with ideological overtones to transform the Russian state into the world's energy superpower.[47] But such a strategy was complicated by a number of potentially serious problems, some of which could even destabilise the Putin leadership at home. Those problems included anti-Russian and pro-European impulses in Ukraine and Georgia, Russia's competition across the CIS with America and China,[48] and the possible rise of Islamic fundamentalism or anti-Russian leaders in Central Asia and the Caucasus. In response, Russian foreign policy documents all pushed the same coherent priorities: safeguard inner cohesion, repel other great powers from Russia's spheres of influence and retain control over the levers of economic modernisation. To achieve those priorities, this Russian leadership determined it needed great power fast. That pointed to the present shortcut.

3rd cause: Ideational factors

As a result of these two pressing requirements for Russian greatness – to resist external pressure on the CIS and bolster Russian central authority across all of Eurasia – Russia's ruling elite and a large part of its populace acquired a great-power mentality. That mentality is now, in itself, a third important source of Russia's quest for greatness. Mentality is hardly of mere epiphenomenal importance,[49] since the way this ideational force interacts with material realities makes it a primary factor. How it does so has to do with national identity. While national identity is mutable, manifold and complex, it acts like national glue, made from shared myths and collective memory by which a nation's people come together in consensus.[50] It informs a nation who it is and is not, in what direction it is oriented and where it seeks to head.[51] It is a nation's *'compass'*,[52] or its Global Positioning System, which not only tells the country where to go, but also indicates the routes to get there. In this way, national identity influences the way national interests are conceived *and* pursued. It affects how a country's elite interprets changes in the world around it, and, in turn, helps frame and narrow the choices for foreign policy reactions.[53]

For Russian national identity, the memory of greatness is profound.[54] In its national imagination, Russia 'is doomed to be a great power'.[55] It is 'predestined' for greatness and 'retains the inherent characteristics of a great power' – whatever the reality.[56] Whether Russia is a great power in technical, statistical or comparative terms is irrelevant. What matters instead is Russia's self-perception as a great power, even if that perception is far more about the *memory* of 'inherent' greatness than the *reality* of actual greatness. As Jan-Werner Müller wrote, '…It is of particular interest how countries which so far have emerged as relative losers of the post-Cold War world – such France and Russia – are recasting their memories of the twentieth century, and reorienting their policies on the basis of particular "lessons from the past". Often this recasting has taken a radical turn, and memory has become shorthand for a glorious national past that needs to be regained in the near future (and the "near abroad").'[57]

Collective memory influences the direction and nature of political change, even when we cannot fully comprehend how.[58] Russia's memory of its 'glorious national past' colours the way Moscow understands and responds to fast-changing events; it has hardened Russia's greatness mentality into a kind of collective default mindset during these extraordinary, transformative decades; and it has encouraged expedient, shorter-term solutions (such as *derzhavnost'*) over longer-term solutions (such as constitutional democracy) to Russia's mounting problems. It helps explain why the Yeltsin and Putin leaderships enshrined great state power as Russia's strategic goal, despite the historical risks of doing so. *Derzhavnost'*, after all, is associated with persistent authoritarianism; it has never brought sustained economic prosperity, nor succeeded in lifting the whole of Russian society out of relative backwardness since Ivan III first sought greatness for Muscovy some 500 years ago.

Russian memories of *derzhavnost'* – as the only form of great power Russia has ever known – strengthened Moscow's preference for multipolar diplomacy without multilateralism. Memories of traditional greatness, emphasising the inviolability of sovereignty, made it particularly difficult for Putin's Russia to sacrifice some sovereignty for mutual benefit within or alongside multilateral institutions, such as the EU, which circumscribe state behaviour.[59] Such memories rendered a kind of unilateral multipolarity as Russia's automatic foreign-policy response to its growing internal and external problems throughout the Yeltsin and Putin eras.[60]

In addition, Russian memories of national greatness informed the way it understood Western behaviour: Western policies towards Russia looked like deliberate, malevolent attempts to limit, contain and encircle Russia's revival. No alternative explanation could seemingly justify the West's relentless expansion into Russian spheres of interest, despite earlier promises not to do so, its triumphalism over Soviet disintegration and Russia's collapse, or its persistent exclusion of post-Soviet Russia from the West's great-power institutions (such as NATO and later the WTO) despite the Soviet Union's peaceful territorial sacrifices in the late 1980s.[61] Indeed, Russian assumptions of Western duplicity explain why the Kremlin *and* many Russian Europeanist-liberals attributed Ukraine's Orange 'Revolution' to Western intervention as 'a long distance controlled popular revolt'.[62] That event triggered a turning point in Russia's perceptions of the West, after which point Russian policy towards the United States, in particular, steadily toughened.

Similarly, Western collective memories and long-held fears of Russia's historical greatness have affected the direction and nature of policy change in Western capitals. Many in the West were predisposed to view Russia in narrow terms of historical and geographical determinism. They assumed that Russia was doomed to return to authoritarianism and hegemonic great-power behaviour.[63] Such preconceptions created a bias against treating Russia as a genuine partner in European security and prejudiced rational cost-benefit analyses against taking the political and economic risks necessary to integrate Russia into Western institutions, even into distant waiting rooms for NATO or even the EU. The result was Russia's effective exclusion from European security architecture. That exclusion increased the chances that Russia would indeed seek solutions separate from the West – such as, Putin's fast-track solution back to great state power, *derzhavnost'*.

By the turn of the millennium, the extreme intensity of these three factors – external pressure, internal requirements and ideational forces – and the way they interacted pushed Russia to re-conceive greatness in its more traditional Russian form of *derzhavnost'*.

But Putin's Russia lacked most measures of modern greatness; it had to *invent* greatness fast. Facing the same problem throughout its history, Russia simply invented greatness through 'social creativity', best demonstrated by 'social identity theory' (SIT).[64] This theory demonstrates how and why Russia often finds itself on risky shortcut paths to greatness, as today.

'Social Identity Theory' and Russia's shortcut to great power

According to SIT, disadvantaged groups will struggle to attain (or re-attain) superior positioning, even if the costs are high.[65] When the group has no immediate hope of materially competing at the top, it finds a unique, third way to frame itself as superior to others; it will turn its deficits into unique advantages in order to take 'shortcuts to greatness'. The Soviet experiment was just that: a shortcut to great power by reframing Russia as the world's unique pioneer of a new Communist order. Gorbachev's 'new thinking' was also a 'shortcut to greatness' – but in quite the opposite sense of state greatness. The Gorbachev leadership reconceived greatness as benefiting the Soviet *people*, not merely the state, and sought to reinvent Soviet greatness by re-branding the USSR as the world's leader in forging a new Kantian world order.[66] His project ended abruptly, however, when the Soviet Union collapsed.

For Yeltsin's bankrupt Russia, inventing greatness was even more challenging. Desperate for means to defend Russian interests on the world stage, Yeltsin sought to invent great power by revising the international structure. Russia would hasten the shift to multipolarity as a means of gaining a kind of virtual and inexpensive greatness.[67] As a pioneer of a new multipolar international order, Yeltsin's Russia would work to erect new poles of power via 'Gorchakovian' politics,[68] leveraging Russia's power by decreasing that of the global hegemon in an effort to reconstitute a Russian 'superpower on the cheap'.[69] Like borrowed power, multipolarity would jack up broken-down post-Soviet Russia on the international stage. But Yeltsin failed: excessive diplomatic leverage atop inadequate economic 'equity' and a crumbling 'management' (i.e. the state), plus a foreign policy de-linked from, and at odds with, domestic and economic policies, could never be an effective path to greatness.

For immediate solutions, the Putin leadership looked to the past for clues about how to constitute power fast. Like Stalin or Peter I, Putin determined that Russia's salvation lay in the *immediate* acquisition of hardpower, which meant re-establishing vertical political control and reclaiming state command over key economic sectors. This demoted the relative value of multipolar diplomacy. Nevertheless, it remained an important tertiary tool. Putin's 2003 anti-US alignment with France and Germany against US position on Iraq, aimed in part at upgrading the EU and post-Soviet Russia to the rank of weighty international actors, is but one example. Not for nothing was Putin dubbed a 'Neo-Gaullist'.[70] The moniker was appropriate, but it was also confusing, underscoring a central ambiguity in Putin's foreign policy during 2000–2004. How could Russia integrate itself into a system while simultaneously working to overturn it? This contradiction emphasised the incoherent character of Putin's first-term foreign policy – a policy Robert Legvold called 'unformed'.[71]

In Putin's second term, Russian foreign policy became more coherent. The Kremlin downgraded its previous stress on westward 'integration', eliminating much of the tension between its integrationist goals and multipolar tactics. Gone was the deliberately pro-Western terminology of 'multivectorism'. Instead, Moscow assertively incorporated multipolarity into the 'shortcut to greatness' as that shortcut's third, crucial dimension, and more assertively stressed the goal of overturning US hegemony. Four new phenomena contributed to that shift. First, the Beslan crisis allowed Moscow to justify strengthening authoritarian control in the name of combating terrorism. Second, Ukraine's Orange Revolution appeared to Moscow as 'the ultimate threat' of Western encirclement.[72] Third, real GDP growth of more than 7% per annum greatly buoyed Kremlin confidence; and last, the Iraqi quagmire revealed America's increasing international fragility.[73]

From then on, Putin's shortcut included state-led economic modernisation fuelled by Russia's energy wealth and rising oil prices, rising nationalism/anti-Westernism to mobilise the population, and authoritarian presidential leadership as the most efficient means of implementing the rest – all bolstered by a forceful multipolar foreign policy to maximise Russian sovereignty over its foreign and domestic interests and guarantee Russia's equal place at the great-power table in a new era of multipolarity in international relations.

Part II   Analysing Putin's multipolar doctrine

How did Putin's Moscow envision the multipolar world it sought to build? What did Russian multipolar policy look like in practice? Four points stand out. First, it was contradictory, despite rhetorical coherence. Second, its main objective was merely political parity with the West, despite claims of revising the world order. Third, it became more ideological and less pragmatic over time. And finally, beneath the confident assertiveness, it was largely reactive.

1.   Contradictions beneath superficial coherence

Moscow's vision was superficially coherent but remained riddled with important contradictions and tensions. These tell us as much about Moscow's multipolarity policy as do official statements. Examples abound: Russian foreign policy sought international *revision* in order to consolidate the Eurasian status quo. And though Moscow's goal was to forge a new, post-Western multipolar global order, Moscow did not really *want* genuine multipolarity: China's vast economic might would translate into its political superiority over any Russian pole, especially over the long term.[74] In response, Russia appointed itself the 'informal spokesman' for the multipolar bushwhackers, the BRICs (Brazil, Russia, India and China), in order to cut the economic queue and situate itself at the political vanguard amongst the emerging powers,[75] much as de Gaulle's France in the 1960s appointed itself political leader of continental Europe to offset West Germany's economic dominance. Moreover, while the Putin Administration confidently presented multipolarity as multiple poles of roughly equal political power, *bipolarity-plus* was a far more likely outcome, with China and the US as the two dominant poles. Moreover, Moscow remained so centred on the West as its main centre of strategic economic and military focus, that all its talk about multipolarity smacked of instrumentalism directed at pressuring the West. Even China remained, in many ways, Moscow's rear theatre for an essentially Western-focused policy.[76]

So, Russia's multipolar campaign was not about multipolarity *per se*; rather it was a struggle for great power via a historical shortcut. But left unanswered is the question: power for what?

2. In search of political parity with the United States

This brings us to the second point. Power was meant to compel the West, particularly the United States, to recognise *political parity* with Russia. Only then could Russia protect its interests and keep threats at bay. Just as in the 1960s, when Moscow struggled to make the United States concede military parity with the USSR and win agreement over post-World War II borders in Europe, Putin's Russia sought to compel the United States to accept Eurasia's political-military-territorial status quo as a matter of Russia's privileged interest. Echoing Soviet diplomatic history, Putin was determined to drive the West to accept international norms on Russian terms. Those norms included the pre-eminence of sovereign state interests over humanitarian or soft principles, non-interference in domestic affairs, and the inviolability of CIS boundaries – that is, no NATO expansion or democracy promotion inside the CIS. But unlike the 1960s, post-Soviet Russia had no hope of attaining military parity with the United States; nor could it attain economic parity in the near future, if ever. It could, however, increase its power via energy sales and multipolar diplomacy. It was in this context that Russia embraced multipolarity with such fervour, especially after 2005, when American pressure inside the CIS (notably, Ukraine) appeared to intensify.

Shortly afterwards, MID published its *Obzor*, a survey of Russian foreign policy goals and interests, which elevated the goal of building a multipolar order to *first place*. The multipolar priority sat on the 4th *line* of the 79-page document. It had appeared only in the middle of the 3rd *page* of MID's Foreign Policy Concept of 2000, trailing behind sections about 'state and society's interests'.[77] By stepping up the multipolar emphasis, Foreign Minister Sergei Lavrov said Moscow was responding to the 'new geopolitical reality', which the West had not yet accepted.[78] 'The emergence of new economic growth centres deprives the West of its monopoly on globalisation processes and leads to a more equitable distribution of resources. The economic potential of these centres is converted into their political influence and thus reinforces multipolarity.... We would like to see all of our Western partners finally give up any illusions about the eternal nature of their domination in all aspects of international affairs.'[79] Lavrov went on to imply that Russia played a leading role in these processes. 'As Russia grows stronger – and, perhaps for the first time in its history, defends its national interests by using all of its competitive advantages – a competitive environment is gradually being re-established in international relations'.[80] Sergei Karaganov, Chairman of Presidium of the Council on Foreign and Defence Policy, whose views often paralleled those of the leadership, pushed the analysis further. Giving this environment the name, 'New Era of Confrontation' or NEC,[81] he painted Russia as a vanguard state leading this competition. For the first time since the Gorbachev era, Russian foreign policy was re-conceived in terms of a competitive struggle with the West. The struggle was to control the global distribution of economic resources and, linked to that, to redefine security along highly traditional 19th century notions of inviolable state interests.

Confident of Russian efforts to regain parity, Karaganov suggested Russia could even gain the upper hand in the struggle: 'Russia is a key state from the point of view of competition between political and socio-economic models, and is, moreover, *capable of tipping the military-political balance in the world.*'[82] By focusing so ardently on regaining political parity with the West, Russian elites got trapped in a Soviet-style *kto-kogo* [who defeats whom] power-struggle with the West. This leads to the third point: the return of ideas and doctrine to Russian foreign policy.

3. The return of doctrine to Russian foreign policy

Though this new Russian struggle with the West was not about ideology, it did accentuate ideas, contradicting the pragmatism that had characterised Putin's first term. At its heart were ideas about the type of the future world order and the kind of political-economic state models dominating that order. As a result, Russia's multipolar foreign policy in Putin's second term developed a doctrinal quality. Russia was re-conceived as an independent power-pole separate from, and implicitly at times superior to, Europe. Official policy documents even went so far as to call for a new *doctrine* in order to codify such conceptualisations of Russia and its new place in the world.[83] This injection of an ideational element diluted the self-consciously non-ideological quality of Moscow's (basically) Western-centric foreign policy during Putin's first term. As Fyodor Lyukyanov, editor of *Russia in Global Affairs*, noticed, 'Moralising tones have crept into some statements, and something messianic has begun to loom behind the concept of multipolarity', as if Russian foreign policy elites were missionaries for multipolarity.[84]

In addition, these new 'moralising tones' represented a conceptual departure from the collective ideas of Yeltsin's second term. That was the era of *officially* declared EU-Russian 'strategic partnership', when Moscow's multipolarity policies flowed from the notion of Russia as a Western-imitation power-pole on the world stage, *alongside* the EU and in roughly equal partnership with the United States. By Putin's second term, all this had changed, and Moscow's multipolarity policy was informed by the competing idea that Russia would be a different kind of pole from the West, an alternative to the West in terms of its economic and socio-political model.[85] The notion of 'sovereign democracy' embodies 'Russia's ideological ambition to be the "other Europe" [once again] – an alternative to the European Union',[86] with a 'different approach to sovereignty, power and world order'.[87] Vyacheslav Surkov even contributed to an edited volume, *Sovereignty*, that described the Kremlin's newfound ideology, sovereign democracy, in 'otherness' terms.[88] Putin embraced that description.[89]

'Otherness' flowed from the non-European half of Russia's historically split identity – the part of Russian identity that animated Slavophilia and the Soviet experiment as alternatives to the Western model. Why *this* half of Russian identity began to speak for Russia, once again, by the 21st century resulted from the way contingency interacted with and reinforced Russia's historical flirtation with 'otherness'. Those contingent events included fall-out from Russia's two decades of torturous 'great state transformation',[90] Yeltsin's failure to continue building democratic institutions, the rise of authoritarian-minded Vladimir Putin as leader, and Western decisions to expand NATO and exclude Russia from crucial Western institutions. 'Otherness' had a circular influence: it encouraged Putin's preference for authoritarian solutions in Russia and Eurasia, which in turn deepened Russia's sense of 'otherness'. This interaction pushed Putin's foreign policy back towards confrontation with the West. From 1996 to 2004, policy was defined by a contradictory, uncertain aspiration for multipolarity within a pro-Western integrationist policy. After 2004, it was defined by an assertive Multipolarity Doctrine meant to take Russia beyond the West. This became the new ideology, of sorts, for Putin's 'shortcut to greatness'.

4. Multipolarity policies in practice: Return to Soviet habits

Moscow's implementation of this Doctrine combined a mix of pragmatic, instrumental tactics with defensive/offensive assertiveness. Business-like instrumentalism was accompanied by a Soviet-style prickly reactiveness, due to the reality of Russia's inferior global economic rank.

Towards Europe, for example, the Kremlin combined assertiveness towards some countries with defensiveness towards others. It merged charm offensives towards cooperative EU countries with belligerent defensive tactics towards the more critical EU members to pressure them into compliant behaviour and undercut their impact on EU policy. This represented a variation on an old theme of 'Soviet instrumental Europeanism',[91] using 'divide and conquer' tactics – especially related to energy – within Europe. While Moscow pursued attractive bilateral deals with individual energy national champions in Europe (such as Germany's E.ON and BASF, Italy's ENI, France's GDF), it simultaneously pressured, harassed or boycotted its threatening critics (such as the UK, Denmark, Poland, Lithuania and Latvia) via trade embargoes, transport blockades, diplomatic pressure and premature renegotiation of energy supply contracts.[92]

This amounted to Putin's abandonment of the last vestiges of 'New Thinking'-era policies towards Western Europe. Since the late 1980s, Moscow had emphatically rejected offensive bilateralism as a diplomatic weapon aimed at dividing European countries, in favour of multilateralism focused on furthering Russia's inclusion into the European Union. But now, the Kremlin made no effort to conceal its return to bilateral diplomatic weaponry. It *explicitly* prescribed bilateralism over multilateralism in MID's *Obzor*, and Putin highlighted Moscow's preference for bilateral deal-making with EU capitals over multilateral haggling with Brussels in his remarks during the EU-Russia summit in October 2007.[93] The reason was clear: EU member-states represented state interests to which Putin appealed, while the EU's pooled interests threatened this sovereignty-obsessed Kremlin. In addition, European countries held Russia's most lucrative economic markets, and their growing dependence on Russia for its gas supplies compelled many European governments to take Russian interests and concerns into account far more than at any time since the end of the Cold War. Russia thus sought to attain 'asymmetric interdependence' with Europe: the EU and its member-states should need Russia more than Russia needed the EU in their new co-dependent energy relationship.[94]

Regarding America, Moscow's reversion to the old Soviet conceptual framework of the world as a struggle with the United States implied the return of a Soviet intellectual (and policy) trap. Given its objective inferiority vis-à-vis the United States (whatever its confident rhetoric), Russia could do little more than react to American actions in angry and defiant ways that betrayed Russia's nagging insecurity. While such reactions may have been justified, they caused the United States and some Europeans to respond in ways that increased Russian insecurity. This 'actively reactive' cycle closed doors to other paths that might have positively changed the US-Russian negative dynamic. For example, the United States rejected or threatened to let lapse all nuclear disarmament treaties except the 1963 Test Ban Treaty and a few other symbolic documents, leaving an unprecedented legal vacuum in this area. In response, Russia reacted to George W. Bush's allergy to disarmament with knee-jerk (yet understandable) tit-for-tats, while providing 'nothing substantial in an intellectual, political, diplomatic, or military-technical sense to counter or change Washington's policies'.[95] Instead, Moscow worsened that vacuum by threatening to withdraw from the 1987 Intermediate-range Nuclear Forces (INF) Treaty and suspending the implementation of Conventional Forces in Europe (CFE) Treaty. In addition, the military increasingly conceptualised its doctrine in 'active reaction' to American attempts to gain a foothold in Russia's traditional zones of influence.[96] For the first time, the military lobbied for the revised doctrine to include 'non-military threats' in the CIS in its definition of threats. (This would have given greater leeway to the military in foreign and economic policy-making – a prospect that caused internal infighting and significant delays).[97] And while the Kremlin increased the Russian military budget from 2.5 to 3.5% of GDP and reinforced its nuclear capacity as part of normal modernisation,[98] those actions were also insecure reactions to American actions in Europe and Eurasia. Adding to the bravado, Moscow exploded the world's most powerful explosive device in September 2007, the 'Father of all bombs', in response to America's 'mother of all bombs'.[99] Moreover, Russian elites had begun to 'worship nuclear weapons as the "ultimate guarantee" of national defence and security' in reaction to the Americans and other threats.[100] Re-embracing nuclear weapons upgraded their political value, which represented a worried response, in part, to American expansionism and Chinese economic might in various parts of the CIS.[101] Finally, Moscow's return to Soviet-style 'active reactive-ness' towards, and obsession with, the United States locked Moscow in a reactive trap and disinclined the Kremlin from taking any of the serious intellectual or diplomatic initiatives required for regulating the global nuclear regime or patching the cracks in the Nuclear Non-Proliferation Treaty. Russia would be left objectively more insecure, not less. Such were the characteristics of Putin's Multipolarity Doctrine in practice.

Part III   Conclusions and consequences of the current shortcut

By the end of Putin's Presidency, Russia's shortcut to greatness appeared successful by some measures. With 6–7% economic growth and a popularly legitimate government, Russia was indeed on its way to re-establishing itself as a great power that could no longer be ignored – if partly out of fear – once again. But many questions posed at the beginning remain unanswered. Will Russia's renewed economic power translate into a capacity to affect international political change in directions that genuinely further Russian interests and ease its problems, both at home and abroad? Might it ultimately lead to a new *kind* of greatness that would be for the sake of citizens, not the state (as mere *derzhavnost'*)? Would it relinquish some sovereignty in exchange for prosperity? These questions remain open. As mentioned at the start, this shortcut is probably the continuation of Russia's 20-year-old 'great state transformation' – not its end. But there are already costs of Putin's shortcut that may affect how history eventually answers these questions.

By taking this shortcut, the Putin leadership built a cohesive authoritarian state with an impressively managed rent-based economy, but not one suited for effective governance, capable of harvesting globalisation's full benefits.[102] By choosing this shortcut, which increased state control over the economy, Putin's Kremlin stifled competition in important sectors, encouraged rampant corruption, reduced the possibilities for continued economic reform, and dampened sources of innovation necessary for Russia to remain an enduring 21st century powerhouse for the sake of its people – at least for the medium term.[103] By selecting this path, the Kremlin controlled televised media, weakened autonomous political parties and groups, and muffled independent thinkers, which put Russia at risk of lacking the creative chaos (flowing from the bottom up) necessary to build a great *nation*, not just a great *state*.

By pursuing this kind of 'Other Europe' greatness via the shortest possible route, Putin's Russia favoured hard-power means to build authority; it eschewed alliances, avoided real political engagement and vacillated over deep integration into the world economy, since that 'would require some relinquishing of control at home and some sovereignty abroad'.[104] Moreover, this shortcut was based partly on a foreign policy doctrine – multipolarity – that resurrected Soviet habits of thought. That doctrine exacerbated Moscow's Cold War-era obsession with the United States. It encouraged a return to zero-sum (*kto-kogo*) thinking, celebrated 'divide and conquer' tactics, and reduced chances for proactive, win-win trade-offs. It strengthened old reflexes to militarise international competition, 'giving it new structure through an arms race'.[105] It was a policy doctrine that missed opportunities to lead on issues, such as nuclear non-proliferation, that could genuinely benefit Russian security for the future.

None of this is irreversible. How Russia will evolve long term, and how it will use its power, will largely depend on a series of contingent factors over the short and medium terms – indeed, the same kinds of contingent factors that pushed Russia down Putin's authoritarian, third-way 'shortcut to greatness' in the first place. That outcome will hinge on the ideological predilections and personal qualities of Russia's leader in the future. It will flow from the way the Kremlin leadership relates to Russia's collective memory and its political culture. It will depend on whether future Russian leaders consolidate or challenge the norms and structures of political institutions that President Putin set up. It will also stem from the quality of future interaction between Russia and the West, the impact of that interaction on how Russia conceives its external threats and national interests, and on whether Russia can resolve its ambiguous identity in more European directions.

What might nudge Russia in such directions? Exogenous forces, such as plunging oil prices and economic crisis, create opportunities for reform – or retrenchment. Further external military developments, including NATO expansion in Georgia, could impel the Kremlin to react sanguinely – or they could continue to drive wedges between Russia and the West. If there are any lessons from the past, it is that material factors, such as economic or external pressures, do not, on their own, provoke reform; nor do they necessarily even encourage reform. The Gorbachev era demonstrates that Soviet economic problems, including the plummeting oil prices of the mid-1980s, did *not* compel the USSR towards radical reform; nor did Reagan's military build-up *force* the USSR towards comprehensive change.[106] Instead, the crucial difference for the USSR came in the form of a strong leader, who was guided by liberal-minded ideas of governance, committed to institution-building for genuine pluralism, and able to defeat entrenched institutional interests. The same will be true for Russia in the future. Until then, the outside world can help by engaging with Russia across many levels. Indeed, European aid to certain Russian regions, as Tomila Lankina shows in this volume, helped those regions become Russia's 'high democratic achievers' over the past two decades.[107]

Hardly 'doomed' to take shortcuts to great state power, Russia could indeed become the kind of major power and great *nation* that rejects *de facto* projects for a Hobbesian multipolar order condoning unregulated competition. It could instead become a power that helps build a global structure based on negotiated international norms and renewed and new multilateral institutions. Whether it becomes *this* kind of great power will depend on the kind of interrelationship that evolves between leadership, ideas and institutions in Russia, and the way the outside world engages with Russia, at all levels.

Notes

1 Phrase, 'shortcut to greatness', attributed to Deborah Welch Larson and Alexei Shevchenko. While their article specifically analyses the Gorbachev era, this article builds on and adapts their idea to the Putin era. From here on, the concept of Russian shortcuts and the expression, 'shortcut to greatness', are credited to them. See: Deborah Welch Larson and Alexei Shevchenko, 'Shortcut to Greatness: The New Thinking and the Revolution in Soviet Foreign Policy', *International Organization*, 57 (Winter 2003): 77–109.

2 Dmitri Trenin stresses Russia's ambivalence about China's potential to dominate Russia. Dmitri Trenin: 'Russia's Threat Perception and Strategic Posture' (25 January 2008), Carnegie Moscow Centre, www.carnegie.ru.

3 On Western mistakes and Russia's luck: Sergei Karaganov, 'A New Epoch of Confrontation', *Russia in Global Affairs*, No. 4 (October–December 2007), http://eng.globalaffairs.ru/numbers/21/1148.html.

4 John Mearsheimer, 'Back to the Future', *International Security*, Vol. 15, No. 1 (Summer 1990): 2–3.

5 Of course, the West (particularly the US) complicated Russia's chances for economic integration into the West, dragging its heels on WTO membership for Russia and refusing to repeal the US Jackson-Vanik Amendment. But Russia's multipolarity policy, even if it were in large part a reaction to Western rejection, merely limited Russia's chances to integrate itself and take full advantage of globalisation.

6 We should point out that China was embraced by the West, while Russia was not. On China's subsequent rejection of multipole diplomacy: Christophe Jaffelot, Jean-Philippe Beja, Julie Newton, 'Cooperation or Collusion?: Russia, India and China in the 21st Century', The American University of Paris, Conference Series (February–April 2008).

7 Sergei Lavrov, 'Forget the Inferiority Complex', *Argumenty i fakty* (13 April 2005), *JRL* (13 April 2005), http://www.cdi.org/russia/johnson

8 Historically, 'Russia's tendency to fall behind in achieving the economic, scientific and technological benefits of globalisation revealed its weaknesses, which Russia's leaders then sought to redress primarily through military and political means in its foreign policy': Celeste Wallender, 'What can Multipolarity', in Robert Legvold, ed., *Russian Foreign Policy in the Twenty-first Century and the Shadow of the Past* (New York: Columbia University Press, 2007), p. 444.

9 Evgeni Primakov, *Gody v bolshoi politike [The Years in Big Politics]* (Moscow: Sovershenno Sekretno, 1999), pp. 212–15.

10 Julie Newton, *Russia, France, and the Idea of Europe* (Basingstoke: Palgrave Macmillan, 2003), p. 239.

11 *Kontseptsiya vneshnei politiki rossiiskoi Federatsii*, Russian Ministry of Foreign Affairs (June 2000), http://www.mid.ru/ns-osndoc.nsf/.

12 'Supercorporation': Wallender, 'Global Challenges', p. 492. Other historical examples of shortcuts to modernisation include Peter and Stalin.

13 Term and question attributed to: Robert Legvold, 'Russian Foreign Policy during Periods of Great State Transformation', in Robert Legvold, ed., *Russian*

Foreign Policy in the 21st Century and the Shadow of the Past (New York: Columbia University Press, 2007), pp. 77–144, esp. 78, 131.

14 Richard Pipes, by stressing the deep roots and strength of Russian authoritarianism throughout its history, offers little hope that Russia can overcome that legacy in order to build enduring great power. Richard Pipes, *Russian Conservatism and its Critics* (New Haven: Yale University Press, 2007). 'Russian mentality and behaviour change slowly, if at all, over time, regardless of the regime in power': Richard Pipes, 'Flight from Freedom: What Russians Think and Want', *Foreign Affairs* (May/June 2004): 9–15.

15 Lilia Shevtsova puts particular stress on institutional weaknesses: Putin's system (the roots laid by Yeltsin) is an 'electoral monarchy' atop 'bureaucratic capitalism', and is unsustainable, she claims. This type of system, if it retains its grasp on Russia, could lead Russia either to dictatorship or decay: Shevtsova, *Lost in Transition: The Yeltsin and Putin Legacies* (Washington: Carnegie Endowment for International Peace, 2007), pp. 107–11, 23. Others agree that this system has deep institutional weaknesses, but do not go so far as to suggest that this system cannot last. On the contrary, writers in this volume such as Ken Wilson, suggest Russia, like Mexico, could go on to be ruled by the same political party for years.

16 Legvold, 'Russian Foreign Policy during Periods of Great State Transformation', p. 31.

17 Dmitri Trenin, *Getting Russia Right* (Washington: Carnegie Endowment for International Peace, 2007).

18 'Gosudar' means sovereign. The term originally designated owners of slaves. Then, the term meant slave owners who became sovereigns after Mongolian sovereigns left Russia in the 14th century. The notion of sovereign-owner then expanded into the idea of the state, which produced the Russian concept of the state as a *'gosudarstvo'* – that is, the state as indistinct from its sovereign leader. Pipes, *Russian Conservatism*, p. 189.

19 'Russian foreign policy is geared to the fundamental goal of redoing Russia as a great power in modern conditions'. Hanna Smith, 'What can Multipolarity and Multilateralism Tell Us about Russian Foreign Policy Interests', in Hanna Smith (ed.), *Russia and its Foreign Policy: Influences, Interests and Issues* (Helsinki: Kikomora Publications, 2005), p. 36. Also: 'Russia has residual superpower mentality'; Dmitri Trenin, 'Russia redefines itself and its relations with the West', *The Washington Quarterly* (1 March 2007), http//www.carnegie.ru/eng/print/75857-print.htm.

20 Vladimir Putin, 'Russia at the Turn of the Millenium', in *First Person: An Astonishingly Frank Self Portrait by Russia's President* (Moscow: Vargrius, 2000), p. 214.

21 Evgeni Bazhanov, quoted in Smith, 'What can Multipolarity', p. 47.

22 Marshall Poe, *The Russian Moment in World History* (Princeton: Princeton University Press, 2003), p. 66.

23 Ibid., p. 70.

24 'thick globalization': Wallander, 'Global Challenges', p. 489.

25 Ibid., p. 491.

26 Michael McFaul, 'New Russia, New Threat', *Los Angeles Times* (2 October 2007), www.carnegie.ru/en/print/76877.

27 Ibid.

28 Vladimir Putin, 'Tver Meeting with Members of Youth Organisation' (24 July 2007), www.kremlin.ru.

29 Vladimir Putin, 'Speech...of National Unity Day', Grand Kremlin Palace (4 November 2007), www.kremlin.ru/eng/text/speeches/2007/11/04/09.

30 Vladimir Putin, 'Speech at the 43rd Munich Conference on Security Policy' (10 February 2007), http://wwwsecurityconference.de/konferenzen.php? sprache+en&id=179. Putin's sharp comments dovetailed with the views of a wide range of elites, who shared his views of the West as actively anti-Russian. Even Alexei Arbatov, a liberal-minded international affairs specialist and former Deputy Chairman of the Duma's Defence Committee, accused the West of meddling in Ukrainian and Georgian politics. He linked the colour revolutions in both Ukraine and Georgia to 'the West's active intervention...in Georgia and Ukraine in support of the most anti-Russian politicians in 2004–2006'. Alexei Arbatov, 'Moscow and Munich: A New Framework for Russian Domestic and Foreign Policies', Working Papers No. 3 (2007), Carnegie Moscow Centre, p. 16.

31 Karaganov, 'A New Epoch'.

32 Ibid.

33 Sergei Lavrov, 'Stenogramma vystupleniya i otvetov na voprosy Ministra Innostrannykh Del Rossii S.V. Lavrova na seminare...v Moskovskom Tsentre Karnegi...21 Iyunya 2007' (21 June 2007), http://www.mid.ru/ brp_4.nsf/2fee282eb6df40e643256999005e6e8c/7d38603flcb584c. Dmitri Trenin: 'Russia's Threat Perception and Strategic Posture' (25 January 2008), Carnegie Moscow Centre, http://www.carnegie.ru.

34 Vladimir Putin, 'Speech at Munich'.

35 Ibid.

36 Cited by: Anne de Tinguy, Conference, 'Le Projet de Puissance de la Russie: Enjeux, Réalites, et Implications Stratégiques', Fondation pour la Recherche Stratégique (2 October 2007), 85.

37 Vladimir Putin, 'Valdai International Discussion Group', Sochi (14 September 2007), www.kremlin.ru/engtext/speeches/2007/09/14/18. Emphasis added.

38 Karaganov, 'A New Epoch'.

39 Alfred Rieber, 'The Reforming Tradition in Russian History', in A. Rieber, A. Rubinstein, ed., *Perestroika at the Crossroads* (M. E. Sharpe, 1991), p. 13.

40 Jeff Kahn, 'What is the New Russian Federalism?', in Archie Brown, ed., *Contemporary Russian Politics: A Reader* (Oxford: Oxford University Press, 2001), pp. 374, 379.

41 Vladimir Putin, 'Address to the Federal Assembly of the Russian Federation' (25 April 2005), http://www.kremlin.ru/eng/text/speeches/2005/04/25.

42 Putin referred to Russia's 'time of troubles' four centuries ago, and suggestively praised those who ended them: Vladimir Putin, 'Speech at the State Reception devoted to National Unity Day', The Kremlin (4 November 2006), http://www.kremlin.ru/eng/text/speeches/2006/11/04. In another speech (quoted in *Moscow News*), Putin referred explicitly to the Yeltsin period as Russia's most recent 'time of troubles' and suggested his (Putin's) leadership had led Russia out of its troubles: Anna Arutunyan, 'Putin Plans for New Role', *Moscow News* (4 October 2007), http://mnweekly.rian. rupoltics/20071004/55280269.html.

43   Vladimir Putin, 'Speech at the Reception on the Occasion of National Unity Day', The Kremlin (4 November 2007), http://www.kremlin.ru/eng/text/speeches/2007/11/04/09.

44   Putin, 'Speech at Munich'.

45   Putin gained popularity not only for the booming economy, but also for the way he handled foreign and domestic politics. A Pew poll showed that in 2003, 76% of Russians expressed confidence in Putin to do the right thing regarding world affairs; by the spring of 2007 (just after Putin's Munich speech), those ratings hit 84%. A 2007 Levada poll showed 86% approved of the way Putin had handled his *entire* Presidency: 'Putin's Popularity Propels Chosen Successor in Russian Election', Pew Research Center (27 February 2008), http://pewresearch.org/pubs/749/russia-public-opinion.

46   On regathering Russia's regions: Eugene Huskey, 'Overcoming the Yeltsin Legacy: Vladimir Putin and Russian Political Reform', in Brown, *Contemporary Russian Politics*, pp. 88–91; Tomila Lankina, 'Local Government, Ethnic and Social Activism', in Brown, *Contemporary Russian Politics*, p. 411. Regarding Russia and the CIS, Russia's Foreign Ministry pledged 'leadership across the CIS': Obzor vneshnei politiki Rossiiskoi Federatsii [Foreign Policy Survey of the Russian Federation], Ministry of Foreign Affairs, RF (March 2007), http://www.mid.ru/ns-osndoc.nsf, pp. 26–32.

47   These efforts consolidated into a political/economic strategy in 2003–2004 as energy prices sky-rocketed. The strategy gained ideological overtones in the wake of Ukraine's Orange Revolution in late 2004, early 2005. Andrei Denisov, 'The Gains and Failures of Russia's Energy Superpower', *Russia in Global Affairs*, No. 2 (April–June 2008), http://eng.globalaffairs.ru/numbers/23/1197.html.

48   For an excellent discussion of Central Asia between the great powers: Robert Legvold, 'Great Power Stakes in Central Asia', *Thinking Strategically: The Major Powers, Kazakhstan and the Central Asian Nexus* (Boston: MIT Press, 2004), pp. 1–38.

49   Jonathan Haslam, *No Virtue like Necessity: Realist Thought from Machiavelli to the Present* (Cambridge: Cambridge University Press, 2002); nuanced realist view: William Wohlforth, 'The End of the Cold War as a Hard Case for Ideas', *Journal of Cold War Studies*, Vol. 7, No. 2 (Spring 2005), pp. 165–73.

50   Jan-Werner Müller, 'Introduction: The Power of Memory, the Memory of Power and the Power over Memory', in Jan-Werner Müller, ed., *Memory and Power in Post-War Europe* (Cambridge: Cambridge University Press), p. 18.

51   Thomas Berger, 'The Power of Memory and Memories of Power: The Cultural Parameters of German Foreign Policy Making since 1945', in Müller, *Memory and Power*, pp. 78–83.

52   Robert English, 'The Sociology of New Thinking', *Journal of Cold War Studies*, Vol. 7, No. 2 (Spring 2005), p. 74; Alexander Wendt, *Social Theory of International Relations* (Cambridge: Cambridge University Press, 2000), pp. 336–43.

53   Julie Newton, 'ForumduFuture' Conference, Assemblée Nationale de France (23 June 2005); English, 'The Sociology of New Thinking', p. 74.

54   Iver B. Neumann, 'Russia as a Great Power', in J. Hedenskog, V. Konnander, B. Nygren, I. Oldberg, Pursiainen, ed., *Russia as a Great Power* (London: Routledge, 2005), pp. 23–5.

55 Andrei Kozyrev, 'Rossiya i SShA: Partnerstvo ne prezhdevremenno, a zapazdyvayet', *Izvestiya* (11 March 1994), p. 3.
56 Andrei Kozyrev, 'The Lagging Partnership', *Foreign Affairs* 73, No. 3 (1994), 62–3; Elin Hellum, 'Identity and Russian Foreign Policy: An Analysis of the Official Discourse, 1992–2004', Mphil Thesis, St Antony's College, Oxford (April 2005), p. 28.
57 Müller, *Memory and Power*, p. 8.
58 Ibid., pp. 1–31, esp. 2.
59 Neumann, 'Russia as a Great Power', p. 25.
60 Hanna Smith agrees: The 'aspiration [for greatness] informs the Russian predilection for multipolarity, and this is a theme that appears in all forms of multipolarity in Russian foreign arguments from Kozyrev to Primakov, and Ivanov til Lavrov.' See: Hannah Smith, ed., *Russia and Its Foreign Policy* (Saarijarvi, Finland: Kikimora Publications, 2005), p. 39 (emphasis added).
61 Dmitri Trenin, 'Russia Redefines Itself and its Relations with the West', *The Washington Quarterly* (1 March 2007), http://www.carnegie.ru/en/print/75857-print.htm.
62 Ivan Krastev, 'Russia as the "Other Europe"', *Russia in Global Affairs*, No. 4 (October/December 2007), http://eng.globalaffairs.ru/numbers/21/1151/html, 3–4.
63 Those such as Richard Pipes, cited above, suggest the dominance of Russia's authoritarian legacy, but they pay insufficient attention to poll data from 1990 linking radical political reforms, the first of their kind in Russia, to change in Russian political behaviour.
64 Larson, Shevchenko, 'Shortcut to Great Power', pp. 77–109.
65 Ibid., p. 90.
66 Ibid., pp. 77–109.
67 Multipolar politics are usually associated with Foreign Minister Evgeni Primakov after 1996, but it was Andrei Kozyrev who began the shift towards multipolar ideas within the context of multilateralism. Smith, *Russia and Its Foreign Policy*, p. 38.
68 Gorchakov's Russia 'managed to produce an international impact incommensurate with [its] internal situation and real weight': 'Roundtable Discussion – Russian Foreign Policy: Amidst the Economic Crisis', *International Affairs* (Moscow), No. 1 (1999), p. 59.
69 'Superpower…cheap': Bendersky, 'Russia's Future Foreign Policy: Pragmatism in Motion', *Power and Interest News Report, PINR* (4 May 2005) in *JRL* (4 May 2005), http://www.cdi.org/Russia/Johnson.
70 Vyacheslav Nikonov, 'Russian Gaullism: Putin's Foreign Policy Doctrine', *Russia Watch*, No. 5, Harvard University (March 2001).
71 Robert Legvold, 'Russia's Unformed Foreign Policy', *Foreign Affairs* (September/October 2001), http://www.foreignaffairs.org/20010901faessay 5570/robert-legvold/russia-s-unformed-foreign-policy.
72 Krastev, 'Russia as the "Other Europe"'.
73 'Obzor', p. 72.
74 CIA World Fact Book, 'Rank Order-GDP', http://www.cia.gov/library/publications/the-world-factbook/rankorder/2001rank.html; Michael S. Bernstam, Alvin Rabushka, 'China vs. Russia: Wealth Creation vs. Poverty Reduction', Hoover Institution (25 April 2005), http://www.hoover.org/research/russian-econ/essays/5084951.html.

75   'Informal spokesman': Dmitri Trenin, 'Russia's Strategic Choices', Policy Brief #50 (May 2007): 3, http://www.carnegie.ru.

76   On Asia as rear guard for Western-centric foreign policy, Bobo Lo, personal conversation. See: Lo, *Axis of Convenience: Moscow, Beijing and the New Geopolitics* (Washington: Brookings, 2008).

77   'Kontseptsiya vneshnei politiki Rossiiskoi Federatsii'; 'Obzor'.

78   Fyodor Lyukyanov, 'The Transition from Bipolar to Multipolar' (23 January 2008), *Moscow Times* in *Russia in Global Affairs*, http://www.eng. global-affairs.ru/engsmi/1167.html.

79   Sergei Lavrov, 'Global Politics Needs Openness and Democracy', *Izvestiya*, in *Johnson's Russia List (JRL)*, #100 (1 May 2007), http://www.cdi.org/russia/johnson.

80   Ibid.

81   Karaganov, 'A New Epoch'.

82   Ibid.

83   'Obzor', p. 3. As the Foreign Ministry urged, 'The main accomplishment of recent years is the re-establishment of Russia's foreign policy independence. This new situation requires a rethinking, including at the *doctrinal* level.'

84   Fyodor Lyukyanov, *Vedomosti* (10 September 2007), 4 in *Current Digest of Post Soviet Press*, Vol. 59, No. 38 (2007): 4.

85   Kravstev, 'Russia as the "Other Europe"', 3.

86   Ivan Kravstev, 'Sovereign Democracy, Russian-Style', *OpenDemocracy* (16 November 2006), http://www.opendemocracy.net/node/4104/print.

87   Mark Leonard, Nicu Popescu, Executive Summary, European Council on Foreign Relations (7 November 2007), http://www.ecfr.eu.

88   Kravstev, 'Sovereign Democracy'.

89   Putin, 'Valdai' (2007).

90   Legvold, 'Russian Foreign Policy during Periods of Great State Transformation', see note 13.

91   On Soviet 'instrumentalism' towards Europe: Newton, *Russia, France, and the Idea of Europe*, Part I.

92   Given the UK's prominence, the Kremlin was extremely sensitive about its criticisms. The 'Obzor' particularly singled out Britain for unusual and angry comment; the British Ambassador was harassed; and BP was squeezed. 'Obzor': 37–8; Mark Leonard, Nicu Popescu, 'A Power Audit of EU-Russia Relations', Policy Paper, European Council on Foreign Relations (November 2007), http://www.ecfr.eu.org, 14–15.

93   'Obzor', p. 32; Vladimir Putin, 'Press Statement and Answers...Following the 20th Russia-European Union Summit', Mafra, Portugal (26 October 2007), www.kremlin.ru.

94   Mark Leonard, Nicu Popescu, 'Russia and Europe', European Council on Foreign Relations (7 November 2007), http://www.ecfr.eu/content/entry/commentary_russia.

95   Aleksei Arbatov, 'Russia and the United States – Time to End the Strategic Deadlock', Briefing, Vol. 10, Issue 3, Carnegie Moscow Centre (June 2008): 2.

96   Daniel Dombey, Demetri Sevastopulo, Neil Buckley, 'Russians Accuse US of Military Expansion', *FT* (9 February 2007), http://us.ft.com/ftgateway/superpage.ft?news_id=fto020920071449264142&page=2.

97 Isabelle Facon, 'Le Projet de Puissance de la Russie', p. 12.
98 'Russia's Upcoming Revised Military Doctrine', *PINR* (26 February 2007), http://pinr.come/report.php?ac=view_printable&report_id=622.
99 Dmitri Litovkin, 'Russia Explodes "Father of all Bombs"', *Izvestiya* (13 September 2007) in *Current Digest of the Post-Soviet Press (CDPSP)*, Vol. 59, No. 37 (2007): 8.
100 Arbatov, 'Russia and the United States', p. 4.
101 'Intelligence Brief: Russia Sends Missile Signal to US and China', *PINR* (1 June 2007), www.pinr.com/report.php?ac=view_printable&report_id=657.
102 Wallander, 'Global Challenges', p. 491.
103 Ibid.; Shevtsova, *Lost in Transition*.
104 Sergei Karaganov, 'The New Era: What is to be Done?', *Rossiiskaya Gazeta* in *CDPSP*, Vol. 59, No. 38 (17 October 2007).
105 Ibid.
106 On these points, see: Archie Brown, *Seven Years that Changed the World* (Oxford: Oxford University Press, 2007), pp. 248–51, 277–94; Archie Brown, *The Gorbachev Factor* (Oxford: Oxford University Press, 1996), pp. 225–30.
107 Vladimir Gel'man and Tomila Lankina, 'Authoritarian Versus Democratic Diffusions: Explaining Institutional Choices in Russia's Local Government', *Post-Soviet Affairs*, 24, 1 (2008): 40–62.

6
The Presence of Absence: Ethnicity Policy in Russia

Peter Rutland

Even though nationalism as an analytical category and political practice has been widely condemned in recent decades, the nation-state remains the predominant form of political structure throughout the world. The break-up of the Soviet Union led to the emergence of 15 states, which began actively promoting national identity as a building bloc of their newly-won independence. The Russian Federation is something of an exception to this trend, since it faces difficult and unresolved questions arising from its multi-ethnic composition. Russian nationalism played an important though somewhat ambiguous role in the break-up of the Soviet Union. Boris Yeltsin used appeals to Russian sovereignty to undermine the position of Soviet President Mikhail Gorbachev. But Yeltsin never subscribed to a clearly-articulated concept of Russian national identity. For Yeltsin, the most important symbol of the new Russian state was – Yeltsin himself. (He was officially described as the 'first president' of Russia.)

Russia inherited from the Soviet state a culturally diverse population, with ethnic Russians only making up four-fifths of the country's population. It also inherited an elaborate structure of ethnic federalism that recognised the rights of certain ethnic groups in their officially designated home territories. Another part of the Soviet legacy was a tradition of political and economic centralisation that had tied the fate of distant regions to decision-making in Moscow – a system that had broken down during the final years of the Soviet Union.

What policies did the state adopt to address these questions of majority and minority ethnic identity? In the 1990s, ethnic policy was overshadowed by struggles over what kind of political system should be introduced, and the pace and character of the economic transition. President Vladimir Putin implemented a clear and coherent policy regarding the reassertion of state power after he came to power in 2000, but he did not resolve the ambiguities in nationality policy that he inherited from Boris Yeltsin. As historian Alexei Miller notes, 'One would be hard pressed to find another country in which there is no consensus on such a broad range of basic topics. There is no agreement on whether Russia should be considered a nation-state or on whether we should strive to make it such a state'.[1] Ethnographer Emil Pain even more provocatively argues that the unwilling birth of the Russian Federation from the ruins of the Soviet Union means that the state sees itself as fundamentally illegitimate. He asks 'How can a single and positive identity form among the inhabitants of a state that is regarded by both the authorities and the public as an unexpected, illegitimate child, a cripple, the victim of a catastrophe or plot?'[2]

The missing link

Throughout the 1990s, Western scholars carried out extensive studies of political mobilisation in individual ethnic republics, most notably Chechnya, Tatarstan and Bashkortostan.[3] There have also been numerous studies of the republics through the prism of federalism: the formal territorial administrative structure of republics and regions, and the ebb and flow of power between them and the federal centre.[4] What is still missing is a study of ethnic policy *per se*: that is, the central government's policy towards ethnicity outside of the federalism framework.[5]

The reason that the subject has not attracted academic attention is simple: the Yeltsin and Putin eras saw no clearly articulated and implemented official Russian government policy towards ethnicity.[6] If there has been no policy since the Soviet collapse, how can one study it?

The absence of a policy was underlined by the absence of a single ministry responsible for ethnic policy. The State Committee for Nationality Questions went through eight name and status changes before its final incarnation, the Ministry for Federation Affairs, Nationalities, and Migration Policies, was abolished in 2001.[7] Its duties were then split between the Interior Ministry (migration); the Trade and Economic Development Ministry (regional development); the Foreign Ministry (the Russian diaspora in the former Soviet republics); and the Justice Ministry (national-cultural associations); among others.[8] There remained only a minister-coordinator without a ministry, a position filled by Valentin Zorin. That post, too, was abolished in September 2004, in the government reshuffle that followed the Beslan school tragedy. A Ministry for Regional

Development was then re-created, headed by former St Petersburg Governor Vladimir Yakovlev.[9]

From Soviet to post-Soviet

This policy vacuum stands in sharp contrast to the Soviet era, when there was an elaborate and intellectually coherent set of policies addressing the 'national question'.[10] Soviet policy combined some rather disparate elements:

a) a recognition of ethnic identity rooted in culture and language, incorporating a primordialist ethnographic model of human development;
b) an ethno-territorial federalism based on Leninist political pragmatism, aimed at turning ethnicity into source of legitimacy and support for the new state, while bringing it under state management and control; and
c) a corresponding territorial and hierarchical compartmentalisation of political bargaining, held together by the state's vertical power structures – the Communist Party of the Soviet Union (CPSU) and Committee for State Security (KGB).

These policies produced regional elites with a strong ethnic identity who were able to use this as a resource to bolster their political power as the USSR collapsed. Territorialisation of ethnicity had been introduced as a tool for state control, but 75 years later it turned out to be the major threat to the integrity of the Soviet and then the Russian state.

In Soviet times the prevailing framework of identity politics was the '*matrioshka*' model, where several layers of identity nest within each other. At the top was the concept of the *Sovetskii narod* (Soviet people) which was supposed to transcend ethnicity, drawing upon common achievements such as the space race and the Great Patriotic War.[11] The Soviet people would speak Russian, but this would be a language of 'inter-ethnic communication' rather than the bearer of ethnic Russian culture. Below the Soviet People were the nations of the 15 union republics, below them smaller ethnic groups, and finally the *malochislennye narody* (the quaintly designated 'small-numbered peoples').[12] Over time, these identities were supposed to 'draw together', but somehow time stood still – or went into reverse – and as the decades passed, ethnic distinctions did not disappear.

With the collapse of the Soviet Union, the category 'Soviet people' evaporated as an instrument of state ideology and policy, living on in a vague popular nostalgia for a lost past. At the same time, the vertical power structures binding the *matrioshka* together also collapsed. Thus, the Soviet framework for theoretically conceptualising and practically managing ethnicity disintegrated. The Russian Federation that emerged as a sovereign state in December 1991 inherited a cumbersome ethno-territorial structure, with 89 federal units or 'subjects', of six different types. A process of mergers from 2005–08 eliminated six small national districts, reducing the total to 83:46 *oblasti* (regions), 21 republics, nine *krai* (districts), four autonomous *okruga* (territories), one autonomous *oblast'* and two federal cities.[13]

Ethnic policy under Yeltsin

President Boris Yeltsin's 'policy' towards the ethnic republics was a by-product of his efforts to secure control of the central state and push through his economic reforms. Yeltsin's approach was driven by his pragmatic encouragement of self-rule for the leaders of the ethnic republics. He famously told them to 'take as much sovereignty as you can swallow' in a speech in Kazan, the capital of Tatarstan, in August 1990.

The leaders of many of these republics eagerly seized their chance, using ethnicity as part of their strategy to secure economic and polit-ical power in their regions.[14] They did this despite the fact that the 'titular' ethnic group formed an absolute majority in only seven of the 21 republics. This strategy was most successful in republics that had enjoyed relatively privileged treatment in Soviet times and/or had natural resources at their disposal – most notably Tatarstan, Bashkortostan and Sakha (Yakutiya). Republic leaders used their control over the media and education systems to build up ethnic pride and identity. The number of languages taught in Russia's schools went from about 40 in 1989 to about 80 by 2003, and according to the 2002 census, the number of people who said they spoke their native (non-Russian) language grew by 2.7%.[15]

In March 1992, Yeltsin drew up a vague federative agreement (an amendment to the 1978 constitution) regulating the relations of the ethnic republics with Moscow. Tatarstan and Chechnya refused to sign. Chechnya declared its independence in October 1991, a path that led ultimately to war. Tatarstan declared itself a sovereign state, and in March 1992 held a referendum in which 61% voted in favor of independence.[16] However unlike Chechnya, Tatarstan is located in central Russia and is physically surrounded by Russian provinces. Independence was not a realistic option. The five million Tatars, predominantly Muslim, were the largest ethnic minority in Russia. Tatars had established a state of their own in the middle Volga region, long before they were conquered by Ivan the Terrible in 1552. The incumbent leader of Tatarstan was Mintimer Shaimiev, who had become head of the Tatarstan government in 1985 and then first secretary of its Communist Party in 1989. Shaimiev's career path was not unusual: in about half the republics, former Communist leaders became post-1991 presidents. Shaimiev was appointed president in June 1991, and would go on to win election in 1996, 2001 and 2005. Appeals to Tatar nationalism combined with an extensive patronage machine enabled Shaimiev to consolidate his grip inside the republic, and hence to strike a hard bargain with Moscow. Tatar was introduced as an official language and soon an extensive state-sponsored mosque-building programme was under way. But Shaimiev had to play a careful game, since Tatars made up only 48.5% of the population in 1989, barely ahead of the Russians at 43.3%. (Those statistics were not accidental: the borders of Tatarstan had been drawn in the Soviet era so that a large part of the Volga Tatar population lay *outside* the Republic, which likewise encompassed a large number of non-Tatars.)

Yeltsin's policy of ethnic *laissez faire* stumbled on through his *de facto* toleration of Chechnya's declaration of independence and a series of bilateral treaties that he signed with the republics in 1994 – a reward for their support during the president's October 1993 confrontation with parliament. It paid off for Yeltsin politically: in the 1996 presidential elections his average vote was 8% higher in the ethnic republics than in the non-ethnic regions.[17] Yeltsin's actions amounted to an implicit policy of recognition of Russia as a multi-ethnic, federal state, with a special status for ethnic groups that happened to be sitting in one of the republics inherited from Soviet federalism.

The new constitution adopted in December 1993 began with the words 'We, the multinational people (*mnogonatsional'nyi narod*) of the Russian Federation...'[18] It established a unified system of executive power in areas of federal competence (Article 77) and declared federal laws sovereign over all others (Article 76), yet at the same time it recognised the legality of bilateral treaties (Article 66.4) and provided a long list of items of joint jurisdiction between the centre and federal subjects (Article 72). It recognised the right of republics to introduce their own official state languages and guaranteed to all the peoples of the Russian Federation the right to maintain their mother tongues and appropriate conditions for their study and cultivation (Article 68).

The official presidential policy on ethnicity was laid out in the 1996 document 'Conception of the State National Policy of the Russian Federation'. However, the secrecy of the deals brokered by Yeltsin and the accompanying asymmetry in the treatment granted to different republics indicate the absence of a principled and logically coherent national policy. By 1999, 46 of the 89 federal subjects had signed bilateral treaties with the Kremlin, most of them unpublished and hence of dubious legality. According to the regional ministry's 1998 report, 42 of the 46 treaties then in operation violated federal laws, and the legality of thousands of pieces of local legislation were appealed by regional prosecutors.

The December 1994 invasion of Chechnya tells us a great deal about the Yeltsin regime – its disrespect for human rights, its disdain for international opinion and its inability to control the military. But what does it tell us about ethnicity policy, beyond the fact that secession would not be tolerated?[19] The ethnic identity of Chechens as Chechens was not challenged; the state merely insisted that they accept Russian sovereignty and remain within the *matrioshka* model.

Who are the Russians?

The keystone in the arch of *Soviet* ethnicity was the concept of the *Sovetskii narod* (Soviet people). In the course of the 1990s, Russian identity did not emerge as a sufficiently coherent and inclusive category to replace that absence.[20] The Yeltsin administration never developed a clear policy on the question of who the Russians were. Yeltsin himself preferred to use the inclusive, civic terms *rossiiskii* and *rossiyane* (pertaining to citizens of the Russian state), rather than the more exclusive and ethnic term *russkii*, as in *russkii narod* (Russian people) or *russkaya natsiya* (Russian nation).

The leading Russian academic theorist of nationalism, Valerii Tishkov, was a Yeltsin advisor and briefly served as head of the State Committee for Nationalities in 1992. He was the most consistent exponent of the idea of developing a 'civic' national consciousness in Russia, based on the notion of *rossiyane* – that is, defining citizenship in inclusive terms, not tied to Russian ethnicity.[21] Tishkov thought that rewarding assertive nationalism in Tatarstan and the other republics was a recipe for endless conflict. He insists that 'the Russian state, regardless of its organisational structure – monarchy/empire, a union of republics and country of Soviets, or a republic/ federation – can and must be classified as a nation-state'.[22] At the same time, Tishkov tied the rise of civic nationalism in Russia to Western scholarship on the transcendence of nationalism in the late 20th century.[23] Similar civic nation-building efforts were also under way in Ukraine, as Alfred Stepan describes later in this volume.[24]

One problem was that democratic institutions were fading fast in Russia in the 1990s – and some kind of democratic participation is central to the notion of a civic political nation. A civic national identity that is dictated from above is arguably a contradiction in terms.[25] A second problem was that the term *rossiiskii* has little emotional resonance, since it usually connotes official state institutions. The term *russkii* is far more common in popular usage, though it usually refers to cultural identity, without any clear political agenda.[26] The term *rossiiskii* was seen as an anti-ethnic term, with some claiming that its use implicitly denied Russians the right to take pride in their ethnic identity. For example, Aleksei Chadaev complained that 'In the official rhetoric of the Russian state, the word "Russian" (*russkii*) has been semi-prohibited'. He went on to argue that '"*Russkii*" is not narrower but in fact broader than "*rossiyanin*". The word "*russkii*" applies today not just to the state of Russia but to the greater Russian world too'.[27] Chadaev's article was endorsed in an afterword by Putin's influential deputy chief of staff, Vladislav Surkov. Arguably, even the concept *rossiiskii* included within it some awareness of *russkii*, since the ethnic Russians were seen as the moving force behind the Russian state. (It was also suggested that a reference to someone as a member of the *rossiiskaya natsiya* could even be a way to signal that person's non-Russian ethnicity.[28]) Tishkov's more radical critics argued that he was putting up an intellectual smokescreen to disguise what the Communists referred to as the 'genocide' of the Russian nation under Yeltsin's rule. Even an academic such as Mikhail Rutkevich could bemoan the 'accelerating extinction of the Russian people' due to demographic decline, the loss of Russians living in the newly-independent states, and the influx of migrants into Russian cities.[29]

Yeltsin encouraged efforts to come up with a definition of the 'Russian idea' (*rossiiskaya ideya*) to put some flesh on the bones of the *rossiiskii* category – there was even a national essay competition on this topic in 1998.[30] But the search for a 'Russian idea', with its emphasis on spirituality and unique collective historical experiences, bore scant relation to Western approaches to 'civic' definitions of national identity, based on individual rights. The intellectual quest for Russian identity came to be dominated by writers in the Eurasianist tradition, a curious school of thought that arose among Russian *émigré* intellectuals in the 1920s and experienced a revival in the 1990s. Eurasianists believe that Russia forms the core of a distinct civilisation, neither European nor Asian.[31] Eurasianism did not easily translate into specific proposals for Russian state policy. It tended to mean support for a more assertive policy of integration with or dominion over the so-called 'near abroad', the former Soviet republics that had become independent states in 1991.

Putin to the rescue?

Things seemed to change with Vladimir Putin's accession to the presidency in 2000. Putin moved decisively to dismantle the *de facto* confederal system that Yeltsin's recognition of republican sovereignty had allowed to entrench itself. Putin insisted on the supremacy of federal laws over the legislation of federal subjects and on the need for a unified legal and fiscal space. He introduced a new system of seven federal districts headed by presidential representatives to ensure the 'power vertical'. By the time of his second address to the Federal Assembly in April 2001, Putin was confidently asserting that trends leading to the 'disintegration' of the state had been reversed.[32] Emil Pain argued that Putin's concern with restoring the 'power vertical' had more to do with a desire to restore central political and economic authority in general than any specific fear of ethnic secession spreading beyond Chechnya – which had undoubtedly been instrumental in Putin's own rise to power.[33]

However, at that point things ground to a halt. Putin's attention was focused on the state rather than the nation: the state needed an anthem, some symbols, some rituals. But Putin showed little interest in weaving these instruments of state into a convincing, emotionally engaging narrative of Russian identity. In his public speeches, Putin was far more accustomed than Yeltsin to use *russkii*, and rarely uttered *rossiyane* or *rossiiskii* – typically, only in connection with matters pertaining to the Russian state (*rossiiskoe gosudartsvo*) and not the Russian people. Moreover, Putin quickly and energetically revived a symbolic repertoire for Russian national identity, pulling up some features from the Tsarist past (for example, new uniforms for the Kremlin guard and regular visits to Orthodox churches), while reviving some Soviet symbols (such as restoring the Soviet anthem, with new words). The innovations enjoyed limited success. In a 2006 survey only 58% of respondents could get the flag colours in the right order and only 34% knew the first line of the new anthem.[34] In his 2005 State of the Federation address Putin talked about the *rossiiskii narod* and *natsiya* as having a 'civilising mission' in the

Eurasian continent. Later that year, the November 7 holiday (marking the 1917 revolution) was replaced by 'Unity Day' on November 4, marking the liberation of Moscow from the Poles in 1612.[35] In his 2007 address, Putin talked about the role of Russians and Russian-speakers beyond Russia's borders – a 'Russian world' (*russkii mir*).[36]

As in many countries around the world, football is perhaps the most powerful indicator of national loyalty. In June 2008 after the defeat of Holland in the European cup quarter final, '700,000 Muscovites poured into the streets in what the official RIA Novosti press agency called the biggest spontaneous street demonstration Moscow has seen since the USSR defeated Nazi Germany'.[37] It is interesting that in a television debate on the eve of Unity Day in 2009, journalist Sergei Dorenko was asked what he thought contemporary Russians have in common, and in response he cited the two iconic achievements of the Soviet era – the victory over fascism and the first man in space.[38]

While state policy was marking time, popular attitudes were shifting. In the 1990s, Russia experienced heavy migration from the former Soviet Union – mainly of ethnic Russians. The revival of the Russian economy under Putin, however, brought an influx of non-Russian migrant workers from Ukraine, Central Asia and the Caucasus. By 2008, they numbered in excess of seven million. Their presence in Russian cities raised ethnic tensions and gave renewed vigour to those calling for the assertion of the 'Russianness' (*russkost'*) of Russian citizens. Popular support for nationalist ideas such as 'Russia for the Russians' grew, with support for that slogan rising from 45% to 55% of respondents between 1998 and 2002, according to VTsIOM polls.[39] However, of that 55%, only 17% supported it unconditionally, while 38% said it should be 'within limits'.[40] Putin did not encourage such sentiments, nor did he use such language himself. He specifically denounced the 'Russia for the Russians' slogan, which was used by the Liberal Democratic Party of Russia (LDPR), in his 18 December 2003 question-and-answer session on Russian TV.[41]

This leads one to suggest that Putin is a statist (*gosudarstvennik*) but not a nationalist. State power – and not national community – is his object of veneration. What Putin sought as President was clearly not bound up with 'ethnic' nationalism. Nor was it about '*civic*' nationalism in the Western sense, since it was not connected to individual rights and democratic participation. Putin made only routine references to Russia as a multi-cultural and multi-confessional state. Pain argued that 'the idea of a multicultural society is absolutely foreign to the current author-ities and to the majority of the Russian population'.[42] Others agreed that 'recognition of difference' was absent from Putin's political idiom.[43]

Putin's Western critics argue that his statist brand of nationalism will not be satisfied with building a state within the current boundaries of the Russian Federation.[44] They suggest that Russia is in its very essence an 'empire-state', one whose leaders' identity is deeply rooted in their capacity to rule over a multiplicity of peoples across the Eurasian land mass. The collapse of the Soviet Union shrank the Russian state to the boundaries it had occupied in the 18th century – before two centuries of steady expansion west, south and east. According to this school of thought, the Russian state will not be content until it once again exercises hegemony over Ukraine, the South Caucasus and Central Asia. Emil Pain shares the concern that the Russian state has a strong imperial component, one which also means that inside the country its inhabitants are treated as subjects rather than citizens.[45]

The anti-national nationalism

Under both Yeltsin and Putin, the state recognised that developing a policy of assertive ethnic Russian nationalism would antagonise the non-Russian groups that according to the 2002 census made up 20.2% of the country's population (up from 18.5% in 1989).[46] Putin ignored, or at times resisted, the clarion calls for Russian nationalism that came from the State Duma or from the ultra-nationalist intellectuals and social movements.

Putin's enthusiastic embrace of foreign partners (German, Chinese, American) during his first term as president was anathema to the nationalists and clear evidence of his statist agenda. Putin was intent on repositioning Russia's identity as an accepted member of the global community. But this strategy, while it persisted, denied nationalists the space to use state policy to define Russians in opposition to the Western or Chinese 'other'.[47] Without such an 'othering', a powerful and assertive national identity would not be forged.

Putin and his PR advisors were obviously aware of the power of appeals to the public invoking nationalist themes. The Kremlin exploited nationalism to build popular support for Putin, using the second war in Chechnya to propel him to victory in the March 2000 presidential election. The Chechens were the obvious target for such a process of identity formation, and judging from opinion polls, the Chechens were indeed feared and vilified by ordinary Russians. Yet government policy has always maintained that Chechens are members of the Russian family, and that the wars were waged to save Chechens from domination by criminal leaders or foreign jihadists. This contradiction grew even sharper in 2003, when Putin switched to a new policy of 'Chechenisation': selecting a loyal Chechen strongman in the form of President Akhmad Kadyrov and devolving responsibility for crushing the rebels to him. From a counter-insurgency point of view this eventually proved successful (despite Kadyrov's assassination in May 2004). But it made it more difficult to build Russian identity on the basis of hatred of the Chechens, as Russian policy was now in the hands of 'good' Chechens. For this reason, even though 'anti-Chechen attitudes and various phobias have been rising steadily,... these campaigns have not led to Russians uniting'.[48]

Apart from consolidating the presidency, Putin's political strategy included the creation of a pro-presidential party of power, in the form of United Russia. This party, too, is more statist than nationalist, in that its appeal is to consensus and order, rather than to division and differentiation, internal or external. Christopher Marsh and James Warhola note that Unity was headed by members of two of Russia's ethnic minorities: Sergey Shoigu (who is from Tuva) and Aleksandr Karelin (whose name evokes Kareliya).[49]

Even if Russian nationalism was not being instigated from above, however, it was flaring up from below, serving as a rallying point for disaffected social groups from skinheads to pensioners.[50] Ramazan Abdulatipov, Chairman of the Assembly of Russia's Nationalities, complained, 'Unfortunately, the state passed the "Russian question" to extremist forces'.[51] Particularly during Putin's second term, there was evidence of a rising xenophobic nationalism that appeared to enjoy at least some support from within the security establishment and other parts of the administration. Street violence against foreigners continued to increase in the 2000s, with at least 87 people killed and 378 wounded in racially motivated attacks in 2008, according to figures compiled by the SOVA institute.[52]

Critics accused the government of fostering radical nationalism in order to create a putative threat that would justify its own increasingly tight control over political life within the country. In any case, the official position of the Kremlin and the government remained hostile to such ultra-nationalist movements. At the same time, the increasingly prickly nationalism that characterised Russian foreign policy during the second Putin administration carefully avoided any real ethnic component. It was a statist nationalism, driven largely by the great-power agenda described by Julie Newton in Chapter 5 of this volume.

To the extent that there was an active state policy, it was devoted more to crushing manifestations of ethnic nationalism than promoting them. The state did not want to use the ethnic nationalist tool for itself – but it did not want anyone else using it, either. There was a series of laws condemning nationalist extremism and incitement to ethnic and religious hatred. More surprising still, these laws were sporadically enforced. Article 63 of the 1997 Criminal Code declares 'motives of national, racial or religious hatred or enmity' in committing a crime to be an aggravating circumstance. The 2002 Law 'On Preventing and Counteracting Extremist Activities' led to bans on Russia National Unity and the National Patriotic Party. Between 2001 and 2004, the press ministry issued 35 warnings to newspapers on grounds of inciting interethnic conflict, a violation of Article 4 of the Law on Media.[53] The 2001 Law on Political Parties barred the establishment of political parties 'on the grounds of professional, racial, national or religious belonging'.

The nationalist Motherland (*Rodina*) Party was created by the Kremlin in 2003 with the goal of drawing support away from the opposition Communist Party. However, Motherland gained in popularity, and its leader, Dmitrii Rogozin, started challenging the Kremlin on issues like corruption. It was banned from running in the December 2005 Moscow city elections on the grounds that its 'Cleanse our city' campaign advertisements were an incitement to ethnic hatred.[54] The party itself was shut down shortly thereafter. Another illustration of how nation-building could slip out of control of the Kremlin's hands is the Movement against Illegal Immigration, founded in 2002, which started using the November 4 Unity Day holiday as an occasion for noisy demonstrations under the slogan 'Russia for the Russians'.[55] Pro-Kremlin nationalists ousted the radicals from the movement in September 2008 and its founder Aleksandr Belov was jailed in May 2009.[56] The 'Russian March' on November 4, 2009 was dominated by the pro-Kremlin *Nashi* youth movement.[57]

Important insights into Putin's thinking on the subject can be obtained from his off-the-cuff remarks during his annual live phone-ins. During Putin's televised press conference in December 2002, Chechnya aside, ethnic issues only came up in a viewer's question about attacks on people from the Caucasus in Moscow markets. Putin condemned such interethnic conflict as a threat to stability: 'We all must understand that we are a single family'.[58] Likewise during Putin's December 2004 press conference, despite the recent horror of Beslan, ethnic issues were mostly sidestepped.[59] Putin brushed aside a question from Kazan about the absence of a nationalities ministry, saying the issue could be adequately tackled by the Regional Development Ministry and by the newly-created Public Chamber. In response to a question about the abolition of gubernatorial elections, Putin invoked the threat of disintegration, and cited the example of Dagestan with its 33 ethnic groups. Referring favourably to Dagestan's tradition of power sharing, Putin said: 'This system has existed for decades and is unlikely to be effective in any other way. Otherwise, representatives of this or that ethnic group will feel slighted and pushed aside from power. However, we cannot develop one system of authorities in one constituent part of the (Russian) Federation and another one in another. We should have a unified (system) for all.'

So Putin, in the same breath, praised the unique arrangements in Dagestan and insisted on a unified system. These statements are logically consistent, if one recognises that the President is the source of the unified system. If he approved the Dagestani leadership, then it was OK. But if they were to choose an arrangement for themselves, without Moscow's approval, then it would not be acceptable. The same logic explains why it was acceptable for Chechnya to sign a bilateral treaty with Moscow, while all the other constituent units of the Federation were being told that such treaties violated the unity of the legal-administrative system.

In 2002, President Putin instructed Nationality Policy Minister Vladimir Zorin to prepare a new version of the state's national policy, issued in 1996. At the same time the United Russia party launched a 'Russian Project' to build national pride, a campaign which the project's leader, Ivan Demidov, explicitly identified with the majority ethnic Russian population.[60] The initial draft of the state policy from the Regional Development Ministry was reportedly rejected on the grounds that it included reference to ethnic Russians as a 'state-forming nation' that were objectionable to other ethnic groups.[61] The new policy did not see the light of day by the end of 2009.

National identity did feature in an influential statement of the philosophy behind Putin's presidency, 'The nationalisation of the future', published by Putin aide Vladislav Surkov in 2006.[62] Surkov wrote that 'People want to live freely in a community based on just foundations. For the majority in a society of a certain scale that community is the nation (*natsii*)', which Surkov defined as 'the supra-ethnic sum of all the citizens of the country'. He continued 'The *rossiisskaya natsiya* (*narod*) unifies all the peoples of Russia in common borders and a common state, culture, past and future.' He later states that '*russkaya* democracy is open and must be welcoming for all *rossiiskikh* peoples'. Surkov's statement clearly shows that the duality of *russkii* and *rossiiskii* concepts of Russianness had not been resolved. In November 2007 United Russia's website posted an article on 'The Russian National Leader Phenomenon', by Abdul-Hakim Sultygov, the party's ethnic policy coordinator, praising Putin as the figure who can unite all Russians.[63] So loyalty to the state, personified in the figure of Putin, seems to be the key factor behind a unified Russian identity.

The individualisation of ethnicity

One important part of Valery Tishkov's promotion of civic as opposed to ethnic nationalism was the idea of shifting ethnicity from ethno-territorial administrative units to the level of individual rights, expressed through voluntary associations of co-ethnics.[64] Tishkov floated the model in 1992, and it was adopted by Nationalities Minister Sergei Shakhrai in 1994, with the creation of a Council of National Associations of Russia. The year 1996 saw the adoption of a Federal Law on National-Cultural Autonomy (NCA).[65] The idea was strongly promoted by Valentin Zorin, Nationalities Minister from 2001 until 2004.[66] This policy sought to detach the provision of ethnic rights from the small number of ethnicities with their own territorial administrative units and root them instead in civil society – allowing groups to request the provision of cultural facilities, media outlets and school classes in the regions where they were based. By 1999, 227 National Cultural Autonomous groups had been registered, rising to 594 by 2004.[67]

This idea had several advantages. First, it took as its starting point the Soviet era understanding of ethnicity as a cultural-linguistic, rather than political or economic, category. This was an advantage because it built upon a conception already prevailing in Russian society and among Russian officials, and did not mark too radical a break from past practice. Second, it addressed one of the major flaws in the old system of ethno-territorial units: the lack of congruence between the ethnic units and the actual distribution of ethnic groups across the territory of the federation. Some 30–40% of Russia's minority population (ten million people) live outside of their titular republics. Their ethnic rights (to education for example) are weakly protected or non-existent. Likewise, there are some ten million people, Russians and others, living in ethnic republics who are *not* members of the titular nationality. Third, the individual concept of ethnicity accorded with contemporary Western theory and practice, as in the US tradition of a plurality of ethnic groups asserting their identity within a common civic identity and shared institutions.

The individualisation approach even fed into post-modern notions of transcending the nation-state.[68] The search for a new policy in Russia happened to coincide with a renewed interest in national minority rights in Europe, for the first time in half a century, in response to the horrors of the Yugoslav wars of succession.[69] It also coincided with a wave of interest in the rights of indigenous peoples, originating in the Native American and Australian aboriginal movements. This was picked up by defenders of the 'small peoples' of the Russian North, and those of the Finno-Ugric group, who have strong backers in the West.[70] But even the Tatars could attach themselves to this movement, regarding themselves as a conquered people (like French Quebecois).[71]

Another example of the individualisation of ethnicity is the policy of seeing ethnicity as the personal choice of an individual rather than an objective, ascribed characteristic, defined according to criteria laid down by the state.[72] The requirement that people list their ethnicity on their passport (paragraph five) was abolished, and in the 2002 census people were given a free choice in self-identifying their ethnicity, rather than being obliged to fit into a pre-arranged list of recognised nations. As a result, the number of recorded ethnic groups rose from 130 to 160.

The new approach, however, also brought problems.[73] For one thing, is the Russian state really willing to leave ethnicity up to the individual? A controversial part of the model is the idea that the state should continue to register, manage and fund these ethnic associations – and only one federal NCA is allowed for each ethnic group. The idea of ethnicity as a voluntaristic, personal choice does not seem to have sunk very deep roots. For example, in a seminar during the 2002 census, Nationalities Minister Valentin Zorin himself seemed reluctant to accept that 'Cossack' was a valid choice as an ethnic identity, preferring to regard it as a 'social' category. And in Tatarstan, the authorities pressed for sub-groups such as Siberian Tatars and *kryashennye* (converts to Christianity) to be counted as regular Tatars.

Likewise, local authorities have often intervened to deny registration to ethnic groups, on the grounds that they might incite inter-ethnic antagonism. For example, in December 1999 the Tatar organisation *Natsional'no-Kul'turnaya Avtonomiya Tatarstana* (NKAT) was denied registration in Ufa, Bashkortostan.[74] Tomila Lankina, writing elsewhere, describes the range of instruments at the disposal of regional elites: registering organisations, granting permission for demonstrations, giving access to premises, and controlling the content of local newspapers.[75] After the upsurge of social activism in 1989–92, Lankina argues, the wave subsided, with control over the new movements shifting from councils to the executive branch in her two cases, Bashkortostan and Adygeya. Civil society traditions in Russia remain too fragile for the pluralistic ethnic group model to flourish.

Managing ethnicity in a global context

Adding to the complexity of the situation is the fact that post-Soviet Russia opened itself to integration with the rest of the world. In the traditional, 19th century world order, nationalism was a domestic affair: it was about building one's nation-state through a process of internal homogenisation and maybe territorial conquest. In the post-1989 world, nationality policy was internationalised. It is no longer solely, or even mainly, an issue of domestic politics. It is about managing borders, defining citizenship, handling migration flows, and generally adhering to international norms regarding protection of ethnic minorities. While the Russian state drifted through the 1990s without a coherent ethnicity policy, it was forced to explain its actions to an alphabet soup of international organisations – the OSCE, the PACE, the Council of Europe and its Commission against Racism and Intolerance, the UNHCR, etc.[76] This forced it, willy-nilly, to articulate a set of policies, in response, for example, to the report of the Advisory Committee on the Framework Convention of the Council of Europe for the Protection of National Minorities.[77]

It is not so much that the international community is forcing Russian policy to conform to its norms: rather, it is a case of Russia's international undertakings obliging the government to articulate a policy which may or may not actually exist. Curiously, the policy process itself has been globalised, even if the practical and normative content of the policy has not. This was not a one-way street. Russia also tried to use the international system to advance its own interests – most notably, regarding the situation of ethnic Russians in the Baltic states. There were widespread fears in the early 1990s that Russia would mobilise to defend the interests of the 22 million ethnic Russians stranded in the now-independent states of the former Soviet Union.[78] Many leading figures, such as Alexander Solzhenitsyn, argued that Russia should reclaim the Crimea (from Ukraine) and the provinces of Northern Kazakhstan, where a majority of the population were ethnic Russians. However, such aggressive nationalist policies never materialised. Though Yeltsin did issue a decree on the subject in August 1994, the focus there was on advancing Russian state interests (military and economic) rather than on protecting the rights of co-ethnics in the 'near abroad'. This policy of passivity in defence of ethnic Russians outside the borders of the Russian Federation continued under Putin. The meek acceptance of Turkmenistan's revocation of dual citizenship in 2003 would be a case in point. Wary of losing their Russian citizenship, many Russians gave up their Turkmen passports, which obliged them to leave the country.

The way in which ethnic politics sits astride and is connected to domestic and international policy and to Russian state goals is most vividly illustrated by the situation in the Caucasus. Russia's backing for secessionist movements in Abkhazia and South Ossetia in 1992 drew Moscow very directly into ethnic politics south of the Caucasus mountains. The Chechen rebellion in turn drew support, psychological and practical, from the south Caucasus, and Islamist radicals sought to spread the insurgency into neighbouring Dagestan, Ingushetiya and North Ossetia. This cycle continued into the Putin era. The Kremlin's encouragement of Abhkaz and South Ossetian secession as a tool to advance Russian state goals in the region eventually culminated in Russia's war with Georgia in the summer of 2008 and Russia's subsequent recognition of the sovereignty of those two break-away republics.

Conclusion

This chapter sketches out some of the diverse factors affecting Russian ethnic policy since 1992. Putin brought stability and order to the Russian political system but made little progress in trying to clear up the ambiguities in Russian ethnic policy. Rather he tried to restructure state institutions to limit any possibility for using ethnicity to challenge Moscow's political power. Putin preferred a 'statist nationalism' that served his interest in consolidating power at home and projecting it abroad, while keeping potential ethnic conflicts in check. In this he was fairly successful, more through guile than through direct confrontation. But Putin largely failed to articulate a clear vision for the future of Russian national identity and the place of the non-Russian peoples within it.

Notes

1　Alexei Miller, 'The Nation as a Framework for Political life', *Russian Politics and Law*, 47, 2 (March–April 2009): 8–29, p. 15.
2　Emil Pain, 'Russia Between Empire and Nation', *Russian Politics and Law*, 47, 2 (March–April 2009): 60–86, p. 82.
3　For example, Dmitry Gorenburg, *Minority Ethnic Mobilization in the Russian Federation* (New York: Cambridge University Press, 2006).

4   For example, Cameron Ross, *Federalism and Democratisation in Russia* (Manchester: Manchester University Press, 2002).

5   Among the exceptions: Bill Bowring, 'Austro-Marxism's Last Laugh?: The Struggle for Recognition of National-Cultural Autonomy for Rossians and Russians', *Europe-Asia Studies*, 54, 2 (March 2002): 229–50; Sven Gunnar Simonsen, 'Inheriting the Soviet Policy Toolbox: Russia's Dilemma over Ascriptive Nationality', *Europe-Asia Studies*, 51, 6 (September 1999): 1069–87.

6   This complaint was frequently raised by North Ossetiya President Alexander Dzasokhov. See: Natalia Ratiani, 'A Generation Growing up amidst Conflict', *Izvestiya* (31 March 2005); and, at the national conference on 'The state's ethnic policy in the 20th and 21st centuries', in Perm: 'Shadow Ethnicity', *Izvestiya* (31 October 2002).

7   Konstantin Smirnov, 'Dolgii put' Minnats ot MVD do MVD' [The long road of the NatsMin from MVD to MVD], *Kommersant-Vlast* (23 October 2001).

8   Virginie Coulloudon, 'New appointment may presage changes in Russia's nationalities policy', RFE/RL *Newsline* (19 December 2001).

9   Yakovlev was appointed presidential envoy to the Southern Federal District in March 2004. He was fired in September 2004 in the wake of the Beslan tragedy, after which he was appointed to head the newly created Ministry for Regional Development. In September 2007 Yakovlev was replaced as minister by Dmitrii Kozak, who was in turn succeeded by Viktor Basargin in October 2008.

10 On the origins of this system, see: Terry Martin, *The Affirmative Action Empire: Nation and Nationalism in the Soviet Union, 1923–1939* (Ithaca: Cornell University Press, 2001).

11 Andrei Okara, 'O subetnicheskoi, etnicheskoi i sverkhetnicheskoi gordosti velikorossov' [Sub-ethnic, ethnic and supra-ethnic pride of the Great Russians], *Politicheskii klass* (18 August 2007).

12 There are now 45 recognised 'indigenous small-numbered peoples', each with less than 50,000 members. Brian Donahoe et al, 'Size and Place in the Construction of Indigeneity in the Russian Federation', *Current Anthropology*, 48, 6 (December 2008), 993–1020.

13 Julia Kusznir, 'Russian Territorial Reform?', *Russian Analytical Digest* (17 June 2008): 8–11.

14 Donna Bahry, 'Ethnicity and Equality in Post-communist Economic Transition: Evidence from Russia's Republics', *Europe-Asia Studies*, 54, 5 (July 2002): 673–99; Dmitry Gorenburg, 'Nationalism for the Masses: Popular Support for Nationalism in Russia's Ethnic Republics', *Europe-Asia Studies*, 53, 1 (January 2001): 73–104. For pro-nationalist views see: Rafael Khakimov, 'Path Forward for the Russian Federation', Network on Ethnological Monitoring and Early Warning of Conflict, *Bulletin*, 2 (2 June 1995), http://federalmcart.ksu.ru/publications.

15 Nationalities Minister Valentin Zorin, quoted in *RIA Novosti* (13 June 2004).

16 Gulnaz Sharafutdinova, 'Chechnya Versus Tatarstan: Understanding ethnopolitics in post-communist Russia', *Problems of Post-Communism*, 47, 2 (2000): 13–22; Dmitry P. Gorenburg, *Minority Ethnic Mobilization in the Russian Federation* (New York: Cambridge University Press, 2003).

17 Christopher Marsh and James Warhola, 'Ethnicity, Ethno-territoriality and the Political Geography of Putin's Electoral Support', *Post-Soviet Geography*

and Economics 42, 4 (2001): 1–14. In 2000 Putin also won a plurality in every ethnic region except the Altay Republic.

18   The Constitution of the Russian Federation, adopted 12 December 1993. http://constitution.ru/en/10003000-01.htm.

19   Matthew Evangelista, *The Chechen Wars: Will Russia Go the Way of the Soviet Union?* (Washington, D.C.: Brookings Institution Press, 2002).

20   Vera Tolz, 'Forging the Nation: National Identity and Nation Building in Post-Communist Russia', *Europe-Asia Studies*, 50, 6 (1998): 993–1022; Vera Tolz, *Inventing the Nation: Russia* (London: Arnold, 2001); Pal Kolsto (ed.), *Nation-Building and Common Values in Russia* (Boulder, CO: Rowman and Littlefield, 2003).

21   Valery Tishkov, 'What Are Russia and the Russian People?', *Russian Politics and Law*, 47, 2 (March–April 2009): 30–59.

22   Ibid., p. 53.

23   Valery Tishkov, 'Forget the "Nation": Post-Nationalist Understanding of Nationalism', *Ethnic and Racial Studies*, 23, 4 (2000): 625–50.

24   On similar debates in Ukraine, see Stephen Shulman, 'The Contours of Civic and Ethnic National Identification in Ukraine', *Europe-Asia Studies*, 56, 1 (2004): 35–56.

25   Emil Pain, 'Russia Between Empire and Nation,' *Russian Politics and Law*, 47, 2 (March–April 2009): 60–86.

26   For example, a search of the language corpus database www.ruscorpora.ru on 20 June 2008 found that *russkii narod* scored 552 hits, *russkaya natsiya* 32, *rossiiski narod* 45, *rossiiskaya natisya* 1, *rossiiyanin* 195 and *rossiyane* 602.

27   Aleksei Chadaev, 'The Return of the Russian and a "Third Russia"', *Izvestiya* (12 June 2006).

28   Miller, 'The Nation as a Framework', p. 18.

29   Mikhail Rutkevich, 'On the fate of the Russian ethnic group', *Russian Politics and Law*, 43, 2 (March–April 2005), 70–82, p. 76.

30   Wendy Helleman (ed.), *The Russian Idea: In Search of a New Identity* (Bloomington, IN: Slavica, 2004).

31   Marlene Laruelle, *Russian Eurasianism: An Ideology of Empire* (Washington, D.C.: Johns Hopkins University Press, 2008).

32   'Poslanie federal'nomu sobraniyu R.F.' (3 April 2001), http://www.kremlin.ru/sdocs/appears.shtml?type=63372.

33   Emil Pain, 'Reforms in the Administration of the Regions and Their Influence on Ethnopolitical Processes in Russia', in Robert Orttung and Peter Reddaway, eds, *The Dynamics of Russian Politics, Volume 2* (Lanham, MD: Rowman and Littlefield, 2005).

34   'Chem gordyatsya rossiyane?' [What makes Russians proud?], VTsIOM press release no. 466, 8 June 2006.

35   Andrei Zorin, 'A New Holiday for Old Reasons' (20 January 2005), http://www.Russiaprofile.org.

36   For data on Russian language use in the newly-independent states, see Kirill Gavrilov et al, 'Status and prospects of the Russian language in the NIS' (11 November 2008). www.eurasianhome.org/xml/t/expert.xml?lang= en&nic= expert&pid=1803.

37   Fred Weir, 'Russia's success in soccer and hockey is credited to petrodollars flowing into sports', *Christian Science Monitor* (27 June 2008).

38 BBC Monitoring, 'Russian TV Talk Show Discusses National Identity', NTV Mir (2 November 2009).
39 Ibid.
40 Yana Amelina, 'What's a Patriot To Do?', *Rossiiskie Vesti* (18 June 2003).
41 Vladimir Putin, 'Excerpts from the President's Live Television and Radio Dialogue with the Nation' (18 December 2003), http://www.kremlin.ru/eng/sdocs/speeches.
42 Emil Pain, 'The Changing Nature of Ethnic Politics under President Putin', Carnegie Endowment Meeting Report, 2, 7 (30 October 2000).
43 David Cashaback, 'Risky Strategies? Putin's Federal Reforms and the Accommodation of Difference in Russia', *Journal on Ethnopolitics and Minority Issues in Europe* 3 (2003), http://www.ecmi.de.
44 'Without Ukraine, Russia ceases to be a Eurasian empire.' Zbigniew Brzezinski, *The Grand Chessboard* (New York: Basic Books, 1998), p. 46.
45 Emil Pain, 'Russia Between Empire and Nation', *Russian Politics and Law*, 47, 2 (March–April 2009): 60–86.
46 'Vserossiiskaya perepis' naseleniya' (2002), www.perepis2002.ru.
47 In Russian parlance, the distinction is between 'our own' (*svoi*) and aliens (*chuzie*).
48 Yevgenii Verlin, 'Emil Pain: There is a Huge Build-up of Ethnic Hatred in Russia', *Izvestiya* (25 March 2004).
49 Marsh and Warhola, 'Ethnicity, Ethno-territoriality': 1–14.
50 Lev Gudkov, 'Xenophobia: Past and Present', *Russia in Global Affairs*, 4, 1 (January–March 2006): 58–66.
51 Pavel Anokhin, 'State of Ethnic Russians is the State of the Nation', *Trud* (31 March 2004).
52 http://sova-center.ru/.
53 There was only one case in 2003, a *Zavtra* interview with Chechen rebel Akhmed Zakaev. ITAR-TASS (2 February 2004).
54 Aleksander Dubovoi, 'Moscow city election cleansed of the Motherland Party', *Kommersant* (28 November 2005).
55 Emil Pain, 'Twilight of the Liberal Empire', *Nezavisimaya gazeta* (15 June 2007).
56 Andrei Kozenko, 'Nationalism with a Human Face', *Kommersant* (13 July 2009).
57 Maksim Selifontov, 'Nashi Gave the Celebration Back to the Russians', *Moskovskii komsomolets* (5 November 2009).
58 'President Putin Answers Questions', RTR via BBC Monitoring (19 December 2002).
59 RTR via BBC Monitoring (23 December 2004).
60 Kira Latukhina and Anastasia Kornia, 'Competing Ethnic Policy Strategies', *Vedomosti* (15 June 2007).
61 Andrei Kozenko, 'Public Chamber Downplays the Role of the Russian People', *Kommersant* (7 March 2006); 'The Fifth Article of Power in Russia', *Kommersant-Vlast* (2 April 2007); Olga Pavlikova, 'Kozak Prompted by the Cossacks', *Gazeta* (21 November 2007).
62 Vladislav Surkov, 'Natsionalizatsiya budushchego' [Nationalization of the future], *Ekspert* (20 November 2006).
63 Dmitri Kamyshev, 'Acting Tsar', *Kommersant-Vlast* (12 November 2007). The article appeared as part of a campaign to persuade Putin to stay on as president for a third term.

64   Valery Tishkov, 'What Are Russia and the Russian People?'
65   Nicky Torode, 'National Cultural Autonomy in the Russian Federation', *International Journal on Minority and Group Rights*, 15 (2008): 179–93.
66   For a profile of Zorin, see Coulloudon, 'New Appointment May Presage Changes in Russia's Nationalities Policy'; Mikhail Vinogradov, 'The Story-telling Minister', *Izvestiya* (7 December 2001).
67   Torode, 'National Cultural Autonomy', p. 186.
68   Valerii Tishkov, 'Zabyt' i natsii (Post-natsionalistichesko e ponimanie natsionalizma)' [Forget about the Nation (A post-nationalist understanding of nationalism)], *Etnograficheskoe obozrenie*, 5, 1 (1998).
69   Bowring, 'Austro-Marxism's Last Laugh?', notes the 1996 United Nations' International Covenant on Civil and Political Rights as a turning point.
70   The Finno-Ugric peoples in Russia numbered 3.1 million in 1989. Unprotected Peoples' Organisation, 'Finno-Ugric Minorities in Russia', conference report (25 August 2004), http://www.unpo.org/news_detail.php?arg=31&par=1124.
71   Khakimov, 'Path Forward for the Russian Federation'.
72   Simonsen, 'Inheriting the Soviet Policy Toolbox'.
73   Elena Filippova and Vassily Filippov, 'National-Cultural Autonomies in Post-Soviet Russia: A Dead-End Political Project', Association for Study of Nationalities conference, Sciences Po, Paris (4 July 2008).
74   Damir Iskhakov, 'Rossiiskii zakon 'O natsional'no-kult'turnoi avtonomii', Seminar Etnicheskii factor v Federalizatsii Rossii, Kazan (18 January 2000), http://federalmcart.ksu.ru/conference/seminar3/index.htm.
75   Tomila Lankina, 'Local Administration and Ethno-social Consensus in Russia', *Europe-Asia Studies*, 54, 7 (November 2002): 1037–53.
76   OSCE = Organization for Security and Cooperation in Europe; PACE = Parliamentary Assembly of the Council of Europe; UNHCR = United Nations High Commissioner for Refugees. See for example the UNHCR reports on Russia, at http://www.ohchr.org/english/countries/ru/index.htm.
77   For the Russian government's response to the Committee's assessment of Russian policy early in the Putin era, see http://www.coe.int/t/dghl/monitoring/minorities/3_FCNMdocs/PDF_1st_Com_RussianFederation_en.pdf.
78   Igor Zevelev, *Russia and Its New Diasporas* (Washington, DC: US Institute of Peace, 2001).

7
Political Parties Under Putin: Party-System Development and Democracy

Kenneth Wilson

This chapter analyses party-system development in Russia during the presidency of Vladimir Putin and considers the implications of this for Russia's political evolution. The party system in Russia in the 1990s was, by the reckoning of most observers, highly underdeveloped in comparative terms. President Putin's time in office, though, saw a number of very significant developments in Russia's party system. For one thing, Putin's administration oversaw the introduction of numerous legislative reforms aimed (ostensibly) at strengthening the party system. The 2003 Duma election also had extremely important implications for the party system. Has the party system in Russia consolidated or not? What were the implications of party-system development under Putin for democratisation? How, in turn, did this inform our understanding of the relationship between party-system consolidation and democracy?

The chapter begins by outlining the condition of Russia's party system in the 1990s. It then examines the relationship between party-system development and democratisation, as purported by the literature. We then consider whether (and how) party-system consolidation occurred under Putin and, if it did, whether this improved the chances for democracy in Russia. The chapter, next, studies the 2007 Duma elections in the context of Putin's second-term party-system reforms. Finally we consider the implications of this analysis for our understanding of the relationship between party-system development and democracy.

Party development in Russia in the 1990s

The underdevelopment of Russia's political parties in the 1990s is illustrated most graphically by their very limited penetration of Russia's

137

state institutions. In the consolidated democracies of Western Europe and the United States, established political parties dominate – in fact virtually monopolise – representative organs of state at national and regional levels. This, as we shall see, was very far from the case in Russia in its first decade as a post-communist state.

Most notably, no party representative occupied the post of president, which is by far the most powerful office in the Russian political system, and only one party candidate (Zyuganov in 1996) even managed to reach the second round.[1] Largely as a consequence of this, given Russia's presidential system, Russia's parties played little role in government or even in government formation. Political parties scarcely penetrated the Council of the Federation, which can fairly be characterised, following Michael McFaul, as having been a 'party-free state institution'.[2] National political parties also played a very limited role in regional politics at both the executive and legislative levels in the 1990s.[3]

The one representative institution in which Russia's political parties played a central role in the 1990s was the State Duma. There were, however, substantial limits to this. Independent candidates won more single-mandate constituency (SMC) seats than any individual party at each of Russia's first three Duma elections.[4] In fact, no party in Russia even nominated candidates in all 225 of Russia's single-member constituencies in any Duma election in the 1990s. Even the Communist Party of the Russian Federation (CPRF), Russia's largest party, contested only 129 single-mandate constituencies in the 1999 Duma election and of the 23 parties on the ballot paper only 11 nominated candidates in more than 30 constituencies.[5] This is a clear indicator of the under-institutionalisation of Russia's parties, as consolidated parties normally contest all of the seats in a polity. (Indeed, there is usually an over-supply of candidates, with stiff competition between prospective candidates to secure the right to run for a party.)

Parties (or what passed for parties) did, however, dominate the contests for Duma seats allocated by proportional representation (PR). This, though, was inevitable, as candidates had no choice but to work through parties, and voters who wished to be represented had to vote for one. The PR system thus ensured the existence of some parties (or party-like groups). Parties in Russia, in other words, only developed to any significant degree in the 1990s where they were legislated into existence.

Even on the PR section of the Duma vote – the one area where parties were predominant – Russia's party system exhibited significant signs of under-institutionalisation. For one thing, the number of parties contesting the Duma PR vote was consistently high and many of the contestants were not what would normally be classed as political parties.[6] Furthermore, there was a conspicuous lack of continuity in terms of the parties contesting elections and gaining representation in the Duma.[7] In Russia, it was not, as with consolidated party systems, the same parties that won seats time after time; indeed only three parties – Yabloko, the CPRF and the Liberal Democratic Party of Russia (LDPR)[8] – won proportional representation seats in each of Russia's first three Duma elections. The way that political parties, both major and minor, have appeared and disappeared between elections is a clear indication of the under-institutionalisation of Russia's party system. There was also pronounced movement of deputies between parties – or more precisely, factions and groups – in the Duma. While the number of defections declined over the course of the first three Dumas[9] the level of 'floor crossing' throughout the 1990s was far higher than in consolidated party systems, where such defections tend to be exceedingly rare.

What, then, were the implications of this 'floating' party system, as Richard Rose has aptly named it, for democracy in Russia?[10] It is a fact of democratic experience, and an axiom of the political science literature, that large-scale representative democracy cannot function without political parties. The question with regard to newer democracies or those in 'transition', however, does not concern the existence of parties so much as the level of development of party systems. Often these polities, and Russia is one of them, have political parties but do not have consolidated party systems. The nature of the link between a consolidated party system and democracy is much harder to ascertain: it is one thing to say that democracy requires parties and quite another to say that democracy requires an institutionalised party system. Many political scientists, however, believe that party-system institutionalisation is important to the process of democratic consolidation.[11] Mainwaring and Scully, for instance, go so far as to claim that, 'It is difficult to sustain modern mass democracy without an institutionalised party system.'[12] There is, though, important evidence that democracy *can* in fact consolidate without an institutionalised party system.[13] While a consolidated party system may not be a prerequisite for the consolidation of democracy, its absence is thought likely to have important implications for the *quality* of democracy.[14]

The experience of Russia in the 1990s tends to support the contention that the degree of development of a state's party system has important implications for the quality of democracy in that polity. The extreme volatility of Russia's 'floating' party system, for instance, undermined accountability. As Rose points out:

> A necessary condition for voters to be able to hold politicians accountable is that the parties remain in business from one election to the next. If each election offers voters new choices, they have no basis for evaluating the past record and credibility of competing parties, or for rewarding or punishing parties on the basis of that past record.[15]

Where a consolidated party system should facilitate accountability, Russia's 'floating' party system thwarted it.

Russia's floating party system also had negative consequences for representation, which is one of the cardinal functions of political parties. For one thing, the excessively large number of (mostly minor) parties competing in elections in the 1990s produced highly disproportional election results. The most egregious instance occurred in 1995. Only four of the 43 parties on the ballot paper managed to gather the 5% of the vote required to enter parliament, meaning that 49.53% of those who cast a vote in the PR section of the election received no representation in the Duma.[16] Results in the SMCs were even less representative: the average plurality of the 225 constituency winners was just 29.3% of the vote.[17] In 1995 many Russians must have cast their two votes and still ended up with no representation in the Duma. In 1999 the problem was considerably less extreme. The average plurality of the SMC winners was up to 34.3%[18] and six parties crossed the 5% PR threshold capturing 81.3% of the vote between them.[19] However, this still left 20 parties with no seats in the Duma and nearly one-fifth of party-list voters without representation. Overall the 1999 results were still far less proportional than in most consolidated party systems.[20]

These representation and accountability problems, moreover, were exacerbated by the heavy traffic between parties within the Duma. This phenomenon – which was particularly pronounced in immediate post-election periods – saw deputies elected as independents joining factions in the Duma or banding together to form new groups (sometimes with the help of deputies lent from other factions), as well as deputies switching from one party to another. In this process many of the small parties that won SMC seats disappeared once in the Duma, while other groups emerged that had not even contested the election.[21] In general, such intra-Duma party-system flux further blurred the lines of representation and accountability. It simply was not clear, for example, who (if anybody) such groups as People's Deputy, Russia's Regions and the Agro-Industrial Deputies' Group were supposed to represent: they had not appeared on the ballot paper in 1999 and, therefore, had not, as such, received a single vote, but they ended up with about one-third of the seats in the Duma. It was also difficult to hold these groups to account, since (with the partial exception of People's Deputy) they did not transform themselves into genuine political parties to contest the 2003 election.[22]

The link between party-system development and the quality of democracy certainly seems to have held in Russia in the 1990s: the 'floating' party system, as we have seen, had clear negative implications for the quality of democracy as it was an obstacle to a more accountable, more representative parliament. This cloud's silver lining, however, was that consolidating the party-system would directly improve the quality of democracy in Russia, if the purported relationship between the two were true.

Party-system development under President Putin

During his time in office, President Vladimir Putin – in stark contrast to his predecessor Boris Yeltsin – repeatedly acknowledged the importance of political parties and expressed a desire to strengthen them. Putin's administration also oversaw the introduction of a number of legislative reforms, aimed – ostensibly at least – at consolidating the party system. Moreover, much of what Putin said in this regard was remarkably consonant with the sort of analyses proffered by political scientists. In his address to the Federal Assembly in July 2000, for instance, Putin said:

> In a democratic society, a constant link between the people and government is provided by political parties. (...) Without parties, it is impossible to carry out the policies of the majority, or protect the position of the minority. (...) Against the background of centuries-old traditions of parliamentarianism and multi-party systems in other countries, the shortcomings of our party system are particularly noticeable. A weak government benefits from having weak parties. It is easier and more comfortable for it to live by the rules of political bargaining. But a strong government is interested in strong rivals. Only in conditions of political competition is serious dialogue possible on the development of our state. (...) Russia needs parties which have mass support and stable authority. And we do not need

parties of officials that are attached to the government, let alone which replace it. Experience has shown, and we have known this for the past several years, that formations like this perish immediately, as soon as they leave their incubator for a competitive environment.[23]

Here, Putin acknowledged the crucial role that parties can play in a democracy and stated that Russia needs stronger parties, which – moreover – should have mass support and not simply be 'parties of power'. In this State of the Nation speech, Putin also called explicitly for a law to regulate political parties and their activities.

The law 'On political parties', which passed into law a year later in July 2001, was the legislative centrepiece of Putin's first-term party-system reforms.[24] The basic principle of this law, as it operated in Putin's first term, was that political parties were the only kind of *organisation* with the right to compete *independently* in elections at the federal and regional levels.[25] Throughout Putin's first term, civic associations were permitted to participate in elections as part of an electoral bloc, so long as the bloc contained at least one party, and independent candidates could continue to contest single-member constituencies.[26]

The law on parties further required parties to register with the Ministry of Justice and in order to do so they had to meet a number of criteria. Most significantly, parties were required to have a minimum of 10,000 members, with no fewer than 100 members in regional branches in more than half of the subjects of the Russian Federation.[27] Additionally, a degree of participation in elections was obligatory.[28] The law also introduced state funding of political parties while requiring parties to submit their accounts to the authorities to be audited.[29]

A number of other amendments pertaining to the activities of political parties, which extended the logic of the law 'On political parties', were also passed in Putin's first term. For instance, a change to the law 'On basic guarantees of electoral rights' made in 2002, introduced the mixed PR/SMC electoral system in the regions.[30] This assigned at least half of the seats in regional legislatures to national political parties (or blocs containing parties), thereby guaranteeing them a much greater role in regional politics than they had had in the 1990s. An amendment to the law 'On the election of Duma deputies' determined that parties, after the 2003 election, would have to win not 5% but 7% of the PR vote to win list seats in the Duma.[31] This law also restricted the number of civic associations that could participate in elections in electoral blocs. It stated, as we have already seen, that a bloc had to contain at least one political party and could consist of no more than three entities. A later amendment ruled that after the 2003 Duma election civic associations would not be allowed to enter into blocs at all.[32]

By making it more difficult to become a political party, this reform package did seem to hold out the prospect of a more stable party system containing fewer parties; it also promised the creation of a party system in the regions where none had previously existed. There was, however, considerable debate as to whether this law was, as its proponents claimed, intended to promote the development of real political parties and to enhance democracy in Russia. Indeed the law's critics argued, to the contrary, that elements of the law were undemocratic and that it would be used to exclude opposition parties from electoral politics. While some of these concerns were justified, many were not, and in practice this package of legislative reforms did produce some positive, if limited, results – whatever the intentions.[33]

Some 44 parties completed the registration process ahead of the 2003 Duma election, which was more than had generally been expected.[34] These parties were joined by 20 civic associations, which were eligible to participate in the election if they joined blocs.[35] This put the maximum number of entities (individual parties or blocs) that could appear on the ballot paper in 2003 at 44. This constituted a very sharp reduction in the number of *potential* participants in the elections: in 1999, 139 civic associations had the right to participate in elections; in 1995 the figure had been 273; 167 civic associations had been eligible in 1993.[36] The vast majority of these civic associations, however, had not exercised their right to take part in elections (or had been unable to). The law 'On political parties', in other words, had succeeded in excluding a large number of tiny, electorally irrelevant parties from the electoral process. Moreover, at 44, the number of parties was still high. Indeed, had all of these parties gone on to take part in the election this would have been the greatest number of participants yet in post-Soviet Russian elections, exceeding even the 43 that had appeared on the ballot paper in 1995. In the event, 23 parties (or, more precisely, 18 parties and five blocs) went on to contest the elections, which only three fewer than had contested the 1999 ballot. In quantitative terms, therefore, the law 'On political parties' had cleared a lot of dead wood from the party system but had made little difference to the number of *actual* (as opposed to *potential*) participants in the election.

The introduction of the law on parties also established a number of important qualitative improvements in the party system. At the very least, the law provided a legal definition of a political party and in doing so clarified – as Sakwa puts it – what is a party and what is not.[37] These reforms also established political parties as the principal subjects of the electoral process. Under the law on parties, moreover, parties in Russia have started to look more like political parties as they are normally understood. Russia's parties now have minimum memberships and nationwide networks of branches. They have written rules and programmes and hold congresses and conferences.

In terms of party-system consolidation, the total number of parties in the party system was greatly reduced and the 44 parties that remained under the new legislation were more like 'real' political parties than most of those that had preceded them in post-Soviet Russia. It was also evident, though, that the institutional sticks and carrots embedded in the law were not sufficient to create a more consolidated *parliamentary* party system; once again, in spite of the legislation passed in Putin's first term, this would depend on the outcome of the electoral process.

Regarding party-system development the election results from 2003 were somewhat mixed. The party system was still highly volatile: two of the parties that had crossed the 5% barrier in 1999 – Yabloko and the Union of Right Forces (URF) – failed to do so in 2003; Rodina (Motherland) – one of the big successes in 2003 – was an electoral debutante. Indeed, strictly speaking, only two of the parties that won list seats in 2003 had done so in 1999 – the LDPR and the CPRF; technically, two of the other 'winners' from 1999, Unity and Fatherland-All Russia, had disappeared; and United Russia – the big winner in 2003 – was a new party that had never appeared on the ballot paper before. United Russia, however, was clearly an expanded version of Unity, which had swallowed Fatherland-All Russia and adopted a new name.

Table 7.1   Results of the 2003 Duma Election[38]

Party	% PR Vote	List Seats	SMC Seats
United Russia	37.57	120	102
CPRF	12.61	40	12
LDPR	11.45	36	0
Rodina	9.02	29	8
People's Party	1.18	0	17
Yabloko	4.30	0	4
URF	3.97	0	3
Agrarian Party	3.64	0	2
Other parties[39]	11.56	0	6
Independents	–	–	68
Against all	4.7	–	3[40]

At the same time, though, there were important signs of consolidation. This was the first time that a party, United Russia, had won more SMC seats than independent candidates. Indeed, fewer independents won SMC seats than ever before and for the first time there were no registered deputy groups (as opposed to factions) in the Duma.[41] United Russia's success in winning 222 seats, moreover, marked the first time that a party had come anywhere near securing a majority in the Duma. The two-thirds majority that it subsequently marshalled (by absorbing independents and representatives of small parties) was unprecedented in the history of post-Soviet Russia and left contemporary Russia with the least fragmented parliamentary party system that it has ever had.[42]

Party-system consolidation and democracy

The question to which we now turn is whether this consolidation of the party system improved the chances for democracy. The answer here has to be that it did not, in terms of either the *means* that were employed to facilitate it or the political implications of the *end* that was achieved.

The party-system consolidation that occurred in Putin's first term was the product of an electoral process that was severely flawed in a variety of ways. It was clear for instance, even before a single ballot had been cast, that several of the parties contesting the election were backed or even formed by the Kremlin. The most obvious example of the Kremlin's activities in this sphere was United Russia. United Russia was openly pro-Putin; indeed this was its main (if not only) electoral selling point. President Putin, in turn, endorsed United Russia, although he declined to become a member of it. Rodina, the Party of Life, the People's Party, the Party of Pensioners and the Party of Russia's Renaissance were also believed to be Kremlin projects. These parties were to serve two main purposes: to act as back-up parties of power for United Russia and to take votes away from the main opposition party, the CPRF.[43]

Evidence of administrative interference in the election campaign was also plentiful. The main issues were captured by the Organisation for Security and Cooperation in Europe (OSCE) observation report on the elections, which found that the campaign 'was characterised by unequal opportunities afforded to candidates and political parties in the media... and use of administrative resources (state infrastructure and personnel on the public payroll) to give advantage to certain candidates and parties'.[44]

Concerning the latter point, most of the complaints, the OSCE found, related to the use of administrative resources by the state apparatus on behalf of United Russia candidates, which, 'to a very large extent, blurred the distinction between the party and the executive administration'.[45] Senior officials, including Putin and numerous regional governors (29 of whom were candidates on the United Russia list, even though they had no intention of taking up seats in the Duma), actively promoted certain parties and candidates. Similarly, governors and other officials were observed in breach of the requirement to suspend their official functions while they were running as candidates. In a number of places, United Russia's headquarters were located within state or government administrative offices.[46]

The media coverage of the election was also consistently uneven. The OSCE monitoring mission found that:

> Overall, the media outlets monitored by the EOM [Election Observation Mission] failed to provide impartial or fair coverage of the electoral campaign. Most media coverage was characterised by an overwhelming tendency of the state media to exhibit a clear bias in favour of United Russia and against the CPRF.[47]

The state TV channels did comply with legal provisions concerning the allocation of free airtime for all contestants; other than this, however, the state broadcasters 'openly promoted United Russia'.[48]

The arrest of Mikhail Khodorkovskii, the Yukos CEO, in October 2003 was a defining moment of the campaign. This politically motivated and highly selective act of law enforcement removed one of the main sponsors of opposition parties from the scene. It also – probably more importantly – framed the entire campaign by fostering a strong anti-oligarch atmosphere in the run up to the election.[49] Allegations concerning the oligarchs' business affairs became a major theme in the election campaign, as did criticism of the parties that were linked to them. All of the main parties were rumoured to be receiving funds from oligarchs and large corporations, and most of them included candidates with clear ties to big business (notably Yukos) on their election lists.[50] However, many of the attacks – made by one party against another and in the media – were targeted at the CPRF, which was probably the principal casualty of the debate. The main beneficiary was almost certainly Rodina, which campaigned on a populist, highly anti-oligarch platform.

While voting on the day was positively assessed overall by the OSCE, a major scandal erupted concerning the count. An alternative count conducted by the CPRF found that the results protocols that had been collected by the election observation mission mounted by the Communists, Yabloko and the URF differed from those used by the Central Election Commission (CEC).[51] The main finding of the alternative count was that both Yabloko and URF had, contrary to the official results, received enough votes to cross the 5% barrier.[52] The CEC denied that electoral falsification had occurred – although the alternative count clearly suggested that it had – and rejected the parties' requests for a recount in areas where the results were disputed, even though this was obviously the only way to ascertain that no fraud had taken place. The CEC's failure to investigate adequately and ascertain that the count *was* accurate left a serious a question mark over the validity of the election results.[53]

The 2003 Duma election campaign, in sum, was systematically unfair in ways that benefited pro-Kremlin parties – principally United Russia – at the expense of opposition parties (or, more precisely, those not favoured by the Kremlin). While the use of these techniques to manipulate elections is not new, their use in 2003 was exceptional even by the standards of post-Soviet Russia.[54] It is also important to note that the election results were the outcome of a complex of many factors: administrative manipulation alone is not sufficient to explain the outcome.[55] It would, however, be implausible to suggest that these machinations did not have a telling impact.[56] The unprecedented degree of electoral manipulation in 2003 *ipso facto* further damaged democratisation in Russia. Party-system consolidation, therefore, did not improve the chances for democracy; indeed, it was achieved – to a very significant degree – *at the expense of democracy.*

The results of the 2003 election also damaged the prospects for *future* democratisation in Russia. The cardinal outcome in 2003, of course, was the scale of United Russia's triumph. Indeed, when discussing the party-system consolidation that took place in Putin's first term we are really referring to the advance and subsequent hegemony of United Russia. To view United Russia's success as positive for democracy in any way, however, would be to misunderstand the nature of that organisation. United Russia is not a normal political party. It is better understood as a cross between the legislative branch of the Presidential Administration and a post-Soviet *nomenklatura*. It has been clear since its formation that United Russia is an ersatz political party. It was founded on the basis of a merger between Unity and Fatherland-All Russia, which was a startlingly cynical and opportunistic exercise given that these parties had been staunch rivals in 1999 and had waged a bitter and dirty campaign against each other. United Russia has little ideology or identity of its own and its main pursuit since its formation was to offer uncritical, weighty support for the President. The party, moreover, has no real power independent of the Kremlin: it is, as Gel'man eloquently puts it 'nothing but the agent of its principals – the top state officials, who keep strict control over its activities and do not permit party autonomy in terms of key decision-making'.[57]

The appointment of Mikhail Fradkov's government was the most telling example of United Russia's subservience to the Kremlin. When this government took office in early 2004, it contained only one member of the party.[58] In addition, as before, it contained some leading figures from United Russia (such as Boris Gryzlov and Sergei Shoigu), who were not formally party members. These, though, were in the minority and continued to owe their positions to Putin's patronage rather than their standing in the majority party. The new Prime Minister, Mikhail Fradkov, was, moreover, a career civil servant rather than a United Russia functionary. It is hard to imagine any normal political party with such a huge majority in parliament approving a government containing so few of its members.

The wider party system was scarcely more encouraging. The liberal-leaning parties, Yabloko and URF, failed to cross the 5% barrier and won just seven seats between them. This left them with minimal influence in the Duma and called their very survival into question. The election results were also a catastrophe for the main opposition party, the CPRF, which won only 52 seats (61 fewer than in 1999), leaving it in a very weak position to oppose Putin and his party of power. The LDPR is broadly supportive of Putin and in any case the LDPR, in spite of its leader's fiery rhetoric, can normally be relied upon to support the executive when necessary. The Rodina bloc was, as we have seen, a Kremlin creation. Its loyal stance was complicated by intra-party splits and intrigues but it could not stray too far from the Kremlin line if it wished to survive, and it never had enough seats to trouble the executive in any case.

In sum, then, while the party system did consolidate in Putin's first term, this process did not constitute *democratic* consolidation in any way. For one thing, as was shown above, United Russia's pre-eminence was achieved through thoroughly unfair elections. Indeed, the electoral violations were so egregious in 2003 that the claim – long dubious – that Russia was an electoral democracy became unsupportable.[59] Furthermore, the party system that emerged after the 2003 election was and remains unlikely to advance the cause of democracy in Russia:

the main democratically-oriented parties, Yabloko and the URF, emerged from the elections gravely weakened, there was no numerically significant opposition, and, most important, the Duma was completely dominated by the Kremlin's legislative proxy, United Russia. The 2003 election, then, signified not the consolidation of democracy, but the consolidation of the Kremlin's hold over the State Duma.

There were also implications, specifically, for representation and accountability. Formally, the PR result was less representative than in 1999, as some 30% of the PR votes cast were wasted (it had been a little under 20% in 1999); the average plurality of SMC winners, however, was up to 41.8% (from 34.3%).[60] More importantly, both accountability and representation were thwarted by unfair elections: voters could only hold politicians to account and have their interests represented only if elections had been free and fair. It must have been difficult for Russia's electorate to make objective decisions concerning voting (and, by extension, accountability and representation) in the absence of reasonably impartial information. Moreover, there was a strong *prima facie* case that 'problems' with the count had denied Yabloko and URF voters the representation to which they were entitled. It is also difficult to see how United Russia, given the vagueness of its platform and its subservience to the Kremlin, was then (or is now) qualified to represent anyone other than the executive. Nor, of course, did (or does) United Russia hold the executive to account, as the party was specifically designed to be accountable *to* the executive, not the other way around. Russia, it seems, has gone from a 'floating' party system to one characterised by 'executive capture', which from the perspective of democratisation is arguably worse than what went before.

In Putin's first term we witnessed a two-pronged process of party-system development. On the one hand, reforms were introduced which were – officially at least – intended to strengthen political parties and which had some beneficial (if limited) effects. Parallel to this, on the other hand, there was extensive electoral manipulation, which actually drove party-system development in practice by securing favourable results for the Kremlin. This pattern should be borne in mind when we consider Putin's second term.

Putin's second term

A number of important part-system reforms were also passed in Putin's second term. President Putin initiated these second-term reforms in his speech to the Government, which was also attended by the heads of regional administrations, in September 2004 following the tragic events in Beslan.[61] The most widely discussed of these reforms, although not the most pertinent to party-system development, was Putin's insistence that regional governors should be appointed rather than directly elected. At the same time, Putin also proposed using PR to elect the entire State Duma (thereby eliminating the single-mandate constituencies). This radical change to the electoral system passed into law in 2005 in the form of a new version of the law 'On Duma elections'.[62] This law also removed the opportunity for parties to compete in Duma elections in blocs, even with other parties: only individual parties would contest parliamentary elections in future.[63]

A change made to the law 'On the Government of the Russian Federation' in October 2004 permitted members of the government simultaneously to hold posts in political parties.[64] The Duma also passed an amendment to the law 'On political parties', which raised the membership requirements made of parties fivefold.[65] This required parties, from 1 January 2006, to have a total of 50,000 members (with at least 500 members in more than half of Russia's regions and no fewer than 250 in other branches). The 7% barrier, which had been approved by the previous Duma, was confirmed in 2005, but the small print was changed making a Duma containing just two parties theoretically possible.[66] Another law passed in 2005 introduced an 'imperative mandate': at subsequent Duma election, any deputies who voluntarily left their factions would lose their seats in the Duma.[67]

Whatever criticisms can be levelled at these reforms – annulling direct elections of governors is, of course, flatly undemocratic, even if few elected governors had done much to advance democracy in Russia's regions, and the 7% barrier is high by international standards – there can be little doubt that they induced further party-system consolidation. The higher membership requirement almost certainly triggered a fall in the total number of parties in the system. Indeed, checks carried out by the Federal Registration Service in 2006 found that only 19 of the 35 registered parties were in compliance with the membership requirements; the other 16 were de-registered. This number later fell to 17 when three parties merged to form a new party called 'A Just Russia'.[68] The parliamentary party system was also more consolidated. It became highly unlikely that more political parties would populate the Duma: the 7% barrier was (and remains) high and it would be very difficult for any party without a faction in the Duma to win seats in parliament in the future unless it were backed by the Kremlin. In particular, it is difficult to envisage either Yabloko or URF winning 7% of the vote. No blocs or independents were allowed to contest the 2007 election, meaning that all of the seats in the Duma were held by individual political parties for the first time in post-Soviet history. Additionally, the imperative mandate cut down on floor crossing, although this phenomenon was greatly reduced anyway in a Duma without blocs and independents.

As in Putin's first term, this new round of *party-system* consolidation hardly contributed to *democratic* consolidation, since the Presidential Administration continued to manipulate elections, successfully promoted pro-Kremlin parties and undermined opposition parties. Given Putin's demonstrable disregard for electoral norms, the very success of the Kremlin's machinations in 2003, and the size of the stakes in the 2007–08 electoral cycle, the Kremlin in 2007 was intent on engineering a rerun of 2003. Indeed, the merger of three Kremlin-connected parties (Rodina, the Party of Life, and the Party of Pensioners) to form a new loyal, left-of-centre 'opposition' party called 'A Just Russia' seemed to reflect just such an ambition. As a result, this continuing pattern of electoral manipulation meant that Russia – by definition – could no longer even be considered in the process of democratisation. Moreover, the consolidation of a parliamentary party system, dominated by forces that were and remain (on the whole) unswervingly loyal to a Kremlin leadership that manipulates elections is unlikely to improve chances for democracy in Russia in the short term.

Conclusion

Earlier in this chapter we saw that many scholars believe that the degree of institutionalisation of a party system has implications for the quality of democracy. By extension, party-system consolidation should be expected to enhance the quality of democracy. In Putin's first term, however, while a degree of party-system consolidation occurred in Russia the means and the end of this occasioned a *deterioration* of the quality of democracy. Furthermore, to return to two of the specific afflictions of Russia's 'floating' party system, this consolidation did not enhance either representation or accountability. Russia's 'floating' party system certainly frustrated representation and accountability in the 1990s, but consolidation *per se* was clearly no guaranteed antidote. These findings call into question the link made in the comparative literature between party-system institutionalisation and the quality of democracy. The Russian case shows that this does not always hold, which suggests that the conditions in which party-system institutionalisation has democratising effects need to be specified more precisely.

It is beyond the scope of this chapter to tackle this issue comprehensively. The analysis, however, yields two important findings concerning party system development and democracy in Russia. The first is that the prospects for democracy in Russia have far less to do with the condition of the party system than with the attitude of the Presidential Administration. What Russia needs, first and foremost, to become an electoral democracy is free and fair elections. It is perfectly possible in principle (although perhaps unlikely in practice) for Russia to become a democracy with an inchoate party system; it is by definition *im*possible to become a democracy unless elections are free and fair. The most proximate cause of the lack of electoral democracy in Russia is that the Kremlin, in the absence of effective checks and balances, is able to manipulate the political process largely without external constraint.

In addition, the composition of the party system was, and remains, a reflection – to a very considerable degree – of the anti-democratic policies of the Putin legacy. In this sense, it is the quality of democracy (or more accurately its absence) that has shaped the party system, rather than the other way around. In the future, however, strong, independent (i.e. non-Kremlin) political parties could potentially perform a crucial role in checking the power of the Presidential Administration; not least, independent political parties could mobilise popular and elite opposition to undemocratic elections. Such parties would also be better placed to facilitate the classical functions of political parties, such as representation and accountability. Party-system consolidation of this type *could* have important positive implications for the future of democracy in Russia.

This brings us to our second main finding, which is that democratisation in Russia will be furthered not so much by a more consolidated party system – and certainly not a more consolidated version of its existing party system – as by one in which political parties that are *actively committed to democracy* predominate: the *number* of parties, therefore, is secondary to their *nature*. Of course it is hard to see how such parties can develop, in spite of the second-term party-system reforms, when the Kremlin is able, to a large extent, to determine the winners and losers of Duma elections. In fact a major fear has to be that United Russia's dominance – achieved via unfair political competition – could persist for decades, as in the case of Mexico's Institutional Revolutionary Party (PRI), in a system where other parties serve only to legitimate (not challenge) its grip on power.[69]

However, if the practices of electoral manipulation cease or fail the party-system reforms enacted during Putin's Presidency could become highly significant. A variety of scenarios are plausible in the post-Putin context. The most optimistic is that President Medvedev would be less inclined to manipulate elections. Moreover, events elsewhere in the former Soviet Union suggest that it is difficult to manage electoral outcomes indefinitely, even in states that are significantly more authoritarian than Russia. It will surely be difficult for the executive to keep repeating the triumphs of 2003 and 2007. If, for whatever reason, there is a backlash, either in the polling booth or on the street, Putin's party-system reforms could serve as the basis for stronger independent parties in the Duma capable of providing greater opposition to the executive. It would be highly ironic if Vladimir Putin, who strived at the expense of democracy to increase the power of the presidency relative to political parties and the Duma – and indeed every other institution in the political system – turns out to have established the institutional framework that helps to strengthen parties, weaken the presidency and foment democracy in the long run.

Notes

1 M. McFaul, 'Explaining Party Formation and Nonformation in Russia', *Comparative Political Studies*, 34 (2001): 1162.
2 Ibid., p. 1163.
3 Ibid., pp. 1168–9; C. Ross, 'Political Parties and Regional Democracy', in C. Ross, ed., *Regional Politics in Russia* (Manchester: Manchester University Press, 2002), pp. 37–56; D. Slider, 'Russia's Governors and Party Formation', in A. Brown, ed., *Contemporary Russian Politics: A Reader* (Oxford: Oxford University Press, 2001), pp. 223–334; K. Stoner-Weiss, 'The Limited Reach of Russia's Party System: Underinstitutionalisation in Dual Transitions', *Politics and Society*, 29 (2001): 385–414.
4 In 1993, 141 independents were elected to the Duma. The figures for 1995 and 1999 are 78 and 114 respectively. (Figures taken from: S. White, R. Rose and I. McAllister, *How Russia Votes* (Chatham, NJ: Chatham House), pp. 125 and 224; Y. M. Brudny, 'Continuity or Change in Russian Electoral Patterns? The December 1999–March 2000 Election Cycle', in Brown, ed., *Contemporary Russian Politics*, p. 170.
5 Based on figures taken from R. Rose and N. Munro, *Elections Without Order: Russia's Challenge to Vladimir Putin* (Cambridge: Cambridge University Press, 2002), p. 122.
6 Thirteen parties contested the PR list in 1993; the numbers for 1995 and 1999 were 43 and 26 respectively: W. A. Clark, 'Russia at the Polls: Potemkin Democracy', *Problems of Post-Communism*, 51, 2 (2004): 28n3. The number of effective parties contesting PR elections in Russia in the 1990s was far higher than in established western democracies using PR (although not exceptional by the standards of the post-communist world). R. G. Moser, *Unexpected Outcomes: Electoral Systems, Political Parties and Representation in Russia* (Pittsburgh: University of Pittsburgh Press, 2001), pp. 45 and 153.

7   Electoral volatility (the change in the vote from one party to others from one election to the next) in Russia in the 1990s was extraordinarily high by comparative standards. Grigorii V. Golosov, *Political Parties in the Regions of Russia: Democracy Unclaimed* (London: Lynne Rienner, 2003), p. 48.

8   The LDPR ran as Vladimir Zhirinovskii's Bloc in 1999.

9   P. Chaisty, 'Party Cohesion and Policy-Making in Russia', *Party Politics*, 11 (2005): 301.

10 R. Rose, 'A Supply-Side View of Russia's Elections: How Floating Parties Frustrate Democratic Accountability', *East European Constitutional Review*, 9, 1/2 (2000): 53–9.

11 Examples include: L. Diamond, *Developing Democracy: Towards Consolidation* (London: Johns Hopkins University Press, 1999), pp. 97–8; P. Hakim and A. F. Lowenthal, 'Latin America's Fragile Democracies', in L. Diamond and M. F. Plattner, eds, *The Global Resurgence of Democracy* (London: Johns Hopkins University Press, 1993), p. 303; T. Huang, 'Party Systems in Taiwan and South Korea', in L. Diamond, M. F. Plattner, Y. Chu and H. Tien, eds, *Consolidating the Third Wave Democracies: Themes and Perspectives* (London: John Hopkins University Press, 1997), p. 137; and J. J. Linz and A. Stepan, *Problems of Democratic Transition and Consolidation* (London: Johns Hopkins University Press, 1996), pp. 7–8.

12 S. Mainwaring and T. R. Scully, 'Introduction: Party Systems in Latin America', in S. Mainwaring and T. R. Scully, eds, *Building Democratic Institutions: Party Systems in Latin America* (Stanford: Stanford University Press, 1995), pp. 2–3.

13 Gabor Toka finds that while the party systems in Poland, Slovakia, Hungary and the Czech Republic remained unstable by any standards in the first half of the 1990s, at least three of the four countries had to be counted as consolidated democracies. The party system of the non-consolidated democracy (Slovakia), moreover, was, in decisive aspects, the most or second most institutionalised of the four. His main finding therefore is that the presence of reasonably institutionalised political parties is not a must for democratic consolidation. G. Toka, 'Political Parties in East Central Europe', in Diamond et al, *Consolidating the Third Wave Democracies*, pp. 93–134.

14 See: A. Hadenius, 'The Development of Political Parties: Russia in Perspective', *Studies in Public Policy*, 365 (2002): 4; Mainwaring and Scully, 'Introduction: Party Systems in Latin America', pp. 21–2; G. Pridham, 'Southern European Democracies on the Road to Consolidation: A Comparative Assessment of the Role of Political Parties', in G. Pridham, ed., *Securing Democracy: Political Parties and Democratic Consolidation in Southern Europe* (London: Routledge, 1990), p. 2; and Toka, 'Political Parties in East Central Europe': 121–2.

15 Rose, 'A Supply-Side View of Russia's Elections': 54.

16 White et al, *How Russia Votes*, p. 227.

17 W. Clark, 'Russia at the Polls', p. 23.

18 Ibid.

19 Based on the figures given by Rose and Munro, *Elections Without Order*, p. 132.

20 For comprehensive comparative evidence, see Michael Gallagher and Paul Mitchell, *The Politics of Electoral Systems* (Oxford: Oxford University Press, 2005).

21 Rose, 'A Supply-Side View of Russia's Elections': 55–6; Rose and Munro, *Elections Without Order*, pp. 106–8.

22 People's Deputy served as the basis of the People's Party, which contested the 2003 election, but there was considerable turnover of personnel. Moreover, most of the People's Party deputies who were elected to the Duma in 2003 quickly joined the United Russia faction.

23 Vladimir Putin, *Poslanie Federal'nomu Sobraniiu Rossiiskoi Federatsii* (8 July 2000), available online at: http://www.kremlin.ru/text/appears/2000/07/28782.shtml.

24 For a more detailed discussion of this law see: E. Bacon, 'Russia's Law on Political Parties: Democracy by Decree?', in C. Ross, ed., *Russian Politics Under Putin* (Manchester: Manchester University Press, 2004), pp. 39–52; and K. Wilson, 'Party-System Development Under Putin', *Post-Soviet Affairs*, 22 (2006): 314–48.

25 'On political parties', 2001, Article 36.1 ('Federal'nyi zakon ot 11 iyulia 2001 g. N 95-FZ O politicheskikh partiyakh', *Rossiiskaya gazeta* (14 July 2001), available online at http://document.kremlin.ru/doc.asp?ID=008011).

26 According to Article 34 of the 2002 law 'On the election of Duma Deputies' an electoral bloc consisted of a maximum of three entities at least one of which had to be a political party: 'Federal'nyi zakon ot 20 dekabrya 2002 g. N 175-FZ O vyborakh deputatov Gosudarstvennoi Dumy Federal'nogo Sobraniya Rossiiskoi Federatsii', *Rossiiskaia gazeta* (25 December 2002), available online at http://document.kremlin.ru/doc.asp?ID=015363. Later amendments, as we shall see, removed the right of independent candidates and civic associations to participate in Duma elections.

27 'On political parties', 2001, Article 3.2. Since January 2006, parties, as we shall see later, have required 50,000 members.

28 'On political parties', 2001, Article 37.

29 For an analysis of the financial elements of this law see: K. Wilson, 'Party Finance in Russia: Has the 2001 Law "On Political Parties" Made a Difference?', *Europe-Asia Studies*, 1465–3427, Vol. 59, No. 7 (2007): 1089–113.

30 'On basic guarantees of electoral rights', 2002, Article 35.16: 'Federal'nyi zakon ot 12 iyunia 2002 g. No. 67-FZ Ob osnovnykh garantiyakh izbiratel'nykh prav i prava na uchastie v referendume grazhdan Rossiiskoi Federatsii', *Sobranie zakonodatel'stva Rossiiskoi Federatsii*, 24 (2002), 6074–216, available online at http://document.kremlin.ru/doc.asp?ID= 012553.

31 'On the election of Duma Deputies', 2002, Article 99.

32 'On the Insertion of a Change to Article 36 of the Law "On Political Parties" and the Insertion of Changes and Additions to the Law "On Duma Deputies"', 2003, Article 2: 'Federal'nyi zakon ot 23 iyunia 2003 g. N 85-FZ O vnesenii izmeneniia v stat'iu 36 Federal'nogo zakona "O politicheskikh partiyakh" i vnesenii izmenenii i dopolnenii v Federal'nyi zakon "O vyborakh deputatov Gosudarstvennoi Dumy Federal'nogo Sobraniya Rossiiskoi Federatsii"', *Rossiiskaia gazeta* (25 June 2003), available online at http://document.kremlin.ru/doc.asp?ID=018068.

33 This argument is fully developed in K. Wilson, 'Party-System Development Under Putin'.

34 For the Central Electoral Commission (CEC) list of these parties see: 'Spisok politicheskikh partii obladavshikh pravom prinimat' uchastiye v vyborakh

deputatov Gosudarstvennoy Dumy Federal'nogo Sobraniya Rossiyskoi Federatsii chetvertogo sozyva (List of political parties with the right to participate in elections to the fourth convocation of the State Duma)', available online at http://gd2003.cikrf.ru/list_34/sx/SelectMode/none/branch_brn/ 1340712/gas_doc_obj/41766493.html.

35 For this CEC list see: 'Spisok obshcherossiyskikh obshchestvennykh ob'yedinenii, obladavshikh pravom prinimat' uchastiye v vyborakh deputatov Gosudarstvennoy Dumy Federal'nogo Sobraniya Rossiiskoi Federatsii chetvertogo sozyva (List of All-Russian civic associations with the right to participate in elections to the fourth convocation of the State Duma)', available online at http://gd2003.cikrf.ru/list_34/sx/SelectMode/none/branch_brn/1340712/ gas_doc_obj/41765493.html.

36 Figures taken from the speech of CEC member Elena Dubrovina, 'Voprosy vydvizheniia i registratsii kandidatov v deputaty Gosudarstvennoi Dumy Federal'nogo Sobraniia Rossiiskoi Federatsii ot politicheskikh partii i izbiratel'nykh blokov po federal'nomu izbiratel'nomu okrugu i odnomandatnym izbiratel'nym okrugam', www.cikrf.ru_1/docl_dubrovina_250203.htm, accessed 31 May 2003. The number of all-Russian political civic associations registered with the Ministry of Justice on the day that the law 'On political parties' came into force (14 July 2001) was 199. See www.fci.ru/WAY/ 203907.html, accessed 27 February 2003.

37 R. Sakwa, *Putin: Russia's Choice* (London: Routledge, 2004), p. 116.

38 Results taken from www.russiavotes.org/2003result.htm, accessed 4 February 2005.

39 Six seats were won by smaller parties, including Rebirth of Russia with three seats, and one each for New Course-Automobile Russia, Development of Enterprise and Great Russia-Eurasian Union.

40 In three districts the number of votes against all exceeded votes for any one candidate. In these cases by-elections were required.

41 Group formation was made more difficult when the Duma raised the minimum number of deputies required to register a group from 35 to 55.

42 For statistical measures of the effective number of parties, which confirm this judgement, see: V. Gel'man, 'From "Feckless Pluralism" to "Dominant Power Politics"? The Transformation of Russia's Party System', *Democratisation*, 13 (2006): 546.

43 A. Ryabov, 'The Evolution of the Multiparty System', in Y. Brudny, F. Frankel, and S. Hoffman, eds, *Restructuring Post-Communist Russia* (Cambridge: Cambridge University Press, 2004), p. 223; and A. Wilson, *Virtual Politics: Faking Democracy in the Post-Soviet World* (London: Yale University Press, 2005), pp. 126–8.

44 OSCE/ODIHR (Organisation for Security and Cooperation in Europe/Office for Democratic Institutions and Human Rights), 'Russian Federation Elections to the State Duma 7 December 2003', OSCE/ODIHR Election Observation Mission Report, Warsaw, January 2004, available online via www.osce.org/ documents/odihr/2004/01/1947_en.pdf, p. 12.

45 Ibid.

46 Ibid.

47 Ibid., p. 15.

48 Ibid., p. 16.

49 D. White, *The Russian Democratic Party Yabloko: Opposition in a Managed Democracy* (Aldershot: Hampshire, 2006), pp. 171–2; K. Wilson, 'Party Finance in Russia: Has the 2001 Law "On Political Parties" Made a Difference?'.

50 K. Wilson, 'Party Finance in Russia: Has the 2001 Law "On Political Parties" Made a Difference?'.

51 A protocol is a record of the votes counted in an electoral district. It is compiled in the presence of observers and authenticated (signed and stamped) by the district election commission. Copies of this document are given to observers while the original protocol is delivered to the CEC. Orkhan Dzhemal', 'Rezul'taty vyborov poddelany', *Novaya Gazeta* (11 March 2004), p. 2.

52 According to this count, Yabloko and URF won 5.88% and 5.04% of the PR vote, respectively. The official results put them at 4.3% and 3.97%. The Communists' share of the vote, at 12.6%, was actually down 0.01% from the official result of 12.61%. United Russia's result, at 33.66% was significantly lower than the official 37.57%. The alternative count found that LDPR had received 11.25% of the vote, slightly lower than the official 11.45%; Rodina's result was, at 10.73%, higher than the official 9.02%. Orkhan Dzhemal', 'Fair Game Ob'yasnyaet', *Novaia Gazeta* (18 December 2003), p. 4.

53 For more on this issue see K. Wilson, 'Party-System Development Under Putin': 333–5.

54 Three prominent American specialists, for instance, have characterised the 2003 election as, 'the most constrained and least competitive since the Soviet period'. H. E. Hale, M. McFaul and T. J. Colton, 'Putin and the "Delegative Democracy" Trap: Evidence from Russia's 2003–04 Elections', *Post-Soviet Affairs*, 45 (2004): 285.

55 For a discussion of these factors see: R. Sakwa, 'The 2003–2004 Russian Elections and Prospects for Democracy', *Europe-Asia Studies*, 57 (2005): 369–98.

56 Not all of the abuses referred to above can necessarily be attributed directly to Kremlin orchestration; what is clear is that the Kremlin did nothing to stop them.

57 V. Gel'man, 'From "Feckless Pluralism" to "Dominant Power Politics"?': 557.

58 This was deputy prime minister Aleksandr Zhukov, who had only joined United Russia six months earlier. Vladimir Fedorin, 'Dvortsovyi perevorot', *Vedomosti* (10 March 2004).

59 Free and fair elections are a *sine qua non* for democracy, according to even the most minimalist definitions of democracy. The 2003 Duma election, as we have seen, came nowhere near qualifying as fair.

60 Calculated from official CEC election results, 'Vote Return in Singles [sic] Seat Electoral Districts', http://gd2003.cikrf.ru/gdrf4_engl.html file, accessed 7 August 2007.

61 Vladimir Putin, 'Vystuplenie na rasshirennom zasedanii Pravitel'stva s uchastiem glav sub'ektov Rossiiskoi Federatsii' (13 September 2004), available online at: www.kremlin.ru/text/appears/2004/09/76651.shtml.

62 'On the Election of Duma Deputies', 2005, Article 3: 'Federal'nyi zakon ot 18 maya 2005 g. N 51-FZ O vyborakh deputatov Gosudarstvennoi Dumy Federal'nogo Sobraniya Rossiiskoi Federatsii', *Rossiiskyia gazeta*, 24 May 2005, available online at http://document.kremlin.ru/doc.asp?ID=027816.

63 This was achieved by omission: the parts of the law that had provided for the participation of blocs in elections were removed.

64 Ministers had previously been allowed to join parties but not to hold party office. 'On the Insertion of a Change to Article 11 of the Federal Constitutional Law "On the Government of the Russian Federation". ('Federal'nyi konstitutsionnyi zakon ot 3 noyabrya 2004 g. No. 6-FKZ, O vnesenii izmeneniya v stat'yu 11 Federal'nogo konstitutsionnogo zakona "O Pravitel'stve Rossiiskoi Federatsii"', *Sobranie zakonodatel'stva Rossiiskoi Federatsii*, 45 (2004): 9737, available online at http://document.kremlin.ru/ doc.asp?ID=024793).

65 'On the Insertion of Changes to the Federal Law "On Political Parties"', article 1: 'Federal'nyi zakon Rossiiskoi Federatsii ot 20 dekabrya 2004 g. N 168-FZ O vnesenii izmenenii v Federal'nyi zakon "O politicheskikh partiyakh"', *Rossiiskaya gazeta* (24 December 2004), available online at http://document. kremlin.ru/doc.asp?ID=025663.

66 The earlier version had stipulated that the 7% threshold would apply only if a minimum of four parties qualified and only if those four parties represented more than 50% of those who voted. (The logic here was that additional parties would be awarded seats in the Duma, even if they had not reached the threshold, until the criteria concerning 4 parties and 50% of the vote were met.) According to the 2005 variant of the law 'On Duma elections' the 7% barrier applies so long as two parties qualify and that they represent over 60% of those who voted (Article 82).

67 'On the Insertion of Changes to Legislative Acts of the Russian Federation Concerning Elections and Referenda and Other Legislative Acts of the Russian Federation', Article 2.1: 'Federal'nyi zakon ot 21 iyulia 2005 g No. 93-FZ, 'O vnesenii izmenenii v zakonodatel'nye akty Rossiiskoi Federatsii o vyborakh i referendumakh i inye zakonodatel'nye akty Rossiiskoi Federatsii', *Sobranie zakonodatel'stva Rossiiskoi Federatsii*, 30 (2005), 7895–8058, available online at http://document.kremlin.ru/doc.asp?ID=028925.

68 A list of the parties registered with the Federal Registration Service of the Ministry of Justice can be found online at: http://rosregistr.ru/index.php? menu=3010050000.

69 On the possible development of United Russia along the lines of the PRI see: V. Gel'man, 'Perspektivy dominiruyushchei partii v Rossii', *Pro et Contra*, 4, 33 (2006): 62–71.

8
The Rule-of-Law Factor

Jeffrey Kahn

The law is a causeway upon which, so long as he keeps to it, a citizen may walk safely.

– Sir Thomas More, *A Man For All Seasons*, Act II

The law is like a wagon shaft; it goes wherever you turn it.

– Russian proverb

Part I Introduction

Nationwide surveys in 1996, 1998, and 2000 revealed strong, albeit abstract, support among citizens of the Russian Federation for rule-of-law principles at levels roughly comparable to those found in Western Europe.[1] But, when Russians were asked to apply those ideals to their own circumstances, a 2004 nationwide survey found that 'an overwhelming majority of Russians do not think that they live under a rule-of-law state'.[2] A 2007 survey continues to support these earlier findings,[3] and recent surveys reveal that few Russians believe this will change during President Medvedev's tenure.[4]

Russian and Western political scientists and area-studies specialists value the rule of law and lament its absence in Russia. There is broad consensus among scholars that the rule of law is as integral to effectively functioning modern democratic states as electoral politics, a workable state bureaucracy, and robust civil and economic societies.[5] It is therefore surprising that this rule-of-law 'factor' – to borrow from the title of Archie Brown's famous book[6] – is rarely subjected to the same rigorous study as those other, more popular political science variables.[7]

Political scientists rightly acknowledge the importance of the rule-of-law factor even if they do not often apply the tools of political science to its study. They should. This essay explores approaches to analysing this important variable. In the remaining two parts of this introduction, I identify flaws in both the rule-of-law definitions advanced by Russia-watchers (when advanced at all) and the metaphors used to describe the normative approach to legal reform that these scholars advocate. Next, I examine facets of the rule of law that are particularly salient and important in a Russian Federation that purports to *be* (not merely *aspires* to be) a 'democratic, federal, rule-of-law state with a republican form of government'.[8] Finally, I defend my own normative preference for a rule-of-law metaphor that dispenses with more common martial or instrumentalist figures of speech in favour of the image of a legal causeway that provides safe transit to Russian citizens through a thicket of state and private obstacles to the exercise of rights and protections of property.

1. Defining (or not) the rule of law

The phrase 'the rule of law' is frequently used by scholars without serious effort to define it.[9] What exactly is its value? How can we measure its existence or effect in a teetering Russian democracy? Are there varieties of 'the rule of law' that, within an identifiable range, satisfy the requirements scholars identify for a democracy? Russia-watchers devote surprisingly little attention to such questions.

When, on rare occasion, political scientists and area-studies scholars do proffer definitions, these tend to be conclusory or imprecise.[10] In the heady days after the Berlin Wall fell and interest rose in 'transitology', research agendas were often driven by the problems that political elites were perceived to face when drafting new and viable constitutional structures. This focus led many to the unexamined assumption that the rule of law would somehow trickle down to the struggles of ordinary citizens after its acceptance by elites negotiating the 'rules of the game'. Others adopted the low definitional bar of legal formalism, the standards for which were deemed to be satisfied by the bare positivist evidence of new laws, codes, or courts standing alone. Thus, one scholar asserted that the rule of law requires only the passage of legislation and the financing of institutions for enforcement.[11] Some scholars briefly acknowledge the broader (and deeper) problems of developing a legal culture, but then prefer to focus on topics like high constitutional politics and election-monitoring.[12] Still others use 'rule of law' simply as a general placeholder to express their criticism of *ad hoc*, non-transparent, corrupt, or other unsavoury types of state action.[13] In short, those who believe that the rule of law is important (and most serious scholars do)[14] tend to assert its existence or absence or marginal effects in Russia in the same way that US Supreme Court Justice Potter Stewart once defined pornography: 'I know it when I see it.'[15]

Why are political scientists more comfortable assessing electoral thresholds, or comparing presidential versus parliamentary political systems, or parsing the criteria for robust civil societies, economic systems and multinational federations, than they are defining the parameters for their inchoate but no less cherished rule-of-law variable? Political scientists seem to prefer to leave that task to the lawyers.[16] This is an artificial academic divide long on history but short on utility.[17] In 1918, the respected American political scientist Thorstein Veblen disdained the academic value of contemporary legal study: 'In point of substantial merit the law school belongs in the modern university no more than a school of fencing or dancing.'[18] Lawyers were practitioners, he said, and thus law schools were trade schools; law professors 'stand in a relation to their students analogous to that in which the "coaches" stand to the athletes'.[19] Almost 40 years ago, Dankwart Rustow asserted that 'our current emphasis in political science on economic and social factors is a most necessary corrective to the sterile legalism of an earlier generation', because, he warned, 'we have been in danger of throwing away the political baby with the institutional bathwater'.[20] This division of disciplines is still a sharp one today, despite renewed attention to the 'new institutionalism',[21] and occasional interdisciplinary crossovers by intrepid scholars.[22] This academic rule of exclusion weakens the ability of Russia-watchers in both disciplines fully to explore such a crucial institution.[23]

2. The value (and danger) of metaphors

Metaphors matter because they affect how scholars think about problems.[24] The metaphors that experts use to describe the rule of law they advocate for Russia are as ill-designed as their definitions. One respected American scholar, for example, argues that 'to build a state that abides by the rule of law, individual Russian judges, lawyers, and citizens must adopt a fundamentally new relationship with the law and make it a tool of defence that emanates from society rather than an instrument of control in the hands of the state'.[25] For this scholar and many others, the law is perceived through instrumental language. Its value thus depends upon who wields this tool and to what end.[26] Instrumentalist metaphors typically take the form of sword or shield wielded by, or turned against, the state.[27]

The law-as-tool metaphor is the wrong one to use when advocating the sort of rule of law needed for a consolidated Russian democracy. It is uncontentious today to critique the use of law as a political tool in late Imperial Russia, or during the Bolsheviks' consolidation of their power, or in an increasingly ossified and stagnant Soviet system. They are sometimes apt *descriptions*. But such an instrumentalist conception of law should not be *advocated* for the institutions and practices so important to an aspiring post-Soviet Russian democracy. Instrumentalism should especially be resisted by scholars in the face of its nearly ubiquitous acceptance among Russia's current leaders and wealthiest private citizens.[28]

I have highlighted the consequences of legal instrumentalism in modern Russian history elsewhere.[29] Here it is enough to note that this conception extends further and deeper into the Russian past than the Bolshevik Revolution. As one Russian area-studies scholar has observed, 'careful research has not revealed a single significant work of Russian literature published prior to 1917 in which lawyers, judges, or the courts are portrayed in a positive light'.[30] Although the Russian bar has always had (and always will have) its leading lights (for example, A. F. Koni in the 19th century, S. A. Pashin in our time), there is no Russian Atticus Finch or Horace Rumpole, no literary theme of 'lawyer as hero' in the popular Russian conception.[31]

I advocate a better rule-of-law metaphor for Russia's first forays into democratic governance, one taken from an unconventional source for contemporary Russian politics. At the climax of Robert Bolt's play, *A Man For All Seasons*, Cromwell plays the part of prosecutor at the show trial of Sir Thomas More. 'I put it to the Court', Cromwell says, 'that the prisoner is perverting the law – making smoky what should be a clear light to discover to the Court his own wrongdoing!' To this attack, More stoically replies, 'The law is not a "light" for you or any man to see by; the law is not an instrument of any kind. The law is a causeway upon which, so long as he keeps to it, a citizen may walk safely.'[32]

Bolt's metaphor captures the essence of my argument. The choice between law as a tool and law as a causeway is, and has always been, a crucial one for Russia's governance. History shows that, with few exceptions, Russia's leaders have chosen the former, instrumentalist metaphor. Russian even provides a proverb, still in use today, for this understanding of law as a tool: 'The law is like the shaft of a wagon; it goes wherever you turn it.'[33]

The causeway metaphor is better for two reasons. First, it suggests useful indicators of the existence of the sort of rule of law desirable in a Russian state ostensibly in transition away from authoritarian rule. Second, for a Russian state of limited economic resources, severe insti-

tutional and attitudinal constraints, and a political legacy of authoritarianism, it is the rule of law envisioned in the metaphor of a causeway – and not in metaphors of weaponry – that reformers should strive
to achieve and scholars should seek to measure.

What the rule of law is, and what metaphors best illustrate it, are
issues now taken in turn.

Part II   The rule of law

The rule of law is not an institution that can be established by fiat,
simply by putting pen to paper or setting bricks on mortar. That has
been a painful, and expensive, lesson for Russian would-be reformers
and an international community of eager legal aid donors to learn.[34]
The rule of law extends far beyond the institutional battles and constitutional conflicts of elites negotiating the boundaries of high politics.
In addition to state institutions (such as a legislature, judiciary, or organs
of law enforcement), the rule of law in a modern state also requires a
variety of non-state institutions: organised legal education, a professional
bar, and a myriad of supporting professions (accountants, investigators,
etc.) and organisations (newspapers, public registries, credit bureaus,
etc.). The rule of law affects the development of mass attitudes and commercial behaviour. It imbeds itself in a country's political culture and in
its civil society. It entrenches expectations about the role and limits of a
state bureaucracy, and the limits of commercial freedom and individual
autonomy. Finally, but most importantly, the rule of law requires some
level of shared expectations by political elites, lawyers, and laypersons
about what *counts* as law, about what are the limits of judicial power, and
about the spheres of life into which the law should *not* be permitted to
intrude. The institutional strength of the rule of law, although difficult
to measure, is perhaps best expressed on a continuum.[35] Thus, when
observers of Russia's transition from Soviet authoritarianism urge the
development of the rule of law, but limit themselves to cramped understandings of its meaning or accept Austinian positivism as sufficient evidence that it has taken root, they are bound to be disappointed in their
expectations, and their predictions for Russian democracy are prone to
error.

Admittedly, defining the full scope of the term is not easy. Successive
legal scholars have debated its theoretical foundations from every vantage
point.[36] It is neither my intent nor is it possible within an essay's constraints to provide exhaustive treatment. My objective is to expose the
depth of meaning and breadth of issues that 'the rule of law' presents to

political scientists, lawyers, and Russia specialists. Standing on the shoulders of giants, I think that the term is of most use to comparativists and Russian area-studies specialists if stated as a set of general principles rather than as a list of specific requirements. I offer three such principles as a starting point.[37]

1. Two caveats and three principles

Two caveats are necessary before introducing these principles.

Caveat No. 1: Government under law

The first caveat is that all principles described below must reinforce one essential meaning: the supremacy of law over government – that is, government under law.[38] The law is binding on the state itself, which remains constrained by it until the law is repealed or changed by some later properly promulgated law.[39] This subordination was justified historically, but with increasing controversy, with the belief in a legal corpus 'beyond the law of the highest political authority'.[40] The continuing debate over this normative belief in a higher law should not distract us here.

Caveat No. 2: Rule of law, not rule by law

The second caveat is that the 'rule *of* law' is not synonymous with 'rule *by* law' or 'rule *through* laws'. These latter phrases describe a political system in which statutes and other legislation are the supreme authority in the state by virtue of adherence to a formal legislative process of passing statutes and other legal acts. In such a system, the state merely subordinates itself to its own rules, which it can change in accordance with the same procedures; in other words, the state is subject to no subordination at all. Such a positivist approach to law is an insufficient guarantee of the procedural and substantive requirements of the rule of law that are explored below.[41] If rule *of* law requires a system in which the state is not the sole *source* of law (see caveat No. 1) and which adheres to procedural formality, these prerequisites are not sufficient. The self-binding notion of government under law does not, by itself, create a *Rechtsstaat*; it does not alone lead to a state ruled through laws. What does is a much deeper and broader set of constraints on state power. These constraints can be identified in the following principles, essential to (if not exclusive or exhaustive of) the meaning bound up in the phrase 'the rule of law'.

Principle No. 1: Nullum crimen sine lege

First, the rule of law, or supremacy of law over government, means that there can be no offence – criminal, civil, political or administrative

– without law. As Lord Dicey expressed it, 'no man is punishable or can be lawfully made to suffer in body or goods except for a distinct breach of law established in the ordinary legal manner before the ordinary courts of the land'.[42] There is a lot packed into this phrase, including an implicit notion of what is law. First, although stated in the negative, the phrase 'no offence without law' has an enormous positive component: unless the law prohibits an action, that action is presumed permissible. As Professor Brown has observed, Mikhail Gorbachev clearly understood that the success of his economic reforms was contingent on a sea change in Soviet legal thinking from the old rule, 'You may do only what is permitted', to 'You may do everything which is not forbidden.'[43] No offence without law thus implies that the law must be publicly accessible and knowable by those whom it would constrain. It promotes predictability and legal certainty. The law should be stated in general terms. And it must not be retroactive in its application.

Principle No. 2: Equal protection under law

A second principle must be that the first principle is universalised: all law applies equally to all citizens. Political elites in the executive and the legislative branches do not enjoy the prerogative to choose when the law applies, or to whom, a feature common to authoritarian regimes.[44] The principle therefore requires that the judiciary treat similar cases similarly, a principle of equality that promotes not just predictability about legal judgements, but also equality of arms between legal combatants regardless of wealth, military rank, or political office that would otherwise immunise against judicial process.[45] It may even imply a judicial mechanism to protect, or at least to give voice to, discrete or insular minorities at risk of permanent political exclusion by entrenched majorities.[46]

Principle No. 3: Enforcement of law

These two principles imply a third: the existence of an independent and politically neutral judiciary that is broadly accessible to aggrieved individuals to enforce legal protections and to remedy violations. But building courthouses is not enough. In a complex modern society, a class of legal professionals is also necessary; so, too, therefore, are supporting institutions like law schools, bar associations, and other non-state organisations. At its most basic level, the tribunals established by the state and open to a professional, non-state class of advocates must be capable of giving legal meaning to rights. From a criminal perspective, that means the rigorous application of established procedures to force the state to meet a standard of proof for its charges. From a civil perspective, it means that rights are not merely hortatory. To quote another ancient maxim: *ubi jus ibi remedium* – for every right there is a remedy.[47] The intrinsic value of judicial process to hear legal claims or present a defence is embedded in this phrase. The Latin word *jus* contrasts with *lex* in much the same way that a 'fundamental right' or higher 'principle of law' contrasts with a simple 'statute' or other positivist expression of parliamentary or executive will. English lacks this distinction, retained in French (*droit* versus *loi*) or Russian (*pravo* versus *zakon*). The ancient phrase is not, nor could it sensibly be, *ubi lex ibi remedium* and retain its meaning for a rule-of-law state.[48]

2. Institutional problems of the rule of law

Political scientists interested in transitions from authoritarianism should explore the problems that the practical application of these prerequisites and principles present with as much vigour as they study elections, parliaments, or civil society. This is not to demand that they descend into the legal minutiae and statutory interpretation that fascinate the law professor.[49] But if comparative politics is to insist – and rightly so – on the rule of law as a *sine qua non* for consolidated democracy, then this insistence can only have real meaning if the full significance of the term is more deeply plumbed and its empirical problems more thoroughly studied.

The overarching principle of law's supremacy over politics is a concept with tangible ramifications that political scientists can observe and measure. As noted above, for there really to be 'no offence without law', the boundaries of the law must be knowable and clearly stated in general terms.[50] Thus, the failure to publish legal acts, or the passage by a parliament of secret laws (such as laws on state secrets), bills of attainder, or laws retroactively criminalising past conduct, are all indicia of a system in which law vies with politics for supremacy. What is more, the boundaries of law's supremacy may have very measurable manifestations connected to problems of competent and equal enforcement of law throughout a country. As Guillermo O'Donnell has demonstrated, these boundaries can be mapped. What is more, reasons for the emergence of 'neofeudalised regions' in the state, or the systemic exclusion of some ethnic groups or classes from the law's protection, can be analysed:

> Let us imagine a map of each country in which the areas covered by blue would designate those where there is a high degree of state presence (in terms of reasonably effective bureaucracies and of the

effectiveness of properly sanctioned legality), both functionally and territorially; the green color indicates a high degree of territorial penetration and a significantly lower presence of functional/class terms; and the brown color a very low or nil level in both dimensions. In this sense, say, the map of Norway would be dominated by blue; the United States would show a combination of blue and green, with important brown spots in the South and in its big cities; Brazil and Peru would be dominated by brown, and in Argentina the extensiveness of brown would be smaller – but, if we had a temporal series of maps, we could see that those brown sections have grown lately.[51]

This conceptual approach to the relationship between the rule of law and democratisation led O'Donnell to note the 'fast and extensive 'browning'' of Russia in August 1993.[52]

That 'browning' is typically associated with the exclusion of disfavoured groups (be they ethnic minorities or unpopular classes) from the law's protection. The rise and fall of the 'oligarchs' under Yeltsin and Putin, however, exposed how even society's seemingly most privileged can find themselves placed beyond the bounds of law.[53] The Yukos affair is only the most widely known example of the dangerous combination of politically malleable judicial and law enforcement institutions with chimerical property rights.[54] Another is the arrest of the oligarch Vladimir Gusinsky, whose media empire was seized following failed debt negotiations with the state-controlled gas giant Gazprom. Shortly after losing his property, Gusinsky lost his liberty, spending four days in police custody on dubious charges before he bought his freedom by signing under duress an agreement to give up to Gazprom his majority stake in his media holdings. The arrangement was brokered by an acting Press Minister, who gave Gusinsky his (*ultra vires*) assurance that in exchange for relinquishing his shares, Gusinsky would be released and the criminal investigation dropped. Gusinsky ultimately petitioned the European Court of Human Rights, which held that his arrest violated the rule-of-law requirement that criminal law not be used as a tool to advance the state's ulterior political or commercial purposes.[55]

Likewise, lawmakers must enact laws in good faith and under an assumption of capacity – that is, laws should not create duties impossible to perform.[56] Russia's tax code, for example, famously violated this fundamental assumption; for much of the 1990s, the tax inspectorate wielded its statutory authority as a tool for rent extraction.[57] During

Putin's presidency, the implementation of heightened registration requirements for foreign-based non-governmental organisations in Russia[58] led
to accusations by those forced to cease their operations in Russia (including Human Rights Watch and Amnesty International) that the new rules
were deliberately made 'so tedious and lengthy as to be almost impossible
to fulfil' and so vague as to permit the pretextual audit or closure of the
Kremlin's opponents.[59] The work-product of parliaments, presidents, and
government agencies – laws, decrees, rules and regulations – is readily
susceptible to such observation.

Another avenue for exploration is the practical application of constitutions and laws, a refrain that will be familiar to sovietologists and
specialists on the satellite states of the former Soviet Union. Are constitutional rights merely aspirational statements without practical effect
or are they cognisable in a court of law? The ongoing battles over residence permits (*propiski*) expose the myth of the constitutional right to
freely choose one's place of residence.[60] Does every right really have a
legal remedy and does every legal person have an equal right to seek
that remedy? Are remedies available both against other citizens and the
state? The inability of Russian courts to ensure the enforcement of
judgements is both relevant and quantifiable.[61] Can the military be
called to account for violation of the law? Are there spheres of state
authority over which the law is suspended or otherwise does not fully
apply? Petitions made to the European Court of Human Rights from
Chechnya have exposed the state's failings in each of these areas.

In addition to assessing the empirical level of equality before the law,
political scientists are well-equipped to hypothesise reasons why equality develops or is suppressed. For example, Stephen Holmes has argued
that equality before the law is correlated with the level of pluralism in
society. Thus, where many groups of roughly equal political strength
exist and compete for leverage vis-à-vis the state, Holmes says that we
should expect the state to be pressured to promote greater equality
before the law. Conversely, when pluralism decreases and there exist
fewer powerful social groups and more opportunity for the state to
play one group against others (or for state co-optation by one group
against others), the society may move away from an approximation
of rule of law and closer to 'rule through law'.[62] These are hypotheses
that political scientists are as well-placed as lawyers to test, if not better
so.

Finally, the extent to which a judicial system follows the rule of law
can be measured with political science methods and standards. The
integrity of the judicial process can be assessed.[63] Do Russian judges

regularly turn to rules of evidence and fixed procedures that govern fact-finding?[64] Do the courts routinely create a written record of their findings? Are there ascertainable signs of fairness in legal proceedings – that is, do tribunals operate in an open forum, treat all parties equally, and adhere to a process designed to facilitate rational inquiry into the relevant circumstances of allegations that the law has been violated?[65] Are court orders practically enforceable?[66] Are 'final' orders subject to reconsideration outside of established appellate procedures with strict time limits for review?[67]

The courts, in order to function, must have institutional guarantees of security regardless of the outcome of cases before them.[68] This raises crucial questions: what is the tenure of judges? How are they removed from office? What protections do judges enjoy against political interference in their work? Are courts provided sufficient resources to function independently? Do necessary supporting institutions exist?[69] Another part of this security, as well as an intrinsic element of a rule-of-law based judiciary, is the requirement of published judicial opinions. Published opinions promote predictability and discourage secret favour by creating pressure to conduct careful analysis of facts and issues to justify with law and reason the decision that is made.[70]

The same methods can be turned to examine the judges and lawyers that staff such a system. How are they trained and chosen? If the judicial institution is to operate in a rule-of-law state, then its legitimacy and efficacy will largely be dependent on its constitution by what Karl Llewellyn called 'law-conditioned' officials, whose legal education, training, and experience combine to generate a particular habit of legal thinking.[71] This professionalisation, in turn, implies the existence of supporting non-state institutions, like a professional bar and law schools.[72]

The political culture that pervades legislative and judicial institutions, like the mass attitudes that exert influence on them, can also be analysed. Do legislators have a basic understanding of rule-of-law principles? Do citizens trust courts to adjudicate their disputes lawfully and dispassionately? Do citizens turn to lawyers to aid them in exercising their rights, or is such an idea considered naive, futile, or even dangerous?

These questions are not an indiscriminate laundry list. Systematic comparisons of Russian law, legal actors, subjects and objects over time (and with other legal systems) can be made by probing the different manifestations of these three principles.[73]

Part III   The rule-of-law causeway

A new metaphor, too, can test our understanding of law's value. 'The law is a causeway', asserts the Thomas More of Robert Bolt's famous play, a causeway upon which, 'so long as he keeps to it, a citizen may walk safely'. Citizens do not walk safely in the Russian Federation. From the most basic transactions of daily life to the most complex commercial affairs, all are subject to arbitrary and capricious interference by the state. Corruption is widespread.[74] The courts are widely mistrusted to resolve either the legal disputes that arise between private citizens or to remedy the wrongs a citizen may suffer at the hands of state officials.[75] If the citizen should seek a political solution to this insecurity, whether through grassroots activism or periodic electoral campaigns, he subjects himself to the state's wide array of what has euphemistically been gathered under the heading 'administrative resources', that is, a canting political playing field of *kompromat* (blackmail), increasingly restrictive election laws, structural fraud, and occasional violence. Whether private individuals or public dissidents, oligarchs or *siloviki* (ranking military or security officials), citizens of the Russian Federation lack the ability to plot a course in private life, business, or politics that, so long as they keep to it, will secure their legal rights and protect them from loss, seizure, or arrest. Such a state of affairs is, to put it mildly, a problem for a would-be consolidated democracy.

The causeway metaphor better expresses the rule of law that should be the focus of a state that purports to desire such a form of government than an instrumentalist metaphor of tool, sword or shield. The value of this causeway lies first in the free movement of citizens that it facilitates among state and non-state institutions in daily life, commerce, and politics. The law is what enables the citizen to know what actions he is permitted to take and what constitutes transgressive behaviour. If the citizen strays from this known path, choosing not to make use of the protections of the law or engaging in unlawful activity, that peril is known, too. These two aspects of the law as a causeway – establishing secure avenues for social interaction and identifiable paths of licit conduct – are of tremendous value to citizens in a state emerging from authoritarian rule into, perhaps, the early stages of democratic government. This conception of the rule of law shifts the initial conception of the state from gendarme to traffic policeman.

Negotiation over the establishment of this legal causeway is exactly the sort of activity in which the political elite should be engaged in the early, critical period of a new or struggling democracy. This process goes hand in hand with establishing the 'rules of the game' for repeated electoral competition. Planning a legal causeway is another way of emphasising that elites should be engaged in establishing the parameters of state power: where it begins, how far it extends, where it stops. Viewing the rule of law as a causeway makes clear that certain spheres of life are simply none of the state's business. There exists a world of private activity and personal choices into which no one would want the law to intrude. What Bernard Rudden has called the 'precious sphere of non-law' is readily identifiable by the metaphor of a causeway: it is what lies off the path in the thicket of human relations that are best left unaffected by the state's legislation.[76]

The direct relationship between the rule of law and individual liberty is also better expressed by the causeway metaphor than by visions of the law as sword or shield.[77] When the state sets forth what activity is protected and what is prohibited, and acknowledges the limits of its own power, it has established for the citizen 'a basis for legitimate expectations,...grounds upon which persons can rely on one another and rightly object when their expectations are not fulfilled. If the bases of these claims are unsure, so are the boundaries of men's liberties.'[78] If, in the words Bolt placed in the mouth of Thomas More, the citizen keeps to the causeway, he may walk safely: no offence against the state is hidden, his rights against all comers are clear. John Rawls stated this relationship well:

> But if the precept of no crime without a law is violated, say by statutes, being vague and imprecise, what we are at liberty to do is likewise vague and imprecise. The boundaries of our liberty are uncertain. And to the extent that this is so, liberty is restricted by a legitimate fear of its exercise. The same sort of consequences follow if similar cases are not treated similarly, if the judicial process lacks its essential integrity, if the law does not recognize impossibility of performance as a defence, and so on.[79]

A stable institutional environment permits the calculation of risk and affords a certain degree of predictability to the results of contemplated social interactions. This is so not only for the citizen vis-à-vis citizen, but also for the citizen in relation to the state. Nowhere is this facet of the rule of law more important, or more easily identified, than in the criminal law that punishes transgression with the deprivation of liberty. But the common law or private civil law that regulates relations between citizens also presents a causeway. It is this area of law that creates a 'legal matrix' that defines who has legal capacity and enables those 'legal persons' to own, trade, contract, and dispose of things and to recognise and enforce the legal obligations of others.[80] Individuals can contract with each other (or with the state for that matter) and know, so long as they stay on this causeway, what routes will secure their interests, with the aid of neutral courts and bailiffs, if necessary.

Instrumental or martial metaphors of the rule of law capture none of these core understandings. The reach of the law as tool or weapon cannot be known in advance. A causeway, on the other hand, can be mapped. A weapon's power, like its reach, is also likely to be unknown until the moment it is tried in some legal contest. The principle that the law applies universally to all is confused by the notion implicit in bellicose metaphors that some individuals or groups seem to have more right to wield the sword of law than others. Thus, the law-as-weapon metaphor necessarily renders suspect the state's capacity to establish a 'neutral judiciary' for the resolution of disputes. How could the law be used as a weapon against the state in the state's own forum? Is not a verdict for the state, then, a blow against the people who would use the law as a sword or shield? These are the loaded questions that Marxist legal theory answers in the negative, a preconception that Bolshevik legal nihilists delightfully embraced to destroy the gossamer threads of the rule of law that existed in the tsarist legal system. The rule-of-law causeway, on the other hand, is a two-way street open to all.

What is more, instrumentalist metaphors of law, even at their most benign, darken the relationship between state and individual. Law as weapon envisions a zero-sum battle between state and the individual: one for the law's power and the other for the law's protection. The state's loss is therefore the individual's gain. What a corrosive set of assumptions in a state seeking to leave behind the oppressive vestiges of authoritarian rule! Given Russia's authoritarian and totalitarian pasts, it is understandable that political scientists should be attracted to the instrumentalist metaphor of law as a tool or weapon in the hands of citizens to protect their rights from an aggressive, intrusive, or feckless state. As Valerie Bunce observed, 'much of the discourse on democratization (and on economic reform) emphasizes arguments that appear to support less, not more, state and thus the notion of state subtraction ... and with the need to rein in the state'.[81] Instrumentalist metaphors of the rule of law implicitly accept this premise of state subtraction. It is the rule of law as *kto kogo* – who over whom, an embrace of the idiom of *zakon kak dyshlo* – law as wagon shaft.

Finally, if the point of electoral politics in a democracy is to provide enough of a guarantee to the losing party that it will have future chances for victory to make fidelity to the 'rules of the game' worthwhile, then it seems strange to adopt an instrumentalist metaphor of the rule of law that implicitly sets the individual at odds with the state. The process of placing constraints on the breadth and reach of a new, putative democracy is not necessarily more effective – and may be more difficult – when framed in an adversarial context of offence and defence. Among the salutary effects of the rule of law on other core features of a consolidated democracy – such as a robust civil society – is the ability of the rule of law to promote conciliation between the state and its citizens. The rule-of-law causeway promotes a conception of the state that instrumentalist metaphors cannot: a state that has the power to conduct what is identifiably its business – securing borders, promoting economic stability, etc. – while limiting the state's power to employ its monopoly on the legitimate use of force against the individual in ways that deprive the individual of his established legal rights.[82] Thus, for example, the codification of private civil law separate and apart from the laws that the state adopts for the health and safety of all (such as, criminal law, labour law, antitrust, etc.) establishes relationships to property and other persons that are largely 'not the State's business….[I]f people act in good faith and stay licit, the State will stay away.'[83]

These metaphors, of course, are not mutually exclusive. In a well-established, consolidated democracy, we may want the rule of law to operate sometimes as causeway and sometimes as sword or shield. My argument is simply that the salutary expectations for the effect of the rule of law on an emerging democracy are best met by those aspects of the concept captured by the causeway metaphor and hindered by those aspects of the concept captured by instrumentalist metaphors of sword, shield, or tool. Thus, like the choice whether to hold nation-wide or regional elections first, the sequencing of rule-of-law objectives is important. In a consolidated democracy with a long history of the rule of law, the law may work simultaneously as causeway, sword, and shield. There may come a time when law is sufficiently embedded in the political culture, institutions, and expectations of a society that the kind of counter-majoritarian legal activism best described by the law-as-weapon metaphor can be tolerated, if not even viewed as an occasional necessary corrective to abusive behaviour by a democratic majority. But in an unsteady system such as Russia's, teetering along a series of tipping points, the causeway should be privileged over all other conceptions of law. The causeway metaphor supports development of other arenas of a consolidated democracy. It is less complicated and possibly less expensive. While Russia's political elites face severe resource constraints on what reforms to conduct and in what order, a metaphor of the rule of law that encourages the simultaneous development of state and society within each's own sphere is to be encouraged.

Part IV   Conclusion

Law as a tool or weapon is not the only metaphor available, and in many ways it is the worst one for a country that only recently struggled for democracy and has not yet reached the end of its great political transformation, which began with the reforms of Mikhail Gorbachev. In an imperfect world, in which reform is piecemeal, partial, and expensive, the causeway metaphor better supports the sort of rule of law that is most important for Russia. It emphasises the essentials of a new form of relationship between state and society in contrast to the hierarchical system of Russia's authoritarian past. It establishes ground rules of the game not just for electoral politics, but for the daily transactions and commercial necessities of individuals and entrepreneurs. It promotes civil and economic societies in which citizens can be secure in their knowledge of which activities are licit and which are prohibited. And it sets certain standards for law beyond its adoption by a majority in parliament. Political scientists are well-equipped to analyse the degree to which Russia conforms to these principles and practices. That study should focus on how the rule of law builds a legal causeway for citizens and the multitude of obstructions that can be placed on that road by the state.

Notes

1   James L. Gibson, 'Russian Attitudes Towards the Rule of Law: An Analysis of Survey Data', in Denis J. Galligan and Marina Kurkchiyan, eds, *Law and Informal Practices* (Oxford: Oxford University Press, 2003), pp. 77, 88.

2   Richard Rose, Neil Munro and William Mishler, 'Resigned Acceptance of An Incomplete Democracy: Russia's Political Equilibrium', *Post-Soviet Affairs* 20 (2004): 200.

3   According to a poll of 1600 Russian residents conducted jointly by the Levada Center and the EU-Russia Center in 2007, 68% of respondents did

not feel that they lived under the defense of law, while almost half of respondents felt that Russia could borrow much that is useful from western democracy and culture. See: http://www.levada.ru/press/2007021501. print.html.

4 'EU-Russia Centre Expert Survey Reveals Priorities For Change in Russia and Doubts about President Medvedev's Ability to Have an Impact', EU-Russia Centre, 6 May 2009), http://www.eu-russiacentre.org/eu-russiacentre-news/ press-releases/eurussia-centre-expert-survey-reveals-priorities-change-russia-doubts-president-medvedevs-ability-impact.html.

5 Thomas Franck, 'The Emerging Right to Democratic Governance', *American Journal of International Law* 86 (1992): 46, 66; Juan J. Linz and Alfred Stepan, *Problems of Democratic Transition and Consolidation: Southern Europe, South America, and Post-Communist Europe* (Baltimore: Johns Hopkins University Press, 1996), p. 10; Thomas Carothers, 'The Rule of Law Revival', *Foreign Affairs*, Vol. 77 (March/April 1998): 99; Valerie Bunce, 'Comparative Democratization: Big and Bounded Generalizations', *Comparative Political Studies* 33 (August/September 2000): 714; Joseph Stiglitz, *Globalization and its Discontents* (New York: W. W. Norton, 2003), p. 139; Francis Fukuyama, 'The Art of Reconstruction', *Wall Street Journal* (28 July 2004): A12.

6 Archie Brown, *The Gorbachev Factor* (Oxford: Oxford University Press, 1996). Brown repeatedly noted the importance of legal reforms pursued by Gorbachev, who was not only a lawyer by training, but the first lawyer to lead the Soviet Union since Lenin: Ibid., pp. 29, 145–6 and 176. Interestingly, a study of 'the father of Russian jurisprudence' was among Professor Brown's first scholarly publications. See: A. H. Brown, 'The Father of Russian Jurisprudence: The Legal Thought of S. E. Desnitskii', in William E. Butler, ed., *Russian Law: Historical and Political Perspectives* (Leyden: AW Sithoff, 1977); Julie Newton, 'An Annotated Bibliography of Published Work by Archie Brown', in Alex Pravda, ed., *Leading Russia: Putin in Perspective. Essays in Honour of Archie Brown* (Oxford: Oxford University Press, 2005).

7 See: Thomas Carothers, 'The Problem of Knowledge', in Thomas Carothers, ed., *Promoting the Rule of Law Abroad: In Search of Knowledge* (Washington: Carnegie Endowment, 2006), p. 27: 'Remarkably little writing has come out of the academy about the burgeoning field of rule-of-law promotion in the last twenty years. And only a small part of that existing literature is written by scholars who have had significant contact with actual aid programs.' Also see: Kathryn Hendley, 'Assessing the Rule of Law in Russia', *Cardozo Journal of International and Comparative Law*, 14 (2006): 347–8. Two notable exceptions are the empirical work of Kathryn Hendley (referenced below) and the theoretical work of Guillermo O'Donnell. Guillermo O'Donnell, 'Human Development, Human Rights, and Democracy', in Guillermo O'Donnell, Jorge Vargas Cullell and Osvaldo M. Iazzetta, eds, *The Quality of Democracy: Theory and Applications* (Notre Dame, IN: University of Notre Dame, 2004), pp. 20, 24–35, note 16.

8 Part I, Chapter 1, Article 1, § 1 *Konstitutsiia Rossiiskoi Federatsii* (1993).

9 Phillippe C. Schmitter and Terry Lynn Karl, 'What Democracy Is…And Is Not', *Journal of Democracy* 2 (Summer 1991): 81; John Lowenhardt, *The Reincarnation of Russia* (Durham, NC, Duke University Press, 1995), pp. 26–8; Vladimir Gel'man, 'Regime Transition, Uncertainty and Prospects for Democratisation:

The Politics of Russia's Regions in a Comparative Perspective', *Europe-Asia Studies* 51 (1999): 939–56; Gordon B. Smith, 'Russia and the Rule of Law', in Stephen White et al, eds, *Developments in Russian Politics 5* (Basingstoke, Palgrave Macmillan, 2001), p. 108; Fareed Zakaria, *The Future of Freedom: Illiberal Democracy at Home and Abroad* (NY: W. W. Norton, 2003); Lilia Shevtsova, *Putin's Russia* (Washington: Carnegie Endowment, 2003), pp. 65–6, 258–9; Francis Fukuyama, '"Stateness" First', *Journal of Democracy*, 16 (2005): 84, 87–8; Thomas Carothers, 'The "Sequencing" Fallacy', and Sheri Berman, 'Lessons from Europe', *Journal of Democracy* 18, 1 (January 2007) (as well as responses by Edward D. Mansfield, Jack Snyder and Francis Fukuyama and replies by Carothers and Berman in Issue 3 of that volume).

10 Even one of the better working definitions, by Linz and Stepan, overemphasises the high politics of constitutionalism and underemphasises the equally important role of an everyday legal culture, non-governmental legal institutions, and the self-binding commitment of the state vis-à-vis ordinary citizens (and not just as against its organised political opponents): Linz and Stepan, *Problems of Democratic Transition and Consolidation*, p. 10. Linz and Stepan refer to constitutionalism as the 'primary organizing principle' of their rule-of-law 'arena'. They focus almost exclusively on the self-binding constraints of politicians. Ibid., p. 248, esp. n.31. In a previous incarnation of this seminal work, the authors use the broader term 'rule of law' interchangeably with the narrower term *'Rechsstaat'*, although it seems unlikely that the authors really intended to limit themselves to the formalistic, positivist implications of the German term. See: Juan J. Linz and Alfred Stepan, 'Toward Consolidated Democracies', *Journal of Democracy* 7 (April 1996): 14–33.

11 Smith, 'Russia and the Rule of Law', p. 112.

12 In a surprisingly ahistorical claim that the rule of law 'rests significantly on democratic institutions and processes', Neil MacFarlane limits his essentially positivist definition of the term with the caveat of judicial independence. S. Neil MacFarlane, 'Politics and the Rule of Law in the Commonwealth of Independent States', in Galligan and Kurkchiyan, eds, *Law and Informal Practices*, pp. 63–6.

13 Even thoughtful meta-analysis is susceptible to this placeholder criticism, and least well-positioned to address it. One respected source defines the rule of law through indicators 'that measure how well agents abide by the rules of society. These include perceptions of the incidence of crime, the effectiveness and predictability of the judiciary, and the enforceability of contracts. Together, these indicators measure a society's success in developing an environment in which fair and predictable rules form the basis for economic and social interactions and property rights are protected.' From: Daniel Kaufmann, Aart Kraay, and Massimo Mastruzzi, 'Governance Matters III: Governance Indicators for 1996, 1998, 2000, and 2002', *World Bank Economic Review*, 18 (2004): 253, 255. (They aggregated data on 'the rule of law' from 25 sources.) These seemingly concrete measures, however, turn out not to be measurements of anything but opinion based on 'polls of experts and surveys of business-people or citizens', the methodological difficulties of which the authors explore at some depth. Ibid., pp. 257, 271–5.

14 A notable exception is Adam Przeworski and José María Maravall, eds, *Democracy and the Rule of Law* (Cambridge: Cambridge University Press, 2003), p. 1: 'The normative conception of the rule of law is a figment of the imagination of jurists. It is implausible as a description. Moreover, it is incomplete as an explanation.'

15 *Jacobellis v. Ohio*, 378 U.S. 184, 197 (1964) (Stewart, J., concurring).

16 The lawyers, on the other hand, lack the perspective and skills that make the contribution of political scientists and Russia specialists so valuable: 'A man who has had legal training is never quite the same again...is never able to look at institutions or administrative practices or even social or political policies, free from his legal habits or beliefs. It is not easy for a lawyer to become a political scientist. It is very difficult for him to become a sociologist or a historian.... He is interested in relationships, in rights in something or against somebody, in relation to others.... This is what is meant by the legalistic approach.' Judith N. Shklar, *Legalism: Law, Morals, and Political Trials* (Cambridge, MA: Harvard University Press, 1964), p. 9, ellipses in citation, quoting J. A. G. Griffiths, 'The Law of Property', in Morris Ginsburg, ed., *Law and Opinion in England in the Twentieth Century* (London: Stevens and Sons, 1959), pp. 117–19.

17 Guillermo O'Donnell reached a similar conclusion: 'I find quite remarkable (and, in fact, one of the negative consequences of the segmenting of disciplines that prevails in the contemporary academic world) that, to my knowledge, the story I have briefly told [about the relationship between democracy and legally defined and protected agency] is largely ignored by democratic, human development, and human rights theories.' See: O'Donnell, 'Human Development, Human Rights, and Democracy', p. 30. See also: Guillermo O'Donnell, 'On the State, Democratization and Some Conceptual Problems: A Latin American View with Glances at Some Postcommunist Countries', *World Development* 21 (1993): 1345–69, 1357.

18 Thorstein Veblen, *The Higher Learning in America; A Memorandum on the Conduct of Universities by Business Men* (Stanford, Academic reprints, 1954 [c1918]), p. 211. For thoughtful rebuttal of this view by a founding member of one of America's newest law schools, see: Thomas E. Baker, 'Reflections on Law Schools and the Idea of the University', *FIU L. Rev.* 1 (2006): 1, 7–11.

19 Veblen, *The Higher Learning in America*, p. 211. Veblen distinguishes the contemporary American law professor from a real 'jurist', who at least could lay claim to 'a grasp of even those quasi-scientific articles of metaphysics that lie at the root of the legal system'.

20 Dankwart A. Rustow, 'Transitions to Democracy: Toward a Dynamic Model', *Comparative Politics* 2 (1970): 343–4. Likewise, A. V. Dicey was hardly immune from these turf battles, asserting that certain subjects of parliamentary procedure and convention were 'not one of law but of politics, and need trouble no lawyer or the class of any professor of law'. A. V. Dicey, *Introduction to the Study of the Law of the Constitution*, 10th ed. (London: Macmillan, 1959), p. 31.

21 B. Guy Peters, *Institutional Theory in Political Science: The 'New Institutionalism'* (NY: Continuum Press, 1999), p. 6. Peters describes law as 'the first defining characteristic' of the 'old institutionalism'.

22   It was not always so. 'If we imagine a late twentieth-century political scientist transposed to the first decade of the century and ask in what direction he might have looked for assistance in analysing the nature of British political institutions, we should find him turning not only to the historians and journalists but to the works of the lawyers, in particular that of Albert Venn Dicey, Frederick Maitland and Sir William Anson.' See: Geoffrey Marshall, 'The Analysis of British Political Institutions', in Jack Hayward, Brian Barry and Archie Brown, eds, *The British Study of Politics in the Twentieth Century* (Oxford: Oxford University Press, 1999), p. 258.

23   An excellent collection of essays on efforts to promote the rule of law in states in various stages of transition from authoritarian rule illustrates this division: Thomas Carothers, ed., *Promoting the Rule of Law Abroad: In Search of Knowledge* (Washington: Carnegie Endowment, 2006). Eight of 11 contributors to the volume self-describe as law professors or lawyers (although one also identifies himself as a political scientist). The book contains wonderfully detailed analyses of what is meant by the phrase 'the rule of law'. But when its authors come to address equally important concepts and theories about democratic transition and consolidation, they expose themselves to the same criticism I make against political scientists and area-studies scholars who engage in rule-of-law sloganeering.

24   Elizabeth G. Thornburg, 'Just Say "No Fishing": The Lure of Metaphor', *University of Michigan Journal of Law Reform* 1 (2006): 40.

25   Michael McFaul, *Russia's Unfinished Revolution: Political Change from Gorbachev to Putin* (Cornell, NY: Cornell University Press, 2001), p. 328.

26   Maravall and Przeworski, *Democracy and the Rule of Law*, pp. 3, 15. 'Rule of law can prevail only when…law is the preferred tool of the powerful…. The conflict between rule of majority and rule of law is just a conflict between actors who use votes and laws as their instruments.'

27   Harold J. Berman, *Law and Revolution: The Formation of the Western Legal Tradition* (Cambridge, MA: Harvard University Press, 1983), pp. 38–9.

28   Gibson, 'Russian Attitudes Towards the Rule of Law', p. 90.

29   'The Search for the Rule of Law in Russia', *Georgetown Journal of International Law* 37 (2006): 353–409.

30   Michael Newcity, 'Why is There no Russian Atticus Finch? Or Even a Russian Rumpole?', *Texas Wesleyan Law Review* 12 (2005): 271, 273 note 5.

31   Ibid., p. 287. The author surmises that 'a central assumption underlying the lawyer-as-hero theme is a faith in the rule of law'. Ibid., p. 288. Although his premise is both empirically and conceptually dubious, Newcity's claims support my argument that in Russia law was and is popularly viewed as a tool, not a causeway.

32   Robert Bolt, *A Man For All Seasons*, Act II 152–3 (Random House, 1990 [1960]).

33   *Zakon kak dyshlo – kuda povernul, tuda i vyshlo.* V. Dal', *Poslovitsy russkogo naroda: sbornik* (Moscow, 1957 [1862]), pp. 245–6; Vyacheslav Kostikov, 'Dva Putina, dve strany', *Argumenty i Fakty* (9 February 2005). The article replaces *zakon* – statute – with *sud* – court – but without meaningful difference.

34   Some scholars place the cost of international rule-of-law projects at over $1 billion since 1986. Rachel Kleinfeld, 'Competing Definitions of the Rule of Law', in Thomas Carothers, ed., *Promoting the Rule of Law Abroad*, p. 31.

The United States alone spent $216 million between fiscal year 1992 and 2000 promoting the rule of law in the countries of the former Soviet Union: U.S. General Accounting Office, 'Former Soviet Union: U.S. Rule of Law Assistance Has Had Limited Impact', GAO-01-354 (April 2001), p. 7. See also: Carothers, 'The Rule of Law Revival': 104; Richard A. Posner, 'Creating a Legal Framework for Economic Development', *The World Bank Research Observer* 3 (February 1998): 13. Not everyone encountered this conceptual difficulty; see: Alexander M. Yakovlev, *Striving for Law in a Lawless Land: Memoirs of a Russian Reformer* (NY: ME Sharpe, 1996), pp. 174–6.

35 See: Kathryn Hendley, *Trying to Make Law Matter: Legal Reform and Labor Law in the Soviet Union* (Ann Arbor, MI: University of Michigan Press, 1996), p. 12. Hendley adopts a rule-of-law continuum between positivism and judicial review for constitutionally entrenched fundamental rights. See: Stephen Holmes, 'Lineages of the Rule of Law', in Maravall & Przeworski, *Democracy and the Rule of Law*, p. 49.

36 H. L. A. Hart, *The Concept of Law* (Oxford: Oxford University Press, 1961); John Rawls, *A Theory of Justice*, revised ed. (Cambridge: Harvard University Press, 1999); Marshall, 'The Analysis of British Political Institutions', pp. 276–8; Dicey, *Introduction to the Study of the Law of the Constitution*, p. vi; William E. Butler, 'Jus and Lex in Russian Law: A Discussion Agenda', in Galligan and Kurkchiyan, *Law and Informal Practices*, pp. 47–8.

37 Dicey argued that the rule of law contained 'under one expression at least three distinct though kindred conceptions'. Dicey, *Introduction to the Study of the Law of the Constitution*, p. 188. Other scholars, notably John Rawls, have ascribed certain principles or precepts to the term that can either be located within Dicey's formulation or that broadly track it. See: Rawls, *A Theory of Justice*, p. 38. My own exposition of the necessary elements of the rule of law, although easily recognisable within Dicey's formulation, do not exactly correspond to his.

38 Dicey, *Introduction to the Study of the Law of the Constitution*, p. 187. For opposing view: Maravall and Przeworski, *Democracy and the Rule of Law*, p. 15.

39 Berman, *Law and Revolution: The Formation of the Western Legal Tradition*, p. 9.

40 Ibid., p. 45. For strong counterargument: Maravall and Przeworski, *Democracy and the Rule of Law*, p. 1.

41 Similarly, many scholars equate the rule of law with constitutionalism. But there exist plenty of examples – the Soviet Union, Nazi Germany, apartheid South Africa – of how such a formalistic *Rechtsstaat* can easily fail to satisfy the other (some would say, normative) criteria of the rule of law discussed below. Harold J. Berman, 'The Rule of Law and the Law-Based State (*Rechtsstaat*)', in Donald D. Barry, ed., *Toward the Rule of Law in Russia? Political and Legal Reform in the Transition Period* (1992), p. 49.

42 Dicey, *Introduction to the Study of the Law of the Constitution*, p. 188; Rawls, *A Theory of Justice*, pp. 209–10.

43 Brown, *The Gorbachev Factor*, pp. 145–6. Gorbachev agreed wholeheartedly with this idea, advanced by one of his advisors, Vladimir Kudryavtsev, then Director of the Institute of State and Law, and soon publicly reiterated it himself. See: Vladimir Kudryavtsev, 'Pravovaya sistema: puti perestroiki',

Pravda Moscow (5 December 1986): 3. Advocacy of such a principle, limiting state action and expanding human liberty was probably as close to the rule-of-law maxim 'no offense without law' as Russia had ever come. It was explicitly incorporated into three early and important pieces of economic legislation concerning individual labour activity (1986), state enterprises (1987), and co-operatives (1988).

44   This aspect of the rule of law has a long lineage. See: Lord Edward Coke, *Prohibitions Del Roy* (1607), reprinted in *The English Reports King's Bench Division*, Max A. Robertson and Geoffrey Ellis, eds, 77 (1979), p. 1342.

45   Dicey, *Introduction to the Study of the Law of the Constitution*, p. 193; Rawls, *A Theory of Justice*, pp. 208–9. This last point is perhaps the most susceptible to variation. Most Western democracies permit themselves some form of sovereign immunity from suits filed against the state and some form of qualified immunity for certain suits filed against individual officials. However, with the growth of the administrative state, the citizen's ability to demand equitable relief, if not money damages, against the state and its agents has generally kept pace with this rule-of-law concept.

46   *United States v. Carolene Products Co.*, 304 U.S. (1938): 144, 152 n.4.

47   It should be noted that even in the United States, a country lacking neither law nor lawyers, application of this maxim is subject to considerable variation in state courts, see: Thomas R. Phillips, 'The Constitutional Right to a Remedy', 78 *N.Y.U. L. Rev.* (2003): 1309, 1313–16; it is even more strictly construed (sometimes to the point of its elimination altogether) in federal courts. See: *Stoneridge Inv. Partners, LLC v. Scientific-Atlanta*, 128 S.Ct. (2008): 761, 779 n.12, 781 (Stevens, J., dissenting). Nevertheless, broad support for the principle is traceable to the country's founding. See: *Marbury v. Madison*, 1 Cranch (5 U.S.) (1803): 137, 147. 'It is a settled and invariable principle, that every right, when withheld, must have a remedy, and every injury its proper redress.'

48   Gianmaria Ajani, 'The Rise and Fall of the Law-Based State in the Experience of Russian Legal Scholarship: Foreign Patterns and Domestic Style', in Barry, ed., *Toward the Rule of Law in Russia?*, p. 5.

49   That said, legal training can lead to different methodological approaches and, thus, different conclusions. Shklar, *Legalism: Law, Morals, and Political Trials*, pp. 15, 72. For example, some legal scholars and social scientists sharply disagree about the level of judicial corruption in Russia. Legal scholars competent to assess judicial opinions tend to view charges of judicial corruption more critically, alleging an over-reliance on the anecdotal accounts of disgruntled litigants and public opinion polls in place of careful legal assessments of judicial opinions and surveys of legal experts and litigators themselves. Compare: Alena Ledeneva, *Unwritten Rules: How Russia Really Works*, Centre for European Reform Essay (May 2001), with: Kathryn Hendley, 'Are Russian Judges Still Soviet?', *Post-Soviet Affairs* 23 (July/ September 2007): 240, 255.

50   For an excellent personal narrative of the harrowing effects of following the urge 'to know what law I have violated', see Aleksandra Sviridova, 'Living in Lawlessness', *East European Constitutional Review* 7 (Winter 1998): 71–5; Masha Gessen, 'A Battle Over A Bicycle', *Moscow Times* (20 October 2005): 10.

51 O'Donnell, 'On the State, Democratization and Some Conceptual Problems', p. 1359.

52 Ibid., p. 1368 n.9. O'Donnell does not theorise other colours, but by 1994 one could well imagine a map of the Russian Federation on which Chechnya appears as a legal black hole, marked by the total absence of state and law.

53 Hendley, 'Are Russian Judges Still Soviet?': 267. 'Russia can fairly be regarded as a dualistic legal state. Many cases are resolved by judges in accordance with the law and without any outside interference. But the political and economic elite can and do interfere when their core interests are in play.'

54 William Tompson, 'Putting Yukos in Perspective', *Post-Soviet Affairs* 21 (2005): 159–81.

55 *Gusinsky v. Russia*, App. No. 70276/01 (Eur. Ct. H.R. Nov. 22, 2004).

56 Lon L. Fuller, *The Morality of Law* 37 (rev. ed. 1969). 'To command what cannot be done is not to make law; it is to unmake law, for a command that cannot be obeyed serves no end but confusion, fear and chaos.'

57 Gerald M. Easter, 'The Russian Tax Police', *Post-Soviet Affairs* 18 (2002): 332–62; Alexander Morozov, 'Tax Administration in Russia', *East European Constitutional Review* 5 (Spring/Summer 1996): 39–47.

58 See: Federal Law of 10 January 2006 'On the introduction of changes to several legislative acts of the Russian Federation', Federal Law 18-FZ, *Rossiiskaia Gazeta* (17 January 2006).

59 C. J. Chivers, 'Russian law forces dozens of foreign organizations to stop work', *International Herald Tribune* (20 October 2006).

60 Article 27, § 1 Russian Federation Constitution. Successive bodies for constitutional adjudication have held the *propiska* unconstitutional since 1991, but with no greater result than inspiring local authorities to greater cleverness in circumventing the holdings of these commissions and courts.

61 Kathryn Hendley, 'Enforcing Judgments in Russian Economic Courts', *Post-Soviet Affairs* 20 (January/March 2004): 46–82.

62 Holmes, 'Lineages of the Rule of Law', pp. 22–3. If Holmes is right, then an extension of that hypothesis suggests that certain procedural rights – notice, confrontation, etc. – indicate the existence of rule of law, since these mechanisms are usable by all interest groups, and especially by the politically weak.

63 Hendley, 'Are Russian Judges Still Soviet?'.

64 For an excellent 'thick description' of everyday courtroom procedures, *see* Karinna Moskalenko and Leonid Nikitinskii, eds, *Basmannoe pravosudie. Uroki samooborony. Posobie dlia advokatov* (Moscow, 2004).

65 See: William Burnham and Jeffrey Kahn, 'Russia's Criminal Procedure Code Five Years Out', *Review of Central & East European Law* 33 (2008): 1–93.

66 The leading scholar in this area is Kathryn Hendley, whose scholarship deftly bridges the divide between political science, area studies, and law.

67 The Russian practice of *nadzor* (supervisory review) is one facet of this issue on which the European Court of Human Rights has expressed serious concern. See: *Ryabykh v. Russia*, App. No. 52854/99 (24 July 2003), esp. paragraphs 51–8.

68 Karl N. Llewellyn, *The Common Law Tradition: Deciding Appeals* (Boston: Little, Brown, 1960), pp. 32–3.

69 For a good comparative analysis of trends in the reform of judicial selection, see: Alexei Trochev, 'Judicial Selection in Russia: Towards Accountability and Centralization', in Kate Malleson and Peter H. Russell, eds, *Appointing*

Judges in an Age of Judicial Power: Critical Perspectives from around the World (Toronto: University of Toronto Press, 2006), pp. 375–94. See generally: Peter H. Solomon, Jr. and Todd S. Foglesong, *Courts and Transition in Russia: The Challenge of Judicial Reform* (Boulder: Westview Press, 2000); Bruce L. R. Smith, 'Constitutionalism in the New Russia', in Bruce L. R. Smith and Gennady M. Danilenko, eds, *Law and Democracy in the New Russia* 1, 14 (Washington: Brookings, 1993) (comments by then-sitting RF Supreme Court Chief Justice Viacheslav Lebedev itemising practical problems for a functioning legal system in January 1993).

70   For reflections on a conversation on this theme between former Constitutional Court Chairman Valery Zorkin and the former Reporter of Decisions for the U.S. Supreme Court, see: Naseem Stecker, 'Reflections of a Modern Scribe', *Michigan Bar Journal* 84 (February 2005): 41.

71   Llewellyn, *Common Law Tradition*, pp. 19–20. Although Llewellyn is interested exclusively in the American law-conditioned judge, his observation is congruent with this rule-of-law requirement.

72   Llewellyn recognised, and we should, too, the dangers of overprofessionalisation. Ibid., p. 23, n. 14. The countermajoritarian hazards of judicial activism also should be considered.

73   Legal scholarship can provide an additional, unorthodox source for evaluating the state of Russian law: the judgements of foreign courts required by the exigencies of litigation before them to assess whether and to what extent to defer to determinations of Russian courts as a matter of comity or conflict of laws. See: *Films by Jove, Inc. v. Berov* et al, 250 F.Supp.2d (E.D.N.Y. 2003), pp. 156, 205–16. This case assesses documentary evidence, affidavits, and the declarations of leading American and Russian experts on Russian law regarding 'allegations of pervasive corruption in the Russian courts' in the course of deciding a copyright dispute involving an American corporation, a Russian joint stock company and a state-owned Russian company. Assessments of Russian law by foreign judges, and the evidentiary submissions by parties before them, may be a surprisingly fecund source for scholars. Ibid., p. 207, n. 47, observing that three judges in a neighbouring federal judicial district had 'recently considered, and rejected, allegations of bias and inadequate procedures in the Russian arbitrazh courts'.

74   Owen Matthews and Anna Nemtsova, 'The New Feudalism', *Newsweek International* (23 October 2006); James H. Anderson and Cheryl W. Gray, *Anticorruption in Transition 3...Who is Succeeding and Why?* (World Bank Publications, 2006), p. 38; *Russian Economic Report – April 2006 (No 12)* World Bank Moscow Office (2006). p. 13; *2006 Corruption Perceptions Index*, Transparency International, (Berlin, 6 November 2006).

75   Robert Coalson, 'Vast Majority of Russians Have No Faith in Judicial Independence', *RFE/RL Newsline* (3 June 2005); Rose, Munro and Mishler, 'Resigned Acceptance of An Incomplete Democracy', but see: Hendley, 'Are Russian Judges Still Soviet?'.

76   Bernard Rudden, 'Civil Society and Civil Law', in George Ginsburgs, Donald Barry and William Simons, eds, *The Revival of Private Law in Central and Eastern Europe: Essays in Honor of F.J.M. Feldbrugge* (Leiden: Martinus Nijhoff Publishers, 1996), pp. 17, 21.

77   Dicey, *Introduction to the Study of the Law of the Constitution*, p. 203.

78 Rawls, *A Theory of Justice*, p. 207.
79 Ibid., p. 210.
80 The phrase 'legal matrix', as well as this understanding of private civil law, is borrowed from Rudden, 'Civil Society and Civil Law', pp. 17, 20–1. As a metaphor, law-as-matrix is broadly compatible with the more literary law-as-causeway.
81 Bunce, 'Comparative Democratization', p. 714.
82 This is not to deny that in some legal traditions the legal process of remedying injury is inherently adversarial. Litigants defend their rights in court, sometimes against the whole world all at once (such as, to settle title to abandoned property). The causeway metaphor does not deny this possibility. It better captures, however, the well-defined boundaries of action understood by all participants.
83 Rudden, 'Civil Society and Civil Law', pp. 17, 21.

9
Ukraine: Improbable Democratic 'Nation-State', but Possible Democratic 'State-Nation'?

Alfred Stepan[1]

The contrasting political evolution of Ukraine and Russia since 1991 poses one of the most intriguing puzzles of the last 20 years. The two countries began the post-communist transition with broadly similar institutional inheritances and comparable levels of socio-economic development. During the 1990s, the economic reforms implemented in the two countries were also similar and generated similar results, although Ukraine was reckoned to lag behind Russia in many areas. These reforms resulted for a time in remarkably similar political economies, often referred to as 'oligarchic capitalism'. In each state, asset ownership was concentrated in the hands of a small number of politically well connected oligarchs and the arbitration of conflicts among rival oligarchs constituted at once a major source of presidential power and one of the president's principal functions. Yet since the end of the 1990s, Russia and Ukraine have taken divergent political paths, the former towards increasing centralisation and authoritarianism, the latter towards a frequently unstable, often corrupt but nevertheless competitive democratic system.

Various explanations have been advanced to explain this divergence, ranging from the personalities of men like Vladimir Putin to the political economy of the so-called 'resource curse'.[2] This chapter will take a different approach. While stopping far short of a comprehensive explanation of Ukraine's admittedly sometimes wobbly democratic evolution, it will suggest that one of the key factors facilitating democratisation in Ukraine was the way the leadership handled Ukraine's ethnic divide – a factor that is more often seen as an impediment to successful democratisation and that, managed otherwise, might well have been so in Ukraine. As this chapter will argue, the choices made by Ukraine's elites in the 1990s about how to define Ukrainian statehood and how to handle the ethnic cleavage have actually served to make democratic consolidation more likely.

This article will be divided into five parts. In Part I, I will attempt to present a new ideal type to supplement, not to replace, the 'nation-state' ideal type. I will call this new ideal type 'state-nation'. Juan Linz, Yogendra Yadav and I think it is particularly useful for political leaders and scholars alike to consider such a model when they contemplate the prospects of democracy in multinational societies. Elsewhere, we have developed and applied the 'state-nation' model to the multinational societies of Spain, Belgium, and India.[3] We are now eager to see how far the model will travel.

In the other four parts of this article, and in a brief summary conclusion, I will use both the 'nation-state' model and the 'state-nation' model to explore independent Ukraine. In Part II, I will examine some conditions and identities that I believe make the implementation of aggressive 'nation-state' policies difficult and dangerous, if the goal is peace and democracy.[4] In Part III, I will examine compromises, conditions, and identities that facilitated the use of some 'state-nation' policies. In Part IV, I suggest some potential reforms, not yet tried in Ukraine, that might do what many theorists of nationalism might think an impossibility; that is, to simultaneously deepen 'nation-state', as well as 'state-nation', democratic loyalties and identities. Part V explores political violence, support for democracy and trust in the state in post-orange Ukraine. In the conclusion, I will give some comparative reflections concerning the questions raised by the title of this article.

Part I The 'nation-state' as an ideal type and the overdue addition of 'state-nation' as an ideal type

At the analytical level of ideal type strategies for fostering identity with and commitment to a democratic state there are two quite different models. The first ideal type is well known, namely the 'nation-state' model. The other ideal type is only now being conceptualised as such. I will call it the 'state-nation' model.

The goal of the nation-state model is for all members of the polity to have a single, powerful, shared identity, as members of the nation, and as citizens of the state. To achieve this goal, the state pursues relatively homogenising and assimilationist policies in the areas of education, culture, and language. In normal electoral politics, autonomist parties are not coalitionable, and secessionist parties are either made illegal or are marginalised. State structures are unitary states or mono-national federations.

A number of polities have been able to pursue such policies, and to craft democracies, such as France, Sweden, Japan, and Portugal. What conditions facilitate such policies? To pursue such policies without ethnic violence or cleansing, enforced assimilation, or international actors playing a dominant role, it would seem to help greatly if, at the time of the creation of representative institutions, there is only one awakened cultural group which sees itself as a nation in the state. If this situation exists, nation-building and democracy-building can be reinforcing logics.

But what happens if at the time of the creation of representative institutions, there is in the territory of the state, more than one territorially concentrated group, each with leaders who consider their group a nation and who are making claims for much more autonomy or even independence?[5] It would seem that in these circumstances, nation-building and democracy-building are conflicting logics. Policies close to the nation-state-building ideal type, would, by definition, privilege and support one of the two or more groups who see themselves as a nation in the state. This is so because the normative goal in the 'nation-state' ideal type is for the cultural *demos*, and the political *polis*, to be overlapping circles.

However, if there are two or more nations with leaders in the territory of the state – as there were in Spain at the death of Franco, in Belgium by the mid-20th century, in Canada when the federation was created in 1867, and in India at independence – democratic leaders face the decision to *reject*, or to *accommodate*, these nationalistic cultures.

All of the above mentioned countries – Spain, Belgium, Canada, and India – in the end, chose policies that are analytically closer to the 'state-nation', than to 'nation-state' ideal type. They decided to recognise, and institutionally give support to, more than one cultural identity, even a national identity, in the state. But, at the same time, they sought to make possible, indeed to nurture, *multiple and complementary identities within the state*. They attempted to facilitate such complementary identities by negotiating a complex series of mechanisms and incentives, such as asymmetrical federalism, consociational practices, multiple state languages, and by allowing the participation of autonomist parties as governments in some regions, and at times, as a member of governing coalitions at the centre.

The goal was to create a network of incentives encouraging the various 'nations' in the state to identify with, and be loyal to, the polit-

Table 9.1   Democracy and Cultural Nation(s). Two Contrasting Ideal Types of Democratic States: 'Nation-State' and 'State-Nation'

	Nation-state	State-nation
PRE-EXISTING CONDITIONS		
Sense of belonging/ we-ness	Awareness of, and attachment to, one major cultural civilisational tradition. This cultural identity corresponds to existing state boundaries with minor exceptions.	Awareness of, and attachment to, more than one cultural civilisational tradition within the existing boundaries. These attachments do not preclude identification with a common state.
STATE POLICY		
Cultural policies	Homogenising attempts to foster one core cultural identity; non recognition of multiplicity of cultures. Unity in oneness.	Recognises, and gives support to, more than one cultural identity. May even recognise more than one cultural nation. All within a frame of some common polity-wide symbols. Unity in diversity.
INSTITUTIONS		
Territorial division of power	Unitary states or mono-national Federations. Federacies possible.	Federal system. Often *de jure*, or *de facto*, asymmetrical. Can even be a unitary state if aggressive nation-state policies not pursued. Federacies possible.
POLITICS		
Ethno-cultural-territorial cleavages	Not too salient.	Salient, and are recognised and democratically managed.
Autonomist and/or Secessionist Parties	Autonomist parties are normally not 'coalitionable'. Secessionist parties are outlawed or marginalised in democratic electoral politics.	Autonomist parties can govern in federal units and are 'coalitionable' at the centre. Non-violent secessionist parties can sometimes participate in democratic politics.
CITIZEN ORIENTATION		
Political Identity	Single identity as citizens of the state and overwhelmingly as members of the nation.	Multiple but complementary identities.
Obedience/ loyalty	Obedience to the state and loyalty to the nation.	Obedience to the state and positive identification with its institutions, neither based on a single national identity.

ical community of the central state, on institutional and political grounds, notwithstanding the fact there was no overlap between the political *polis* and the various cultural *demoi*. Table 9.1 illustrates how both ideal types aim to create identification with a democratically useable state, but how they do this by systematically different policies toward cultural communities.

With Juan Linz and Yogendra Yadav, I have developed in much more detail the 'state-nation' argument for Spain, Belgium, and especially for India. I believe we have raised serious doubts as to whether these three democracies could have been constructed and sustained as democratic nation-states, and we also have documented that the modal self-identification in all three countries is a pattern of 'multiple and complementary' identities.

In the rest of this article I will explore whether the ideal type distinctions between 'nation-state' strategies and 'state-nation' strategies might be useful in analysing the situation confronting the Ukraine at Independence in 1991.

Part II   Conditions and identities making the pursuit of aggressive 'nation-state' strategies difficult and dangerous

For a newly independent country to opt for aggressive, but peaceful and democratic, nation-state strategies, it is very useful if three con-

Table 9.2   Self-identification in Catalonia, the Basque Country and Galicia in Spain

	Catalonia	The Basque Country	Galicia
Only Spanish	8.5	5.5	3.2
More Spanish than Cat/Basque/Gal	4.1	5.7	6.3
As Spanish as Cat/Basque/Gal	40.9	34.5	57.6
More Cat/Basque/Gal than Spanish	27.2	23.4	27.1
Only Cat/Basque/Gal	16.4	27.1	4.8
Don't Know/Don't Answer	2.8	3.8	1.0
	100	100	100
N	(1200)	(1800)	(1200)

Source: Sondeo de Opinión del Observatorio Político Autonómico 2003.

Table 9.3   Subjective National Identity in Belgium

	All of Belgium	Flanders	Wallonia	Brussels
Only Belgian	14.2	10.6	17.7	23.5
More Belgian than Flemish/Walloon	20.5	17.0	24.8	26.7
As Belgian as Flemish/Walloon	43.2	44.6	43.8	31.5
More Flemish/Walloon than Belgian	17.4	22.8	09.8	11.3
Only Flemish/Walloon	02.9	03.5	01.8	02.6
Don't Know/Don't Answer	01.9	01.4	02.2	04.5
	100	100	100	100
(N)	(3651)	(2099)	(1258)	(311)

Source: 1995 General Election Study Belgium.

ditions are present: 1) a near overlap between the cultural *demos* and the political *polis*, 2) a relatively unified, electorally-based, political elite that is in agreement about pursuing such policies, and 3) a geopolitical situation that is supportive of, or at least not dangerously hostile to, the pursuit of such strategies. At independence, Ukraine met none of the three criteria.

1. Cultural *Demoi*, not *Demos*

In a 2005 public opinion survey in Ukraine, 81% of the respondents self-identified themselves as being of 'Ukrainian nationality', and only 17% self-identified themselves as being of 'Russian nationality'.[6] But identities and everyday language use in Ukraine create many more obstacles for aggressive nation-state-building strategies than the above figures indicate. In 1995, for example, in the five eastern provinces close to Russia, 59% of the population defined themselves as 'ethnic Ukrainian', but only 15% spoke Ukrainian as their 'language of preference'.[7]

Ukraine's history has created an especially complex multinational society. The territory that is now independent Ukraine has only existed since 1954, when Soviet leader Nikita Khrushchev assigned Crimea, the home of the Soviet Black Sea Fleet, to Ukraine. The majority of the population in Crimea is made up of ethnic Russians and there is a sizeable Islamic Tatar population. As late as 1994, only 6% of the total Crimean population completely supported Ukrainian independence.[8]

In contrast, important cities in Western Ukraine, such as L'viv, until their annexation by the USSR at the end of the second World War, had for hundreds of years been a part of the Polish-Lithuanian Commonwealth, the Austro-Hungarian Empire, and later Poland, while Eastern Ukraine was under Imperial Russia or the USSR.

Strong nation-state strategy advocates would have had to put great emphasis on making the Ukrainian language *de facto*, as well as *de jure*, the dominant language throughout the territory. This would have been difficult because, even if we exclude the Crimea, only 44% of Ukraine's population shortly after independence used Ukrainian as their 'language of preference'. This percentage varied from a high of 92% in the West, to 24% in the capital of the country, Kiev, to less than 15% in the East and South.[9]

Religion is not a homogenising factor, or even a cross-cutting cleavage in creating a common cultural *demos*. Indeed, in many parts of Ukraine religion contributes to compounding cleavages. Since the Union of Brest in 1596, many Orthodox bishops in the West, virtually alone among the Orthodox in the world, broke away from Orthodoxy and pledged allegiance to the Pope in Rome as Uniates (in return for which they were allowed to retain their Eastern Rites). Orthodoxy itself is probably more fragmented (or pluralistic) in Ukraine than it is in any country in the world, with three intensely competing Orthodox rites. Some bishops accept the Moscow Patriarchate, while others accept the Kiev Patriarchate. There is also a Ukrainian Autocephalous Orthodox Church. Finally, and very importantly, a third of the population self-identify as 'not religious'.[10]

From 10 August to 29 September, 1991 Richard Rose, in collaboration with the All-Russian Centre for the Study of Public Opinion (VTsIOM), conducted a survey among the Russian minorities in 11 of the 15 Republics of the USSR. The responses from *self-defined* ethnic Russians in Ukraine graphically document just how, in some critical attitudinal areas, only a few months before independence they were very far from feeling that they were members of the Ukrainian 'nation-state', or 'demos'. In answer to the question, 'With what nationality do you define yourself', 89% answered 'Russian', and only 7% answered 'Ukrainian'. In answer to the question, 'When you say "in our country" what do you most often mean?', 79% answered 'Soviet Union', 11% answered 'this Republic'. Concerning the inquiry as to the language spoken by their children and grandchildren, 67% said it was Russian, 2% said it was Ukrainian, and 29% said it was both. Significantly, 52% of the ethnic Russians felt that knowledge of the Russian language should be compulsory for ethnic

Ukrainians. In an important political sense, the ethnic Russians were happy if the USSR, or the new state of Russia, retained some political responsibility for protecting the Russian diaspora in Ukraine. In answer to the question, 'Who should be responsible for protecting Russians' interests in the republic?' (with multiple answers allowed), Russians in western Ukraine indicated Republican leadership (74%), USSR leadership (44%), Russian leadership (40%), and the Soviet Army (7%).[11]

2. A key division among political elites

Nationalism and the demand for Independence had an early champion in Rukh, initially a movement, and later a political party. Among the early nationalists, there were certainly many who would have liked to have pressed for strong nation-state promotion policies. However, unlike Poland's Solidarity, Rukh had trouble building a strong active constituency outside of its original base, which was in the 90% Ukrainian-speaking, pro-European, anti-communist, Western part of Ukraine, centred around Lviv (with some strong followers in the capital Kiev in the center of the country). Rukh was close to the zenith of its powers in 1989, but at its First Congress, 85% of its members were from the West and the Center, and only 6% from Eastern Ukraine.[12] In the 1991 Presidential elections, the Rukh candidate came in second with 23% of the vote. In the first two competitive elections for the Parliament, in 1990 and 1994, Rukh and its allies only managed to win slightly more than a quarter of the seats.[13]

The other major political elite group came from the Ukrainian Communist Party (CPU). The former ideological secretary of the Communist Party, Leonid Kravchuk, won the first presidential elections in 1991 with 62% of the vote. In the first parliamentary elections of 1990, the CPU won 86%. In general, the partisan composition was incredibly unclear in the first parliament, because while most MPs were Communist Party members, such membership mostly reflected their elite status rather than their ideological views (since CPSU membership was required to get any kind of high position). Most scholars of this period refer to the dominance of what became known as the conservative 'group of 239' – that is, the number of deputies who voted for Kravchuk to be chair of parliament in mid-1990.[14] In fact, while many of the 450 members of the Ukrainian parliament in 1990 were formally listed as independents, Wolczuk asserts that 'only 68 deputies were not CPU members' (this puts the percentage of Communists in parliament at about 85–6%).[15] With a strong base among Russian speakers, especially in the Eastern parts of Ukraine, the Communist party and its allies had very few incentives to champion aggressive nation-state policies that would lead, *de facto*, to a marginal-isation of the Russian language.

There were in fact some disincentives. A rapid movement toward Ukrainian being the only usable language in parliament may well have hurt the careers of members of the largest party in the Parliament, the CPU. A content analysis of speeches in the parliament reveals that only 30% of CPU deputies spoke Ukrainian in parliamentary debates in the early 1990s.[16]

3. Geo-political constraints to aggressive nation-state policies

At the time of Russian independence it was by no means clear how strong Russian nationalism might, or might not, become. However, what was clear is that by far the largest number of ethnic Russians who were 'lost to Russia' (11.3 million) were in the Ukraine.[17] Russia also still had a large military presence in the Ukraine. At independence, Ukraine had a 'soldier-to-inhabitant' ratio of one soldier to every 98 inhabitants, where as Russia only had one soldier to every 634 inhabi-tants – and many of these soldiers in Ukraine were still under Russian commanders.[18] Moreover, prominent Russian citizens from elite insti-tutions again and again referred to Ukrainian independence as 'tem-porary'. Numerous public opinion polls by the Moscow-based Public Opinion Foundation found that 'Russians could not accept Ukrainian independence'.[19]

In comparative terms it is important to stress that geo-politically, none of the multinational societies that Stepan/Linz/and Yadav consider close to the state-nation pole, such as India, Belgium, Spain, Canada, or Swit-zerland, has a potentially hostile *irredentist* relationship with a powerful neighbouring country. Ukraine, at independence, potentially had such a politically significant irredentist relationship with Russia. Now, after the Russian invasion of Georgia, and Russia's recognition of their sponsored breakaway states of South Ossetiya and Abkhazia, the threat of Russia as an irredentist power towards parts of Ukraine is more evident than ever.[20]

Ukraine has a mutually dependent energy situation, with most of Russia's exports to Europe passing through Ukraine, but in a short-term crisis, Ukraine is extremely vulnerable to Russian retaliation. Estimates are that probably as much as 90% of Ukrainian oil, and 60% of Ukrainian gas, comes from Russia, at once highly subsidised prices.[21] On occasion, Russia has literally turned the lights out in parts of Ukraine.[22]

International, as well as domestic, power balances therefore made aggressive nation-state policies in the aftermath of independence both difficult and dangerous, then in 1991, and now in 2008.

Part III Conditions and compromises that facilitated the use of state-nation policies

Two months after the Orange Revolution I asked one of the leading political science specialists on Ukraine, Dominique Arel, the following question: 'If, at independence, a full 19th century French style 'nation-state' strategy had been attempted, what are the chances that Ukraine would have remained united and peaceful?' His answer was 'Nil'.[23]

There was certainly no conceptually conscious effort to follow strategies close to what I have called the 'state-nation' ideal type, but there were conscious efforts to avoid the nation-state dangers.[24] I first became aware of this in the mid-1990s in conversations with Ukrainian politicians. I had been invited to Kiev by Ukrainian parliamentarians when they were discussing the draft constitution. My major expertise that interested them concerned how to avoid loop-holes in presidential decree legislation that might facilitate presidential authoritarianism. They were also interested in my thoughts on how Spain handled its multinationalism peacefully and democratically. In informal discussions, a frequent cautionary theme among Russian and Ukrainian participants alike was that, if they were careful, they could build a state, but if they allowed themselves to get into irresolvable fights over particular identities, or divisive symbols, they could easily lose their historic opportunity. State-building, not nation-building, was their essential effort. How did they do this? Let me briefly discuss seven important conditions and compromises, with state-nation overtones, that helped state-building.

1. Some positive Russian attitudes towards living in an independent 'state-nation' of Ukraine (as long as their rights were protected)

As we have just seen, many Russian (and even some self-defined Ukrainians) had attitudes and language preferences that would have made them resistant to nation-state-building policies at independence. The utility of our 'state-nation' supplementary ideal type is that it directs attention to the possibility that within the set of attitudes that might be hostile to nation-state-building policies, there could be a politically useable set of attitudes that might be quite supportive of 'state-nation' building policies. A key claim of our 'state-nation' ideal type is that 'multiple and complementary identities' are not only useful in multinational societies, but possible. The Richard Rose/VTsIOM study supports this thesis. Since our purpose is to expand our understanding of different ways to build commitment and loyalty to a democratic state, let us examine these Russian attitudes carefully. In those areas outside the Ukrainian nationalist stronghold in western Ukraine, the following sets of Russian responses to questions reveal attitudes, three months before independence, quite supportive of state-nation policies.[25]

- 'All people in the republic, both Russians and titular residents, share the same hardships now' (Agree, 96%).
- 'Russians in this republic are being discriminated against' (Agree, 3%).
- 'I don't feel alien in this republic' (Agree, 86%).
- 'How would you evaluate relations between different nationalities in the republic?' (Cordial, 28%, Normal, 58%, Tense, 9%, Hostile, 0%).
- 'Do you intend to emigrate from this republic or do you intend to stay for the rest of your life?' (Firmly decided to emigrate, 2%).
- 'Pogroms of Russians are possible in the foreseeable future' (Agree, 3%).[26]

Attitudes, of course, are highly malleable. What is impressive in Ukraine is that, by and large, both the Ukrainian majority, and the Russian minority, made a series of compromises and decisions that built upon, rather than eroded, attitudes that were supportive of state-nation policies.

2.   The wording of the declaration of independence

As Roman Szporluk argues, 'it is essential to remember that the independent Ukraine proclaimed in August 1991 did not define itself as an ethnic state. It was a jurisdiction, a territorial and legal entity....The new state declared that all power in it derives from "the people of Ukraine"'.[27]

3.   The inclusive law on citizenship

Unlike Estonia and Latvia, which at independence passed exclusionary citizenship laws that disenfranchised many Russians, Ukraine, in October 1991, passed a very inclusive citizenship law. In her important account of negotiations concerning the constitution, Wolczuk argues that this law, 'adopted a territorial definition of citizenship and membership in the new state was granted automatically to almost everyone who was living in Ukraine at the time the law was passed (the so called "Zero Option"). As no category of the population was formally excluded from the political community, citizenship based on *ius soli* became one of the fundamental attributes of the new political community'.[28]

Timing helped secure this compromise. The Referendum on Independence was scheduled to take place in a month. Ukrainian nationalists accepted this inclusive wording as a way to encourage a positive vote for independence in Crimea and in the Russophone East. The compromise was also deliberately crafted as a way of blunting the warnings by Communist Party hardliners on the dangers of ethnic exclusion modelled on the Baltics.[29]

4. Growing strategic cooperation between Rukh and the Communist leadership over statehood

As the Rukh-based nationalists began to realise that their electoral upper base was probably only between 20% to 30% of the vote, and that they needed some cooperation with Communist leadership to win, and sustain, an independent Ukrainian state, they increasingly shifted from an exclusive, 'nation-based', to an inclusive, 'state-based' discourse. As Alex Motyl and Bohdan Krawchenko note, 'Rukh's language was palatable to the Communists such as Kravchuk because it was nationalist, but neither chauvinist, nor racist; it had at its core the attainment of statehood for the Ukrainian people, whom Rukh carefully defined in non-ethnic terms that permitted Russians, Jews, and Poles, and others to take part in and support its cause. Such a nationalism was at least as potentially appealing to Communists, as it promised them the opportunity of continuing to serve as an elite, if not the only elite, within a future Ukrainian state'.[30]

With the two major political elite groupings cooperating strategically in their advocacy of independence, and with an inclusive citizenship law already passed on 1 December, 1991, a Republic-wide Referendum approved the independence of Ukraine by 90% , including 80% support in the heavily Russophone Eastern Oblasts, and 54% in Crimea.[31] On the same day, the once anti-nationalist, but now nationalist, Kravchuk, was elected president of the Ukraine with 62% of the vote.

5. Partial compromises over the constitutional preamble

As in many countries with a multinational society, there was a heated constitutional debate over the preamble. Who are the people? The preamble to the constitution adopted in 1996 was indeed a partial victory for the nationalists, but in the same long sentence, there is a partial compromise for all nationalities. The parliament voted for the constitution 'on behalf of the Ukrainian people – citizens of all nationalities, expressing the sovereign will of the people, based on the centuries-old history of Ukrainian state-building and on the right to self-determination realised by the Ukrainian nation, all the Ukrainian people...adopts this Constitution'.

As a trade-off for this partial compromise with the nationalists, the constitution went on in its next 15 chapters to embed one of the most rights-protecting (but often not enforced) constitutions of any post-communist European state. As previously mentioned, Ukraine created one of the most inclusive citizenship laws of the countries in post-communist Europe. Article 55 also gives citizens the right to seek redress for the violation of their rights from any international judicial organisation of which Ukraine is a member. Article 15 also created a Human Rights Representative located in the parliament, not the executive. Dominique Arel implicitly affirms the 'state-nation', as opposed to 'nation-state', policies that Ukraine pursued after Independence. 'Ukraine strove to convince the world that, unlike many of the successor states of the former Soviet bloc, its state was being built on territorial and civic principles, eschewing any privilege for the titular Ukrainian group...In terms of civic rights, one can hardly disagree with the assertion that Ukrainian state policy has been all-inclusive...It is difficult to disagree with the contention that the Ukrainian state-building project is resting on territorial, as opposed to ethnic, foundations'.[32]

6. The *de facto*, if not *de jure*, compromise over language

As late as 1968, only 17% of the post-secondary textbooks in Ukraine were in Ukrainian.[33] However, in 1989 the Ukrainian parliament, still under Gorbachev's USSR, passed the 'Law on Language' establishing Ukrainian as the state language of Ukraine, and stipulated that Ukrainian be introduced in higher education and state bodies within ten years. At independence, some Ukrainian nationalists wanted to push for 'Ukrainian Only', but a strong group of Russophones in Crimea and Eastern Ukraine wanted then, and want now, for Russian to be established as the second official state language.

Article 10 of the constitution adopted in 1996 opens in *de jure* 'nation-state' language. The first two clauses read:

- The state language of Ukraine is the Ukrainian language.
- The state ensures the comprehensive development and functioning of the Ukrainian language in all spheres of social life throughout the entire territory of Ukraine.

However, the third clause of Article 10 (especially if one substituted the word 'nationalities' for 'minorities') has some state-nation tones:

- In Ukraine, the free development, use and protection of Russian and other languages of national minorities of Ukraine, is guaranteed.

Article 53 further constitutionally entrenches Russian and makes any aggressive nation-state, homogenising, 'Ukrainian only', state policies difficult, and indeed illegal.

- Citizens who belong to native minorities are guaranteed in accord-ance with the law the right to receive instruction in their native lan-guage, or to study their native language in state and communal educational establishments and through national cultural societies.

An ideal type state-nation strategy would probably call for Russian to be one of the two official languages of Ukraine. The countries closest to the nation-state ideal type, such as Switzerland, Belgium, Spain, India and Luxembourg all of course have more than one official language in the state. India has 22 official languages.

The key question for us to analyse is how much the *de jure* language of Article 15 actually impeded some core state-nation values such as 'multiple and complementary identities' and polity-wide access to public and private careers.

When Sri Lanka made Sinhalese the only official state language, and eliminated English as a vital link language, this nation-state policy virtually precluded important polity-wide public sector careers, or state-nation identities, for Tamil speakers, very few of whom spoke Sinhalese. Within a decade, almost no Tamil speakers were important state bureau-crats. Sri Lanka at independence had many conditions that would have facilitated state-nation policies and the prolongation of its unified and democratic polity. However, the aggressive pursuit of nation-state policies in Sri Lanka's multinational society helped produce a 25 year long civil war that has threatened the country's democracy and physical integrity.[34]

The situation in Ukraine has some quite important differences with Sri Lanka that make state-nation identities possible notwithstanding the fact that Ukrainian is the only official language of the country.

The pattern of the everyday use of language in Ukraine helps defuse the issue. In a 1995 poll, 32% of respondents said they used Ukrainian as their sole language at home, 33% used Russian as their sole language, and 35% used *both* Ukrainian and Russian.[35] In any case, in Ukraine, the lan-guage of preference is not necessarily a marker of self-identity.[36] Although only 32% of the population said that Ukrainian was the sole language they spoke at home, 70% of them nonetheless self-identified as ethnic Ukrainians.[37] You might add that the languages are sufficiently close that frequently in parliament and elsewhere, conversations go on between one side that speaks exclusively Russian and the other side that speaks exclusively Ukrainian. Thus, whatever language is spoken, there is rarely a problem of mutual comprehension (at least in the narrow linguistic sense).

Self-identified ethnic Ukrainians who are in fact Russophones understandably might not want to jeopardise their careers by having to speak Ukrainian at the workplace or to use it in exams for entry into the public service. However, while only 40% of self-identified Ukrainians in Kiev spoke Russian at home, in the same sample, 98% said they wanted their children to be 'fluent' in Ukrainian.

Most important for the long-term possibility of 'multiple and complementary' identities in a possible 'state-nation' polity in Ukraine, is that 91% of self-identified ethnic Russians in Kiev, and 96% in Lviv, expressed a desire that their children be fluent in Ukrainian.[38]

State policies toward teaching the Russian language are still quite permissive. Ukrainian language instruction is not, as Article 10 stipulates, available 'throughout the entire territory of Ukraine'. Indeed, in parts of Southern and Eastern Ukraine, it is still difficult to get Ukrainian-language textbooks.[39]

7.   The use of some key common symbols

Citizens and political leaders in a multinational society, if it is to have a political community close to the 'state-nation' ideal type, need to have, and to appeal to, some common symbols.

In Ukraine, there are more facilitating conditions concerning non-polar identities than the huge literature on the 'two Ukraines' indicates. Fortunately, an important longitudinal study of the supposedly polar opposite cities, Lviv in the so-called nationalist West, and Donetsk in the so called pro-Russian East, has been carried out by the Ukrainian scholar, Yaroslav Hrytsak. In these studies, the overwhelming percentage of people polled agreed that the medieval Kyivan Rus period was the starting point of Ukraine. There are thus not competing, but complementary, founding myths about Ukraine. Also, throughout all of Ukraine, the most popular historical figure is the Cossack leader, Bohdan Khmelnytskyi, whom ethnic Ukrainians, as well Russians in Ukraine (unlike Russians in Russia) see as a major state-builder. Indeed, even President Kuchma, often accused of pro-Russian leanings, made a major speech on the 400th anniversary of Khmelnytskyi's birth implying his 'we-feeling' with him. 'Today, carrying on Bohdan's work, we are realising the third attempt at the revival of our state.'[40]

The theoretical literature on nationalism often points to the utility of an 'other' in forging some common identities. In Ukraine, ethnic Ukrainians, Russians, and Crimean Tatars have a shared historical 'other'. The famine in Ukraine, which led to millions of deaths, and also the expelling of the Tatars from Ukraine in 1944, are directly seen as policies of Stalin. Thus, ethnic Russians and Ukrainians alike 'both in the West and East, are unanimous in their negative evaluation of Stalin and his acts of repression; they see him as the main villain in Ukrainian history, the number one anti-hero. And this is exactly what makes them different from Russians [in Russia]: a majority of the Russian population [in Russia] considers Stalin in rather positive terms, as a great state builder, who turned the Soviet Union into a world superpower.'[41] A recent pre-independence 'othering' factor that forged some commonalities among virtually all citizens of Ukraine vis-à-vis Russia was the Chernobyl disaster itself and its callous handling by Moscow.[42]

Understanding three different types of polarisation: Voter, identity and issue

Too many observers conflate voter, identity and issue polarisation. To understand the possibilities of a state-nation in Ukraine it is imperative that we disaggregate polarisation. 'Voter polarisation' is by comparative standards very high. But 'identity polarisation' is less so, and there is far less 'issue polarisation' than the vast majority of the literature indicates.

To be sure, there are strong voting differences between Lviv and Donetsk, and what would appear to be dangerous voter polarisation between East and West.[43] For example, in the third and final round of voting for the president during the Orange Revolution, the pro-Orange Yushchenko won 93.7% in Lviv, but only 4.2% in Donetsk.[44]

But a few years earlier, when a hard question was asked of the population of the two cities if they should become divided into several different countries, only 1% in Lviv, and 5% in Donetsk, chose the option of radically dividing the political community.[45] My point is that voter polarisation may not necessarily reflect polarisation about desired future political identities.

Fortunately for the political community of Ukraine, 'voter' polarisation, is only one type of polarisation. Conceptually and empirically we can also speak (and measure) 'identity polarisation', and 'issue polarisation', as well as 'voter polarisation'. 'Identity polarisation' is substantially less in Donetsk than 'voter polarisation'. For example, on a three-point scale of identity, 28.5% of respondents in Donetsk said they were 'only Ukrainian', 20.2% said they were 'only Russian', and the modal response was bi-ethnic, 47.8%. Thus, 76% of respondents in

Donetsk have some degree of Ukrainian in their self-definition of identity.

'Issue polarisation' is also strikingly less than 'voter polarisation'. The North-West (where Lviv is located and which voted overwhelmingly for Yushchenko) was presented in the Russophone media during the 2004 elections as being in favour of extreme 'Ukrainianisation only' language plans, and of being against good trade relations with Russia. In fact, 68% of those surveyed in the North-West, far from being for *more restrictive* policies toward the status of Russian, are for *more permissive* policies toward the Russian language than the constitution presently prescribes; 45% were in favour of Russian being made an official language at the local level if people want it, and 23% were in favour of Russian being made the second official language. In terms of Ukrainian government relations with the Western Europe and with Russia, there was surprisingly little issue polarisation in North-West Ukraine. On a five point scale, 56.5% of respondents in the North-West chose the middle position, 'equal orientation toward the West and towards Russia'. This was also – barely – the modal position (36.5%) chosen in the South-East.[46]

These data offer some prospect that, if future electoral campaigns are waged in a context of a freer press, and there is less government controlled 'administrative resource' used to generate polarisation than there was in the 2004 elections, and as the pro-Orange and anti-Orange opponents of the 2004, 2006, and 2008 struggles die out, new politicians might find it increasingly productive to devise policies that appeal to citizens on issue areas where there is in fact not overwhelming polarisation . If so, voter polarisation could diminish, and multiple but complementary identities of a state-nation sort could increase.

Part IV   On the possibility of simultaneously deepening 'nation-state' and 'state-nation' democratic identities and loyalties

The above sub-title may strike some readers as a contradiction in terms because they may think the two ideal types are always in an either/or relationship. Let us see why this is not necessarily so, theoretically or empirically.

The goals of both ideal types include the creation of a useable state, without which a democracy is impossible. Both ideal types can also have policies that may help develop commitment and loyalty to the democratic institutions of the state. I have argued that Ukraine has more of a chance to create a democratic political community if it does not pursue aggressive nation-state policies. However, theoretically, there can be policies that may look like nation-state policies, but which, if implemented softly and widely, also might facilitate the multiple and complementary identities that are crucial both for state-nations and for democracies in multinational societies. Let us explore this proposition in the case of Ukraine.

Adult Russophones do not want to be forced to speak Ukrainian in the workplace or for the exercise of their full rights of citizenship. Nonetheless, the overwhelming percentage of them wants their children to have the opportunity to speak Ukrainian fluently. However, in many schools in the East and South, there are not enough Ukrainian-speaking teachers, and many of the textbooks are not only in Russian but were written in the Soviet era in what is now Russia.[47] If Russophone parents see that state policies are improving their children's capacity to function successfully in Ukraine, these same Russophone parents might well increase their trust in the state-nation policies of the Ukrainian state. If in two generations, virtually every adult in Ukraine speaks Ukrainian (even though many of them will continue also to speak Russian), the policy would also have been a good 'nation-state' policy.

A somewhat more complex question is Russian language news on television. For a combination of financial constraints and sensitivity to nation-state sensibilities, the Ukrainian government state TV channels, such as UT-1, are in Ukrainian. This meant that most Russophones, especially in Eastern Ukraine, watched Moscow-originated programmes during the 2004 Presidential elections and during the Orange Revolution. The production of high-quality attractive television news programmes in Russian may be seen as a linguistic compromise on nation-state goals, but it would probably be a plus for building a political community in Ukraine that is at ease with Ukraine as a viable democratic nation-state for some of its citizens, and a viable democratic state-nation for other of its citizens. Certainly the goal of having Russophones with complementary, as well as multiple, identities would be served.

Another major issue raised during the Orange Revolution concerns presidential powers. Yushchenko and his loyalists, who would have been happy with a stronger nation-state focus, were unhappy that, in exchange for the outgoing pro-Russian government of Kuchma agreeing to fairer election rules and a re-run of the presidential election, Viktor Yushchenko agreed to transfer some presidential powers to the parliament and to the prime minister within a year. Not withstanding the self-serving intentions of outgoing President Leonid Kuchma, this historic pact, if it can survive the transitional crisis that contributed to intense 'dual government' conflicts between President Yushchenko and his first Prime Minister, Yulia Tymoshenko, may in the long run produce positive results for Ukraine's democracy and prospects for joining the European Union.

The Ukrainian Constitution of 1996 adopted a model of governance close to the French-style, dual executive, semi-presidentialism created by Charles de Gaulle for the Fifth Republic: a directly elected president with significant executive powers and a prime minister responsible to parliament. This system works best when the president and the prime minister come from the same political party or coalition, have a majority in parliament, and where the president is what Cindy Skach calls a 'party-person'. In the classic theory of semi-presidentialism, if the president does not have a parliamentary majority, political power should pass to the prime minister if he or she controls a majority in parliament.[48]

However, classic theory, and the modern French experience, is virtually silent on how the system should work if neither the president nor the prime minister has a majority (as in Yeltsin's Russia).[49] In the case of Russia under Yeltsin – and in many of the post-Soviet cases – the president in the absence of a party majority often rules on the margin of constitutionality by decree, or goes out of the democratic box entirely by closing the parliament, tightly controlling the rewriting of a constitution in which presidential powers are greatly enhanced, and then holding a plebiscitary ratification of a model that is most aptly called 'super-presidential semi-presidentialism'.[50]

Something like the above occurred in post-independence Ukraine, except for the very important facts that no president ever dissolved the parliament or was able to completely rewrite the constitution.[51] There are two key points about 'super-presidential semi-presidentialism' that are central to our inquiry as to whether Ukraine can become a democratic state-nation. First, no stable democracy in the world, and certainly no European Union member country, has a constitution that is remotely close to being 'super-presidential semi-presidentialism'. Second, 'state-nations' are facilitated if there is some degree of a 'shared executive', but by definition 'super-presidential semi-presidentialism' is an 'indivisible good'. Let me elaborate.

A look at the eight post-communist countries admitted to the European Union in 2004 is instructive. Five – Hungary, the Czech Republic, Estonia, Latvia and Slovakia – are parliamentary. The other three – Slovenia, Poland and Lithuania – have directly elected presidents, but none comes constitutionally and politically close to Kuchma's Ukraine. Like Portugal in the 1980s, they adopted semi-presidential systems that so reduce presidential authority, and so increase the parliament's powers, that they are most accurately described as 'parliamentarised semi-presidential' systems.[52]

This is the 'shared power' model towards which Ukraine could theoretically be (but is not actually) moving towards. If Ukraine ever began to practice parliamentarised semi-presidential politics, the presidency could become less of a potential source of ethnic polarisation, thereby strengthening the common identity that many ethnic Ukrainian, and ethnic Russian, citizens of Ukraine are committed to upholding. This is so because all the countries closest to the state-nation pole in the world (Spain, Belgium, India, Luxembourg, and even Switzerland with its collective executive) are in essence parliamentary. Because a parliamentary regime requires a majority, or at least a supported minority government, parliamentary regimes are often 'coalition-requiring' and 'coalition-sustaining'. However, President Yushchenko, and his first Prime Minister, Yulia Tymoshenko, constructed the cabinet as a near 'winner take all' majoritarian government. Yushchenko's core party, 'Our Ukraine', only won 102 seats in the 450-seat parliament, but according to Dominique Arel's analysis, 13 of the 17 cabinet members were drawn from 'Our Ukraine'. More importantly, the cabinet did 'not include a single [political] representative of the eastern and southern industrial elites'.[53] If, the 'parliamentarised semi-presidentialism' rules come fully into play, it would be important for the government, which may well not have a majority, to seek out some allies in the parliament from the East and South, and this would probably entail some cabinet seats as well.[54]

This might increase the incentives for polity-wide cooperation that could help overcome the current polarisation both of regions, and to a lesser extent, between ethnic Ukrainians and ethnic Russians. Two months after the triumph of the Orange Revolution, in answer to the question, 'Are you proud of being a citizen of Ukraine?'; 83% of ethnic Ukrainians answered 'Very' or 'Somewhat', whereas only 52% of ethnic Russians did so. Concerning the Orange Revolution, 58% of the ethnic Ukrainians, but only 17% of the ethnic Russians affirmed that the Orange Revolution would be 'Definitely good', or 'Probably good' for the development of Ukraine.[55]

My final comment concerns federalism. Every country close to the state-nation pole (with the exception of tiny Luxembourg) is federal. Must Ukraine become federal to maintain itself as a country with many 'state-nation' qualities? Most of the scholars I have asked were worried in 1991, and after Russia's invasion of Georgia in 2008, they are more worried, about territorially concentrated power under the existing conditions of polarisation and policy conflicts with its large neighbour Russia. As I discussed earlier, Ukraine – unlike the near state-nations of Spain, India, Belgium, or Canada – had a potentially threatening irredentist situation on its borders in 1991. Federalism might not have been prudent in these circumstances. However, is federalism nonetheless the only solution? Not necessarily. But serious decentralisation should be considered, as well as centre-regional development projects. Many of the East-West conflicts have a strong economic as much as cultural component. For example, part of the reason Yanukovich received 93.5% of the vote in Donetsk in the third round of the 2004 presidential election was that industrial production in Donetsk had declined from a base of 100 in 1990 to 43.6 in 1998. However, after Yanukovich was appointed governor of Donetsk in 1997, he worked with the central government on a series of industrial promotion policies, and created two new 'special economic zones'. By 2003, Donetsk's industrial production base had risen to 69.4, the unemployment rate had declined, and Yanukovich received much of the credit. Correctly or not, Yushchenko was presented in the 2004 elections as opposed to these regional development plans.[56]

Much of the East is dominated by heavy state-owned Soviet-era mines and factories. At the moment every governor is appointed directly by the president and municipal budgets are small. A model for Ukraine possibly to consider is the Scandinavian countries, which combine unitary states with much greater budgets for cities than the federal states of Europe.[57]

Scandinavia is also a leader in how unitary states have been able create highly decentralised 'federacies' to respond to the special needs and wants of peoples who are not ethnically, historically, or geographically part of the nation-state (or indeed even the unitary state itself), but who are citizens of the state. Federacies allow an otherwise unitary state, to negotiate constitutionally embedded federal-type relationships, with a relatively isolated and distinct community, without making the entire polity a federation. Some possible federacy models to examine for the Crimean Tatars might be Greenland's relationship to Denmark, or the Aland Islands relationship to Finland.[58]

The major thing for modern democratic thinkers and policy-makers is *not* to abandon the nation-state where it is appropriate, but to *increase* the repertoire of viable democratic alternatives for those conditions where it is inappropriate. The Ukrainian case is useful in that it helps expand our political imagination about new alternatives for situations where it might be democratically difficult, or even dangerous, to try to make a robust effort to create a nation-state.

Part V What are post-Orange responses to violence, polity-wide support for democracy and trust in institutions?

Let me now look at three areas in post-Orange Ukraine that are crucial for Ukraine's chances of becoming a democratic state-nation.

1. Violent conflicts between national groups?

There is a strong consensus in the literature that in the 18 years since independence, in contrast to many post-Soviet states, there has been virtually no politically motivated violence by ethnic groups or nationalities against each other in Ukraine, and no state support for such activities. Since democracy is very difficult to construct if there is widespread political violence in the state this is a supportive condition for democracy.

It is always difficult to prove a counterfactual, but key Ukrainian specialists that I have cited, such as Dominique Arel, José Casanova, and Roman Solchanyk, as well as much of the evidence I have presented in this article, leads to the conclusion that such peaceful supportive conditions would have been much less likely if robust nation-state-building policies had been applied.

2. Growing and complementary support for democracy among the national groups?

Good political and state practices, as much as good citizen's attitudes, are involved in a possible democratisation. But supportive attitudes might help drive some practices to be democratic and might maintain pressure against corrupt practices. In 2005, the last year for which I have good survey data, Ukrainian attitudes toward democracy were still well below our three democratic state-nations of Spain, Belgium, and India, somewhat similar to Chile but better than Russia or Brazil. See Table 9.4.

For our concern with multiple but complementary attitudes as being necessary for a democratic state-nation, the data underlying Table 9.4 yield a disturbing fact that: within Ukraine, where around 57% of respondents expressed support for democracy, ethnic Ukrainians' support for democracy was 60%, while that of ethnic Russians was only 43%. However, it should be noted that this 43% by ethnic Russians in Ukraine was 19% higher than the support for democracy of Russians in Russia, so we cannot say that low support for democracy is an intrinsic consequence of historic Russian political culture *per se*. It is also useful to note that ethnic

Table 9.4 Percentages Affirming that 'Democracy is Preferable to any other Form of Government': In Two Democratic State-Nations, in early Democratising Ukraine, 'Competitive Authoritarian' Russia, and Selected Latin American Democracies. (Number in parenthesis shows the percentage of those who answered the question and excludes 'don't know/no' answer)

	Consolidated democratic state-nations			Early democratising versus competitive authoritarian		Troubled Latin American democracies	
	Spain	Belgium	India	Ukraine	Russia	Chile	Brazil
Democracy is preferable to any other form of government	78 (83)	70 (78)	60 (83)	57 (66)	29	52 (54)	41 (48)
In some circumstances an authoritarian government can be preferable to a democratic government.	9	10	6	18		18	21
For someone like me, a democratic or a non-democratic regime makes no difference	7	10	6	11		25	23
Don't know/ No answer	6	10	27	14		4	15
N	(1000)	(1036)	(8133)	(2000)	(?)	(1200)	(1240)

Sources: The data for India are from the *National Election Study, 1998*, coordinated by Yogendra Yadav of the Centre for the Study of Developing Societies, Delhi. The data for Russian and Ukraine come from Richard Rose, 'Divisions within Ukraine: A Post-Election Opinion Survey', *Studies in Public Policy* # 403 (2005): 29, question D7. The data on Russia is from Richard Rose, 'New Democracies Barometer' (2001), Data for Brazil and Chile are from the *Latino Barometer 1996*, directed by Marta Lagos. The Spanish and Belgian data are from the *Eurobarometer 37* (1992).

Russian support for democracy in Ukraine was 2% higher than the support for democracy by Brazilians.

Unfortunately, we do not have for Ukraine previous years of the classic question in Table 9.4, so we can not say anything about trends on this question. However, we do have an important battery of related questions that Richard Rose frequently asks in post communist countries. Rose calls a respondent a 'confident democrat' if they 'disapprove of the suspension of parliament and considers suspension unlikely'. In 1996, only 30% of Ukrainians were 'confident democrats', which was the lowest of the ten post-communist countries surveyed, whose average was 59%. However, in 2005, 'confident democrats' in Ukraine had more than doubled to 63%. Just as important for our concern with multiple and complementary identities in possible state-nations in multinational societies is the fact that both ethnic Russians, and ethnic Ukrainians, alike score an identical 63% (see Table 9.5).

Democracy is more likely to become 'the only game in town' the more citizens 'become habituated to the fact that political conflict will be resolved according to established norms and that violations of these norms are likely to be both ineffective and costly'.[59] Table 9.5 indicates that some such habituation may be starting in Ukraine.

So do some important political practices, such as the routine involvement of thousands of electoral observers at the elections of 2004, 2006, and 2007. Such observers, many from Central European member states of the European Union such as Poland, Hungary, and Lithuania, by and large have been accepted as legitimate and important by all major Ukrainian political parties.[60]

Table 9.5 Percentage of 'Confident Democrats' in Ukraine and 10 other Post-communist countries in 1996 and in Ukraine in 2005

	1996			2005		
	10 post-communist countries	Russia	Ukraine	Ukraine	(Ethnic Ukrainians)	(Ethnic Russians)
% 'Confident Democrats'	59	36	30	63	(63)	(63)

Sources: The definition Richard Rose uses for 'confident democrats' in all the surveys above is the same as he used in the ten-country survey, that is, a respondent ' disapproves suspension of parliament' (Q.29) AND 'considers suspension unlikely' (Q.28), see Richard Rose and Christian Haerpfer, 'New Democracies Barometer IV: A Ten Nation Survey', *Studies in Public Policy*, #262 (1996): 86. For Russia see Richard Rose, 'Getting Things Done With Social Capital: New Russian Barometer VII', *Studies in Public Policy*, #303 (1998): 44. For Ukraine in 2005 see Richard Rose, 'Divisions within Ukraine: A Post-Election Opinion Survey', *Studies in Public Policy*, #403 (2005): 32.

3.   Still low trust in institutions?

A major 'democratisation' attempt – and no democratisation attempt is ever certain – probably only really began in Ukraine with the victory of the Orange Revolution in December 2004. Thus, while part of the government has been democratised, much of the former non-democratic state apparatus and routines remained, as this survey indicates, not deeply changed, although there is pressure for improvement from a critical press.

What this means in terms of citizen's opinions is that there is still virtually the same low trust in the state's courts and police, somewhat more trust in democratic institutions such as parties and parliament. The substantial increase in the trust of the president in the 2005 survey was not sustained throughout the 2006–2008 period, given the president's involvement in conflicts with two of his prime ministers.

Since ethnic Russians are still somewhat worried about their treatment by the Orange Revolution (which by and large they did not vote for), they score lower on all these increases of trust. The temptation of some Orange Revolution ideologues to take an aggressive turn towards building a 'nation-state' would exacerbate, rather than ameliorate, these ethnic Russian worries.

Better democratic governance for all citizens, more democratic shaping of the state, and implementation of some of the policies I suggested in the last section, is necessary to continue and broaden the slight upward trend in trust indicated in Table 9.6.

Conclusion: The comparative state of democracy and peace in Ukraine in 2008

Ukraine, as we have seen, has a number of serious problems with the quality of its democracy. However, let us analyse the state of democracy in the 12 countries that were members of the USSR since the 1920s to see where Ukraine stands comparatively within this set.[61] One of the most cited annual reviews of the state of democracy in the world is the Freedom House Survey. This survey ranks countries on a seven-point scale (with 1 being the best score and 7 being the worst) for 'political freedoms' and an identical seven-point scale for 'civil liberties'. Of the 12 countries in the set, Ukraine has the best total of the two scores; 3 on political freedoms, and 2 on civil liberties, for a total of 5. The average total of the other 11 countries in the set is 9.7. Russia receives a 6 on political rights and a 5 on civil liberties, for a total score of 11.[62] In a number of my writings I use a combined score of 5 or less as one of the many

Table 9.6 Percentage of Respondents Expressing Trust in Institutions in Ukraine and Twelve Other Post-Communist Countries in 1998, and in Ukraine in 2005

	1998			2005		
	Twelve post-communist countries	Russia	Ukraine	Ukraine	Self-defined (Ukranian Nationality)	(Self-defined Russian Nationality)
Courts	29	24	15	16	(18)	(10)
Police	30	18	12	10	(11)	(5)
Parties	13	7	8	12	(13)	(9)
Parliament	22	13	8	25	(27)	(11)
President of Country	44	14	13	48	(54)	(20)

Sources: For the 12 post-communist countries see, Richard Rose and Christian Haerpfer, 'New Democracies Barometer V: A Twelve Nation Survey, *Studies in Public Policy*, # 306 (1998): questions 27a, b, c, and p. The 12 countries were the Czech Republic, Slovakia, Hungary, Poland and Slovenia (now all in the European Union), but also Bulgaria and Romania, and the then non-democracies of Serbia and Montenegro, Croatia, and Ukraine, and the dictatorship of Belarus. Even in this very mixed company Ukraine in 1998 had the lowest score on each one of the six variables listed above. For Russia see Richard Rose, 'Getting Things Done with Social Capital: New Russian Barometer VII', *Studies in Public Policy*, # 303: questions K3 a, b, c, f and i. For Ukraine in 2005, see Richard Rose, 'Divisions Within Ukraine: A Post-Election Public Opinion Survey', *Studies in Public Policy*, #403 (2005): questions D4 a, b, d, e and f. The definition of nationality Rose uses in these surveys is not essentialist but self-definition. The self-definition question was posed as 'what do you consider your nationality now?'. 81% answered 'Ukrainian', 17% answered 'Russian', and 2% answered 'other'. See question C2b.

indicators of a country that is above the threshold of a democracy. On this indicator Ukraine in 2007 was the only democracy of the 12 countries.

I began this chapter with a question. If the goals are peace and democracy – for a country like Ukraine with a multinational quality to its society and a potential irredendentist neighbour – is a 'nation-state' policy, or a 'state-nation' policy, more likely to contribute to peace and democracy? With all its failings, Ukraine is a democracy and, internally and externally, Ukraine has been peaceful.

I believe that the evidence marshalled in this chapter indicates that if Ukraine had followed aggressive nation-state policies, the quality of its democracy would now be worse, and its peace, indeed its territorial integrity, would have already been threatened.

One hopes that this credible post-independence past is taken into consideration in future choices by Ukraine's leaders and citizens. Georgia, a multinational society, pursued nation-state policies and strove to join NATO. Georgia's peace and democracy suffered. It would appear that a majority of citizens in Ukraine are not enthusiastic about embracing the nation-state policy of joining NATO but are comfortable pursuing a more state-nation policy of good economic and political relations, for domestic and international reasons, with both the European Union and Russia.

Notes

1   The author would like to thank the Ford Foundation for their support of his work on federalism and decentralisation and Dominique Arel and Lucan Way for their helpful comments on an earlier draft. A significantly different version of this paper was published in *Post-Soviet Affairs*, 21, 4 (2005): 279–308. The editors are grateful to V. H. Winston & Son, Inc, for permission to print this revised and updated version in the present volume.

2   For an examination and rejection of the 'resource curse' hypothesis as an explanation of Russia's political evolution, see William Tompson, 'A Frozen Venezuela? The "Resource Curse" and Russian Politics', in Michael Ellman (ed.), *Russia's Oil: Bonanza or Curse?* (London: Anthem, 2006).

3   For the argument and documentation see Alfred Stepan, Juan J. Linz, and Yogendra Yadav, *Democracy in Multinational Societies: India and Other Polities* (Baltimore and London: Johns Hopkins University Press, forthcoming, 2009). Also see my 'Comparative Theory and Political Practice: Do We Need a "State Nation" Model as Well as a "Nation State" Model?', *Government and Opposition* (Winter 2008): 1–30.

4   Concerning the status of democracy in Ukraine before the Orange Revolution, Lucan A. Way nicely analyses the formal, and especially informal, 'limitations on democracy [but also] the reasons why authoritarianism never became consolidated in Ukraine'. He asserts that 'Ukraine under Kuchma's presidency was

a model case of "competitive authoritarianism" – a civilian nondemocratic regime with regularly held elections that are competitive but extremely unfair'. See his 'Ukraine's Orange Revolution: Kuchma's Failed Authoritarianism', *Journal of Democracy*, 16 (April 2005): 131. It is probably also useful to note that on Freedom House's seven point scale of political rights (1 being the best score) Ukraine is the only one of the 12 non-Baltic former members of the Soviet Union never to have had a political rights score in 1992–2005 worse than 4. To be sure, it also never had a score above 3. Also, the constitution was deeply debated, and was not designed only by the President as Russia's was in 1993, and some features of this constitution were useful to the Orange Revolution activists. On constitution-building in Ukraine see, Kataryna Wolczuk, *The Moulding of Ukraine: The Constitutional Politics of State Formation* (Budapest: Central European University Press, 2001).

5 In above cited book by Stepan, Linz and Yadav we call such a situation 'politically robust multinationalism'. Ukraine is a multinational society, but (with the occasional exception of Crimea which could possibly be a federacy), not a 'politically robust multinational' polity. Data contained in this article would suggest that if aggressive nation-state policies had been pursued in Ukraine at independence, Russians would most likely have (as in Sri Lanka) become 'politically robustly multinational' and more ethnically conflictual and possibly even secessionist. The literature on nationalism is filled with warnings about the 'slippery slope of ethno-federalism', with which in the case of Yugoslavia (but not in India, Belgium, and Spain) we are in complete agreement. However, much less studied, and equally prevalent, is the 'slippery slope towards violence and secession' in cases of aggressive nation-state-building in societies that are multinational. We analyse such a case, Sri Lanka, in Stepan, Linz and Yadav, *Democracy in Multinational Societies*, Chapter 4. This article hopes to be a contribution to that under-theorised issue.

6 Richard Rose, 'Divisions within Ukraine: A Post-Election Opinion Survey', *Studies in Public Policy*, No. 403 (2005): question C 2a, p. 23.

7 See table 6.5 in Dominique Arel, 'Ukraine: The Temptation of the Nationalizing State', in Vladimir Tismaneanu, ed., *Political Culture and Civil Society in Russia and the New States of Eurasia* (Armonk and New York: M. E. Sharpe, 1995), p. 170. In all of his work Arel draws the important distinction between 'native language' and 'language of preference'.

8 See Roman Solchanyk, 'The Post-Soviet Transition in Ukraine: Prospects for Stability', in Taras Kuzio, ed., *Contemporary Ukraine: Dynamics of Post-Soviet Transformation* (Armonk and London: M. E. Sharpe, 1998), especially, pp. 30–3.

9 Arel, 'Ukraine', p. 170.

10 See José Casanova, 'Ethno-Linguistic and Religious Pluralism and Democratic Construction in Ukraine', in Barnett R. Rubin and Jack Snyder, eds, *Post-Soviet Political Order: Conflict and State Building* (New York and London: Routledge, 1998), pp. 81–103, especially see Table 5.2. In the 2004 presidential election followers of the Kiev and Autocephalous Orthodox churches tended to support the Orange Revolution whereas priests and monks from the Moscow Patriarchate often paraded in support of Yanukovich. See 'Ukrainians Threaten Orthodox Split', *The Ukrainian List*, # 355: 17–20.

11 See VTsIOM (with Richard Rose) 'Russians Outside Russia: A 1991 Survey', and 'Russians in the Baltic: A 1991 Survey', *Studies in Public Policy*, Numbers

283 and 287 respectively, Centre for the Study of Public Policy, University of Strathclyde, Glasgow, both published in 1997.

12 Wolczuk, *The Moulding of Ukraine,* p. 96.

13 For the 1990 elections see Dominique Arel, 'The Parliamentary Blocs in the Ukrainian Supreme Soviet: Who and What Do They Represent?' *Journal of Soviet Nationalities,* Vol. 1, No. 4 (Winter 1991): 108–54. On the limits these elections presented to any ethnic-based nationalism see Roman Szporluk, 'Reflections on Ukraine after 1994: The Dilemmas of Nationhood', *The Harriman Review* (March–May 1994): 2.

14 Szporluk, 'Reflections on Ukraine after 1994'.

15 Wolczuk, *The Molding of Ukraine,* p. 96.

16 See Arel, 'Ukraine: The Temptations of a Nationalizing State', p. 186, footnote 45. Indeed, Arel states that these deputies denounced Ukrainian language nationalists as 'linguistic fundamentalists'.

17 Alexander Motyl and Bohdan Krawchenko, 'Ukraine: From Empire to Statehood', in Ian Bremmer and Ray Taras, eds, *New States, New Politics: Building the Post-Soviet Nations* (Cambridge: Cambridge University Press, 1997), p. 244.

18 Bremmer and Taras, *New States, New Politics,* p. 294.

19 See detailed citations and analysis in two articles on the Ukrainian security situation; James Sherr, 'Ukrainian Security Policy: The Relationship between Domestic and External Factors', and Taras Kuzio, 'National Identity and Foreign Policy: The East Slavic Conundrum', both in Kuzio, ed., *Contemporary Ukraine,* pp. 221–44 and 245–66, respectively.

20 See for example George Friedman, 'Georgia and the Balance of Power', *New York Review of Books,* Vol. LV, No. 14 (25 September 2008): 24–6.

21 See the discussion by Sherr, 'Ukrainian Security Policy', p. 263.

22 Communication with an IDB official based on his personal observations in Eastern Ukraine (London, June 2005).

23 Dominique Arel, is the Chair of Ukrainian Studies at the University of Ottawa and the coordinator of *The Ukraine List* newsletter, which has published over 350 issues, is the author of numerous works on Ukraine and comparative nationalism, and coordinated the Ukraine section of the overall project on *Identity Formation* led by David D. Laitin. The interview with Arel was in February 2005 at the University of Ottawa. I should note that a standard assertion in the literature on Ukraine is that there has been virtually no ethnic or political violence during, or after, the drive for independence. In 1994, there was a rash of articles about the possible break-up of Ukraine. Thus the formulation of my question.

24 However, the article I have footnoted previously by José Casanova explicitly cites an early discussion by Juan Linz of our 'state-nation' concept, and agues that it was the most appropriate strategy for Ukraine to follow and that many of the policies actually negotiated, and implemented, were close to 'state-nation' policies, see especially, pp. 87–8. Also, the previously footnoted article by Roman Szporluk, does not use the terminology 'state-nation', but the entire tone is consistent with my argument.

25 A separate sample was made for Russians in Western Ukraine to which I shall make occasional references.

26 'Russians Outside Russia', *Studies in Public Policy,* # 283: questions, 43, 44, 41, 81, 31, and 48 respectively. In Latvia and Estonia, the titular populations were

attempting nation-state policies and Russian minority answers on these six questions were much more wary. The only area where Ukrainian 'nation-state' advocates were in the majority at the time of the survey was in Western Ukraine and Russian attitudes in Western Ukraine were substantially more sceptical of the neutrality and fairness of a potential Ukrainian state.

27 See his 'Reflections on Ukraine in 1994', p. 1.

28 Wolczuk, *The Molding of Ukraine*, p. 89.

29 Ibid.

30 In their previously cited article in Bremmer and Taras, *New States, New Politics*, pp. 250–1. Casanova is in agreement. He writes that 'Rukh had incorporated explicitly such an inclusive policy in its platform', p. 86. The fact remains however that the core membership and electorate of Rukh retained a Ukrainian ethnic base.

31 The incentives for strategic cooperation by the Communist elites were enhanced by the fact some of them supported the failed putsch of August 1991 and wanted to be protected from Yeltsin.

32 Arel, 'Ukraine', pp. 167–8.

33 Motyl and Krawchenko, 'Ukraine: From Empire to Statehood', p. 243. Historically the key issue was enrollment in Ukrainian courses. In a private communication, Dominique Arel wrote that such enrollment 'was almost nil in Imperial Russia, very high in the 1920s–30s, decreasing after World War II, and near extinction in urban areas of East and South Ukraine, as well as in Kiev, from the 1960s on'.

34 See the chapter on Sri Lanka in Stepan, Linz and Yadav, *Democracy in Multinational Societies*, Chapter, 4. Since 1997 I have made three research trips to Sri Lanka. Virtually all the key participants I have interviewed, from the Prime Minister on down now think that their aggressive nation-state policies, especially toward the privileged place of Sinhalese and Buddhism, and their complete hostility to decentralisation, contributed directly to the crisis.

35 See table 5.1 in Casanova, 'Ethno-Linguistic and Religious Pluralism and Democratic Construction in Ukraine', p. 89.

36 See for example the subtle analysis of this point in Dominique Arel, ' La face caché de la Révolution Orange: l'Ukraine en négation face à son problème régional', *Revue d'ètudes comparatives Est-Ouest*, Vol. 37, No. 4 (Décembre 2006): 11–48.

37 Ibid. This is a standard finding in surveys in Ukraine.

38 See table 12 in Ian Bremmer, 'The Politics of Ethnicity: Russians in a New Ukraine', *Europe-Asia Studies*, Vol. 46, Issue 2 (1994).

39 See Nancy Popson, 'The Ukrainian History Textbook: Introducing Children to the "Ukrainian Nation"', *Nationalities Papers*, Vol. 29, No. 2 (2001): 325–50.

40 Wolczuk, *Building of Ukraine*, p. 177.

41 Yaroslav Hrytsak, 'On the Relevance and Irrelevance of Nationalism in Ukraine', The Second Annual Cambridge-Stasiuk Lecture on Ukraine (20 February 2004): 8. For example, in the year 2000, when asked in Russia to name the 'most outstanding' politician to have headed the state in the 20th century, Stalin emerged as number one; see Archie Brown, 'Cultural Change and Continuity in the Transition from Communism: The Russian Case', 'Culture Matters' Project Final Conference, Tufts University (26–28 March 2004). Survey conducted by VTsIOM.

42   Currently in Ukraine, another 'othering' factor is that mothers of whatever nationality would see unification with Russia as incurring the risk of having their sons drafted and killed in the war against Chechnya.

43   For an excellent review of the extensive literature on the polarisation debate in Ukraine, and a very informative quantitative analysis that leads the authors to the conclusion that it makes more sense to speak of eight , as opposed to two, regions, see Lowell W. Barrington and Erik S. Herron, 'One Ukraine or Many? Regionalism in Ukraine and its Political Consequences', *Nationalities Papers*, Vol. 32, No. 1 (March 2004): 53–86.

44   See the extremely useful work by Richard Rose 'Divisions Within Ukraine: A Post Election Opinion Survey,' *Studies in Public Policy*, # 403 (2005): 49–50. In the 2004 US presidential elections the most polarised state was Utah (Bush, 71%, Kerry 26%), however the District of Columbia resembled Donetsk in that the overall losing presidential candidate won overwhelmingly (Kerry 90%, Bush 9%). One of the leading Ukraine analysts, Andrew Wilson, after a July 2005 visit to Donetsk, wrote that polarisation was declining somewhat and that 'most east Ukrainian elites are regrouping under party labels that accept the agenda set by the new regime.' See: *The Ukraine List* #354 (15 July 2005): 11.

45   See the fascinating studies by Yaroslav Hrytsak, 'National Identities in Post-Soviet Ukraine: The Case of Lviv and Donetsk', in Zvi Gitelman, Lubomyr Hajda, John-Paul Himka, and Roman Solchanyk, eds, *Cultures and Nations of Central and Eastern Europe* (Harvard Ukrainian Studies, Vol. 22, 1998), pp. 263–82, and 'Ukrainian Nationalism, 1991–2001: Myths and Perceptions', Austrian Institute for Eastern and South-Eastern Europe, Vienna (15 October 2001).

46   All these data are drawn from the above cited work by Arel and Khmelko, 'Regional Divisions in the 2004 Presidential Elections in Ukraine'.

47   See Popson, 'The Ukrainian History Textbooks'.

48   For an important new work on the theory of semi-presidentialism with a pioneering analysis of why it contributed to the breakdown of the Weimar Republic, and its functioning in the French Fifth Republic, see Cindy Skach, *Borrowing Constitutional Designs: Constitutional Law in Weimar Germany and the French Fifth Republic* (Princeton: Princeton University Press, 2006).

49   On these silences and the very exceptional conditions that allowed this model to function reasonably well in France, see Alfred Stepan and Ezra Suleiman, 'The French Fifth Republic: A Model for Import? Reflections on Poland and Brazil', in Alfred Stepan, *Arguing Comparative Politics* (Oxford: Oxford University Press, 2001), pp. 257–75.

50   See Timothy J. Colton and Cindy Skach, 'The Predicament of Semi-Presidentialism', in Alfred Stepan, ed., *Democracies in Danger: Diagnoses and Proposals* (Baltimore and London: The Johns Hopkins University Press, 2009). A shorter version of their argument appeared as 'The Russian Predicament', *Journal of Democracy* 16 (July 2005): 113–26.

51   For Kuchma's augmentation of his powers see Wolczuk, *The Molding of Ukraine*, pp. 205–9. Oleh Protsyk, who wrote his 2000 PhD at Rutgers on semi-presidentialism in Ukraine, argues that both Russia and Ukraine are what Shugart and Carey would call 'president-parliamentary', but that Russia's version gives the president more powers than in Ukraine. Nonetheless, he writes

that for most of his time as president Kuchma tried to 'increase the formal powers of the presidency' and that he 'consistently played the role of a challenger to the existing constitutional status quo'. See Protsyk, 'Troubled Semi-Presidentialism: Stability of the Constitutional System and Cabinet in Ukraine', *Europe-Asian Studies*, Vol. 55, No. 7 (2003): 1077–95, quotes from 1087. Also see Andrew Wilson, 'Ukraine: Two Presidents and their Powers', in Ray Taras, ed., *Post-Communist Presidents* (Cambridge: Cambridge University Press, 1997). In the same volume see the thoughtful essay by Juan Linz, 'Introduction: Some Thoughts on Presidentialism in Post-Communist Europe', pp. 1–14. On attempts to measure presidential powers in post-communist Europe see Timothy Frye, 'A Politics of Institutional Choice: Post Communist Presidencies', *Comparative Political Studies*, Vol. 30, No. 4 (1997): 523–52. Whereas Frye scores presidential powers in Slovenia, Slovakia, Latvia, the Czech Republic, and Estonia as all in the 4.5 to 5.5 range, he scores Ukraine 15, and Yeltsin's super-presidential Russia 18. Due to politics, however, unlike Putin's Russia, there was often grid-lock under the first two directly elected presidents in Ukraine.

52 Steven D. Roper, in his combined score of presidential powers – in each of the ten regimes in Europe he classifies as 'premier-presidential' – gives Slovenia and Lithuania the lowest scores, that is, he considers that they have the weakest presidents. See his 'Are All Semi-presidential Regimes the Same? A Comparison of Premier-Presidential Regimes', *Comparative Politics* 34 (April 2002): 260, Table 3. Roper does not give a score for Ukraine because he classified its regime as 'presidential-parliamentary'. For the reduction of presidential powers in Poland and Portugal see Colton and Skach, 'The Predicament of Semi-Presidentialism', in Stepan, ed., *Democracies in Danger*.

53 See the first three articles in *The Ukraine List*, No. 338 (8 February 2005), which list all the cabinet ministers and discuss their backgrounds. The invaluable *Ukraine List* is coordinated by Dominique Arel and came out almost daily during the Orange Revolution. I supplemented the three *Ukraine List* articles with conversations with Arel at Ottawa University the day the cabinet was announced. It should be noted that both Yushchenko and Tymoshenko were born in the East, and both speak Russian, but politically, they are not seen as representing the East.

54 Any semi-presidential system, even what I call a 'parliamentarised semi-presidential' variant, has some of the potential problems of a 'dual executive' that by definition would not be found in a pure parliamentary system. The transition to 'parliamentarised semi-presidentialism' is being attempted in a more difficult context in Ukraine than in Portugal or Poland. In Portugal, the transition was helped by the fact that the sitting Prime Minister, Mário Soares, was a very active member of West European social democratic parliamentary circles, and felt that Portugal's normalisation within Europe, would be helped by creating a weaker president, and he became the first incumbent of the new post. In Poland, the transition was made when the ex-communists controlled both houses of Parliament and the presidency, and they consensually decided that a stronger Prime Minister was a safer long-term model for democracy and for the communist party. In Ukraine, the dual executive potential was exacerbated because the party system was weaker and democratic procedures less established, than they were at the

time of the transition in either Portugal or Poland. The potential for 'dual executive' conflict was also exacerbated in Ukraine because the two leaders of the Orange Revolution, Viktor Yushchenko, who became the directly elected president, and Yulia Tymoshenko, his first prime minister, were leaders of the two major competing political groups that contested the 2006 parliamentary elections that were supposed to produce the new effective head of government, the prime minister. The 2005 crisis between president Yushchenko and Prime Minister Tymoshenko has much to do with the fact that they intended to compete against each other in the presidential elections of January 2010. For a statement by President Yushchenko about the origins of the 2005 crisis, see *The Ukraine List*, #357b (8 September 2005): 1–3. On the next day the sacked Prime Minister gave her account, see *The Ukraine List*, #359 (12 September 2005): 1–15.

55   These responses are from the previously cited February 2005 survey, Richard Rose 'Divisions within Ukraine', questions C3 and E9.

56   These figures on Donetsk come from Svitlana Kalinina, Alexander Lyakh, Galina Savchenko, and Adam Swain, 'Regional 'Lock-in' or Local Hegemonic Bloc? Industrial Restructuring in the Ukrainian Donbas', paper prepared for the Danyliw Research Seminar in Contemporary Ukrainian Studies at the Chair of Ukrainian Studies, University of Ottawa (29 September–1 October 2005). For the non-ethnic reasons for the Eastern regions, and Donbas in particular, to support failing heavy industry, and economic relations with Russia, see the previously cited article by Barrington and Herron 'One Ukraine or Many', especially pp. 70–1. From a comparative viewpoint of political symbols, it should be noted that in Donetsk, the Ukrainian flag is flown (unlike Kurdistan where the Iraqi flag is not flown) and no one has reported a Russian flag flying in Donetsk, as some were briefly flown in Crimea.

57   For example, in 1992–1996 municipalities in the four democratic federal systems of Western Europe spent 14.3% of total public expenditures, whereas municipalities in the 11 unitary states spent 24.6% of total public expenditures. In Denmark, Finland and Sweden, municipal expenditures in this same period accounted for 44%, 37%, and 35% of total public expenditures respectively. For the data, see *Government Finance Statistics* (Washington, DC: International Monetary Fund), various issues. For an analysis of these robust municipal expenditures in unitary states, see Juan J. Linz and Alfred Stepan, 'Inequality Inducing and Inequality Reducing Federalism: With Special Reference to the "Classic Outlier" – The USA', Paper given at the XVIII Congress of the International Political Science Association, Quebec City, Canada (1–5 August 2000): especially table 2.

58   On federacy type arrangements in Finland, Norway, Italy, Portugal, and Indonesia, see Chapter 7, 'On "Federacy" as a Formula for Democratically Managing Multinational Societies in Unitary States', in Stepan, Linz and Yadav, *Democracy in Multinational Societies*, forthcoming.

59   See Linz and Stepan, *Problems of Democratic Transition and Consolidation*, p. 5.

60   There were about 9000 observers in 2004, 3500 in 2006, and 3000 in 2007. The largest group of observers in 2007 came from the European Network of Election Monitoring Organisations (ENEMO) with observers from 16 countries including many Central European members of the European Union. See 'Election Observers Descend on Ukraine', in *The Ukraine List* #421,

entry 7 (28 September 2007). The decline in observers was due, according to that report, because of 'Ukraine's success in conducting a free and fair election in 2006'.

61 I therefore omit the three Baltic countries that only became part of the USSR via the Molotov-Ribbentrop Pact of 1939. All three of these countries had, unlike any of the 12 countries in our set, substantial experience with democracy in the interwar period, and all have been members of the European Union since 2006.

62 For the raw data for 193 countries see, 'The 2007 Freedom House Survey', *Journal of Democracy*, Vol. 19, No. 2 (April 2008): 66–7.

10
Explaining European Union Aid to Russia[1]

Tomila Lankina[2]

Since 1991, Russia has received a large volume of funding from Western donors to aid its political and economic transformation. The European Union accounts for a substantial share of this funding, amounting to over 2.6 billion euros. Therefore, it is surprising that virtually no systematic scholarship exists on the pattern of aid choices and allocations, or indeed, on their longer-term impact on targeted actors. Although there are a number of case studies and policy papers on the various dimensions of aid or concrete projects, we still lack a comprehensive picture of the EU's technical assistance. Such an exercise would allow us to begin to explain and to theorise about the reasons – economic, strategic, bureaucratic, political, cultural or other – behind the EU's and its member states' aid choices. This chapter presents findings from statistical analysis of a dataset that the author compiled of *all* EU projects conducted in Russia's regions between 1991 and 2005. The analysis is complemented by interviews with European Union and Russian officials involved with TACIS (Technical Assistance to the CIS) projects as well as by an examination of key EU policy and strategy papers on Russia.

The chapter is structured as follows. The first section discusses comparative and theoretical scholarship on Western aid in various national and international contexts and, based on the literature review, outlines a number of hypotheses about donor intentions and choices. These hypotheses are then tested in the chapter's second section in an effort to explain the motives behind EU aid to Russia's regions. The last section concludes.

Explanations of foreign aid choices

Despite the diversity of national and international contexts in which donors operate, it is possible to group the various approaches that have been advanced to explain Western aid flows into several broader explanatory variables. Peter Schraeder, Steven Hook, and Bruce Taylor provide a useful framework for analysis, on which I rely as a starting point to generate my hypotheses.[3] Their study of humanitarian assistance found that foreign-aid flows could be explained largely by the recipient country's economic potential, perceived strategic importance and cultural similarity with the donor. The humanitarian-need hypothesis that the above scholars advanced for analysing aid to Africa will not be tested here because the context we are investigating and the nature of the aid given are both different from the African context. In place of the recipients' humanitarian needs, I substitute democratic performance, which, in the post-Cold War international context, is what many donor programmes have targeted both in post-communist states and in other countries. I also add a 'bureaucratic' hypothesis to the analysis, suggesting that aid choices may be influenced by factors related to bureaucratic expediency and efficiency in aid project implementation. Each of these hypotheses is explained and discussed in greater detail below.

The most straightforward and easily testable hypothesis relates to economic factors. The choices of donor governments are arguably often motivated by existing or potential economic opportunities in recipient countries. Although such aid may also have beneficial consequences for those on the receiving end, its actual motives are instrumental in nature to the extent that its primary concern is the furthering of trade or investment interests or the satisfaction of aid providers' needs for cheap labour, raw materials, and natural resources. The logic is as follows: if faced with the option of channelling aid to an area or country with little economic attractiveness or one with trade or investment potential, donors would be more likely to provide aid to the latter than to the former even if their aid needs might be equal. Schraeder et al found that this was the case with Japan, a country pursuing an active 'business interests' aid policy.[4]

Moreover, even nations with an established reputation for generous need-based aid have been shown to pursue economic interests as a key motive.[5] Sweden, for example, was found to have acquired a tendency in recent years to tie aid to exports of Swedish products and services.[6] Where economic interests are at stake, donors would arguably be less likely to channel money to local actors that might undermine the furthering of such interests. The United States Agency for International Development (USAID), in particular, has been criticised for such practices. Erika Weinthal and Pauline Jones Luong convincingly demonstrate, for example, how in Kazakhstan, US donors, mindful of American oil company interests, deliberately refrained from supporting local environmental NGOs that might challenge the environmental costs of oil projects.[7] This was despite the fact that support for civil society organisations has been an avowed goal of American democracy promotion in the region. In the Russian regional contexts, some European developmental programmes were likewise seen as instruments for the advancement of European states' economic interests. 'The Northern Dimension should be seen in the context of the strategic importance of Russia for the energy sector of the EU. The resources of North-West Russia, including gas, oil, coal, forest and minerals, are vast and can hopefully be harnessed for European use as well', declared one European official.[8] Echoing him, a scholar in a key European policy think tank wrote about the regional dimension of EU involvement in Russia in the context of an EU-Russia 'strategic partnership': 'The issue is the EU's possible diversification away from Gulf oil supplies'.[9]

The second group of explanations of aid motives could be labelled strategic. According to such explanations, aid is likely to be channelled to countries or regions of strategic, security, military or geo-political significance. For example, the rivalries and strategic calculations of major powers were arguably the main motivating factors behind aid during the Cold War. Although in the post-Cold War world, other factors have come to play a much stronger role in aid choices, strategic calculations continue to feature prominently in aid allocations in particular geographic regions. A case in point is Uzbekistan, which received a substantial volume of aid from the United States after 11 September 2001 in return for allowing the US to set up military facilities on its territory. Arguably, security concerns were also behind aid allocations to particular Russian regions bordering the EU. Scholars using discourse analysis have shown how the stress on 'de-securitisation' or 'avoiding the language of security' and substituting this language with the vocabulary of peace, democracy and cooperation actually has security motives behind it.[10] Other have shown how, within the same geographical area, such as the highly militarised Barents Sea region, different donors chose to support different actors – NGOs versus governmental agencies – based on their underlying security concerns.[11]

Schraeder et al found that cultural factors also played a role in aid allocations. Examples are the large amounts of aid allocated by France to Francophone former colonies or by Britain to English-speaking countries of the Commonwealth. Another cultural factor could be ethnic ties between donor and recipient nations, which could motivate aid allocation decisions.[12] Generally, over the last two decades, both the practice of international relations and how scholars theorise it have undergone a dramatic shift from more *Realpolitik*, instrumental issues to normative concerns for democracy and human rights.[13] It would be difficult to deny that such concerns have become more important in the aid allocations of major Western actors, such as the United States, the European Union and individual European countries.[14] In Uzbekistan, for example, pressure to democratise was brought on the Uzbek dictatorship by the United States, which risked losing a strategic ally. The US's normative concerns drove the former client to look for patrons among other, less democratic nations, such as Russia.

Finally, bureaucratic factors may have a significant impact on aid allocation patterns. Studies show how pressures to exaggerate project-implementation success rates, or the peculiarity of reporting requirements, determine which actors receive aid and which do not. So do such factors as knowledge of English or recipients' greater capacity to achieve successful outcomes or to implement programmes efficiently.[15] This middle point in the chain of donor-recipient interactions, at which entirely practical concerns of getting a particular project done figure strongly, is remote from the grand policy calculations of the wider donor community, be they economic, strategic, cultural or other. At this point, the actors who are already more 'capable' in relative terms to begin with are more likely to obtain aid because they would make the donors look good and effective.[16] In post-communist contexts, these considerations would also explain why 'larger, urban-based, more cosmopolitan' NGOs were found to be beneficiaries of many EU civil society-building programmes.[17] They would also explain why in Russia some regions with more developed democratic institutions enjoyed a particularly high concentration of aid beneficiaries, while in others, Western aid levels were very modest.[18]

Aid to Russia

The regional dimension of aid to Russia offers a unique opportunity for testing the above hypotheses. Russian regions are extremely diverse along a number of dimensions. In economic terms, inter-regional diversity is one of the highest in the world among developed industrial nations.[19] The regions range from natural resource-rich provinces and industrial giants to poor regions that depend on massive federal transfers. They therefore offer Western actors a wide variety of conditions for investment and trade. Some of the regions, such as those in the northwest, also have a strategic significance for external donors because of their border location or access to major ports. Many of the regions also are diverse culturally and ethnically, allowing us to test the extent to which ethno-cultural factors have motivated the aid allocation decisions of major Western actors. For example, Finland, a central EU player in shaping policy towards Russia, shares similar ethnic and linguistic features with populations in several of Russia's regions, such as Kareliya, Komi and Udmurtiya.

The data

The data presented here come from the regional component of EU technical assistance to Russia. EU technical assistance to Russia distinguishes between federal and regional components. In regional projects, federal agencies were present as partners only in such areas of federal significance as building border-crossings or natural parks in federal jurisdiction, or broader umbrella projects covering several regions, in which the Federal Envoy's office might play a coordinating or supervisory role.[20] Most regional project activity did not involve federal actors, although federal agencies sometimes tried to vet or influence it.[21]

As of August 2005, an astonishingly large number of EU projects – 1147 in all – were completed or in the process of implementation in Russia's regions. Their financial volume ranged from several hundred to several million euros. The sheer volume of aid notwithstanding, there was little effort throughout the 1990s and early 2000s on the part of the donor itself (that is, the EU) to systematise project aid records, according to TACIS officials' own admission. Finally, in December 2004, an Internet database accessible to the public was set up with links to project data for each of the nine TACIS Local Support Offices (LSOs). The data were not always complete. For example, in some project records key local or Western partners were not specified. In others, where there were multiple recipient regions, not all regions were listed. The vast majority of projects that were listed, however, had the basic data on project start dates, key regional and foreign partners, and volume of funding. The available data therefore allowed an observer to come up with a relatively comprehensive picture of the regional dimension of aid to date and changes in aid patterns over time. Because a new set of programmes and regulations entered into force in 2007, and previous funding programmes were subjected to re-evaluation and restructuring in 2005–2006, the year 2005 also offers a convenient cut-off point for data analysis.[22]

Descriptive statistics

Initial descriptive statistics reveal that on the recipient side, several regions have been over-represented throughout the 15-year aid period that we are investigating. Among the winners are north-western regions, but also regions in the Volga, Urals, and Siberian federal districts. Even within the federal districts, the picture is mixed: some north-western regions, including those, like Novgorod *Oblast'*, known for their openness towards the West, have modest records of project cooperation. Likewise, within the Volga, Urals, and Siberian federal districts, there are regions that participated in only a handful of projects, while others were involved in many projects and were beneficiaries of millions of euros in aid (Table 10.1). On the external side, EU countries with a disproportionate share of project cooperation on record are Finland, Germany, France and the United Kingdom (Table 10.2).[23]

The volume of technical assistance steadily increased between 1992 and 1998, experiencing a dip in 1998, presumably because of Russia's 1998 financial crisis. By 2002, aid volumes reached levels similar to those of 1998. Between 2002 and 2004, there was an apparent decline in project activity.[24] This could be related to changes in cooperation arrangements between the EU and Russia and the introduction of the European Neighbourhood Policy, which replaced TACIS with a new set of funding instruments, implemented in 2007. But from 2004 to 2006, according to TACIS officials, the number of applications from the Russian side actually increased by about 1.5 times.[25]

Data analysis

How do we begin to make sense of the complex picture of technical assistance involving a plurality of Western and local actors? In order to test for the possible influence of economic factors on technical assistance decisions, I used several regional economic indicators from the Russian State Committee on Statistics, *Goskomstat*, for 2002.[26] These are the volume of foreign investment in the region, regional trade with non-CIS states and the volume of gross regional product (GRP). Regression exercises, using logged values for economic indicators and aid volumes, however, reveal that these factors were not statistically significant (Table 10.6).

Strategic/security calculations – or what in the EU is referred to as the 'proximity agenda',[27] our second hypothesis – appear to feature prominently in regional partnership choices. This pattern is confirmed

Table 10.1   **Number of Projects Conducted per Region**[a]

Rough ranking based on number of projects with region as key partner region	Region	Projects in which region served as key partner	Total, including projects with region listed as one of several partner regions	Aggregated aid volume in euros for projects in which region served as key partner
1	St. Petersburg	264	289	138,219,497
2	Kaliningrad	79	87	47,157,995
3	Novosibirsk	65	74	72,796,659
4	Kareliya	64	70	45,012,204
5	Leningrad	45	64	24,301,832
6	Moscow City	36	47	45,006,756
7	Nizhegorodskaya	32	37	28,365,861
8	Sverdlovsk	25	28	28,236,643
9	Perm	24	26	13,413,111
10	Kemerovo	23	30	28,719,595
11	Pskov	19	24	83,499,75
12	Murmansk	18	27	16,537,457
13	Udmurtiya	17	22	2,170,197
14	Tomsk	17	31	3,899,723
15	Arkhangelsk	16	23	12,094,267
16	Samara	15	21	571,597
17	Saratov	14	20	8,002,558
18	Chelyabinsk	14	17	6,875,573
19	Altay *Kray*	14	19	10,352,575
20	Novgorod	13	24	6,702,765
21	Krasnoyarsk	13	19	6,762,229
22	Vologda	12	13	6,948,761
23	Tatarstan	12	17	2,514,537
24	Irkutsk	12	15	4,080,834
25	Komi	8	9	10,464,808
26	Omsk	8	11	6,698,841
27	Moscow *Oblast'*	6	8	1,024,0138
28	Kirov	6	8	127,800
29	Rostov	5	11	6,650,348
30	Penza	5	5	276,948
31	Mariy El	5	6	721,944
32	Ivanovo	4	9	7,097,499
33	Buryatiya	4	6	3,016,236
34	Vladimir	3	7	4,280,000
35	Orel	3	4	17,000
36	Yaroslavl	3	7	239,346
37	Khabarovsk	3	5	19,924

Table 10.1   **Number of Projects Conducted per Region**[(a)] – *continued*

Rough ranking based on number of projects with region as key partner region	Region	Projects in which region served as key partner	Total, including projects with region listed as one of several partner regions	Aggregated aid volume in euros for projects in which region served as key partner
38	Altay Republic	3	6	38,992
39	Astrakhan	3	5	486,480
40	Bashkortostan	3	3	47,194
41	Chuvashiya	3	5	53,293
42	Orenburg	3	4	46,660
43	Tyumen	3	7	13,968
44	Voronezh	2	9	700,000
45	Kostroma	2	4	16,018
46	Kursk	2	3	328,110
47	Lipetsk	2	2	45,870
48	Tver	2	8	95,000
49	Primorskiy	2	5	94,035
50	Belgorod	1	3	56,843
51	Bryansk	1	1	200,000
52	Kaluga	1	1	0
53	Ryazan	1	1	53,000
54	Tula	1	7	99,860
55	Nenetsk	1	3	0
56	Kabardino-Balkariya	1	1	90,000
57	Krasnodar	1	5	7000
58	Stavropol	1	1	0
59	Ulyanovsk	1	3	8840
60	Kurgan	1	1	3500
61	Taymyr-Dolgano-Nenetsk	1	1	9499
62	Yamalo-Nenetsk	–	1	N/A
63	Yakutiya	–	1	N/A
64	Adygeya	–	1	N/A
	Unspecified	179	9	24,837,952
	Total	1147		93,577,724

[(a)] *Source*: For information on the sources for data in this and other tables, see endnote 23.

Table 10.2   Number of Projects in which an EU-country Organisation Served as External Partner[a]

Country	Country listed as first or key partner	Other projects with country listed as one of several EU partners	Total
Germany	176	27	203
Finland	162	19	181
United Kingdom	128	31	159
France	117	24	141
Netherlands	51	19	70
Italy	49	19	68
Belgium	40	11	51
Sweden	35	10	45
Denmark	36	10	46
Greece	18	2	20
Spain	14	14	28
Austria	14	16	30
Ireland	13	3	16
Estonia	4	2	6
Lithuania	3	1	4
Poland	3	1	4
Portugal	2	9	11
Consortium or company, country not specified	175		
External partner unspecified	106		

[a] *Source*: See endnote 23.

if we add to the regression the logged values for 'distance from the West' measured in kilometres between Russian regional capitals and the EU's closest European capital, Helsinki. In the regression, greater distance from Europe is negatively correlated with aid (Table 10.6). The geographical map of the density of aid is a good visual representation of this pattern (Figure 10.1). Despite this fact, cross-border cooperation was but one aspect of project activity, with eligibility not limited to border regions in most EU programmes. We still need to explain why several of the top ten project regions were located in Russia's *glubinka*, far away from western borders.

While security concerns related to border areas were apparently important in technical assistance, the above project record calls for a more nuanced investigation of additional factors that are at work. Why

Figure 10.1 Density of EU Aid to Russia's Regions

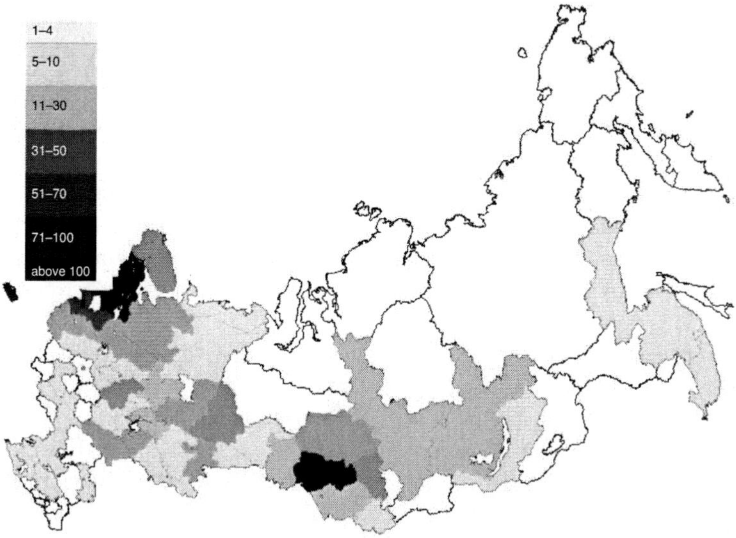

Source: Author's calculations based on EU data on the number of projects conducted per region; see note 23.

Nizhniy Novgorod and not Saratov? Why Leningrad and not Pskov? How does our third hypothesis – namely, concern for democracy promotion – fare in explaining regional aid patterns? On a declarative level, democratic institution-building was one of the key motives behind the EU's technical assistance. In practice, too, the EU was known to devote a large share of its overall aid – more than the US, for example – to democracy promotion.[28]

There are several issues, however, that might have conflicted with the EU's declared motives in the actual day-to-day project decision-making and implementation. The EU was known to be very *étatiste* in its choice of local implementation partners. This fact arguably stems from the peculiarity of continental Europe's domestic institutional cultures, where the role of the state was greater in social welfare in general than, for example, in the United States.[29] Furthermore, like such multilateral institutions as the World Bank, the EU often has to work with government agencies, or secure their approval for project activity. This might lead to the EU's aversion to dealing with non-state actors critical of the government, such as human rights organisations, a stand that would conflict with the EU's own declared commitment to democratic pluralism. Moreover, technical assistance covers a wide range of projects, such as the building of sewage facilities, which on the face of it may have little to do with normative concepts like democracy and civil society.

In order to answer the question about the role of democracy in regional aid volumes, I added available measures for levels of regional democracy to the regression analysis. The measures are taken from scores that the scholar Nikolai Petrov compiled on the basis of an analysis of regional political processes over roughly the same time-period that we investigated and using the Freedom House method.[30] The analysis revealed a statistically significant relationship with aid flows. This relationship was positive, however, suggesting that aid went to areas that were more democratic to begin with. The regression shows that even controlling for distance from the West, democracy levels were important predictors of aid (Table 10.6).

In order to test in a more nuanced way the hypothesis that democracy promotion guides aid choices, I differentiated several project partners on the Russian side. On the governmental side, one could identify federal, regional and municipal bodies, and on the non-governmental side, there were actors, such as NGOs, universities, think tanks and private businesses. Contrary to expectations, non-governmental actors were key partners in an overwhelming majority of projects. Universities accounted for the largest share of project activity, followed by regional bodies and NGOs, with federal actors involved in a modest 12% of project work. Taken together, non-state actors accounted for as much as 60% of all project activity (Table 10.3). Furthermore, initial bivariate

Table 10.3   Agencies Identified as Key Russian Partners and their Overall Share in Project Activity[a]

Type of partner	Number of projects	%
Federal	139	12.1
Regional	246	21.4
Local self-government	124	10.8
University	283	24.7
Think tank	9	0.8
School	2	0.2
NGO	184	16
Private	137	11.9
Unspecified	23	2
Total	1147	100

[a] *Source*: See note 23.

correlation exercises show that aid to non-state actors correlated with scores for societal pluralism in the respective regions that were likewise drawn from Petrov. The correlation was significant at the 0.01 level (at 0.337). Like our findings on democracy levels, the relationship between aid to non-state actors and levels of civil society development was positive, suggesting that aid flowed to areas where there were greater levels of openness and pluralism to begin with. While support for civil society or other non-state organisations was easily attributable to genuine concern for democracy and pluralism, motives behind aid to governmental actors may not so easily be attributed to such concerns.

According to one approach in international relations scholarship, we may consider the availability and capacity of local actors to provide 'access points' as the main factor facilitating external influences.[31] We may extend this logic to test the 'strategic' and economic hypotheses further. Perhaps it was not concern for democracy *per se* that drove EU aid-flows to Russia, but an interest in influencing sub-national areas for economic or strategic reasons in order to bypass the federal centre? Such an interpretation would be in line with the speculative and populist pronouncements of Russia's right-wing politicians who accused Europe of preparing the ground for annexation of Russia's territories, using them as a source of cheap natural resources or labour, or plotting 'coloured revolutions'. EU support for regional and local governments *could* be seen in this light because the degree of their power and independence from federal authority may affect their relations with external players.[32] There are two possible ways of establishing how the strength of regional and local governments affected aid patterns in the Russian regional contexts. One is the measure of local government strength and independence available from the Petrov data. Because local government independence varied substantially from region to region, we may speculate that it had a significant impact both on the capacity of municipal actors for external cooperation and on the willingness of external agencies to work with them as key partners. In fact, bivariate exercises do not reveal a very strong statistical relationship in this respect, with the correlation significant at the 0.05 level (at 0.231).

It is also possible to test for relationships between regional institutional independence vis-à-vis the federal centre and aid. Before President Vladimir Putin embarked on his federal reforms, some regions, such as the ethnically defined republics, had substantially greater amounts of formal power vis-à-vis the centre than others. Under President Boris Yeltsin they also acquired authority to conduct external relations and dispose of their natural resources.[33] An examination of project activity in the republics over the course of the 1990s does not show greater levels of aid. In fact, most of the republics – both the weaker ones like the North Caucasus entities and the powerful ones like Bashkortostan – were conspicuously absent or under-represented. Tatarstan, the leader in the 'parade of sovereignties', occupied a modest 23rd place in project activity (Table 10.1). In order to test further for relationships between more 'decentralist' regions and aid-flows, I devised a dummy for *oblasti* and also for regions with republic status. Again, adding the republic dummy to the regression, or testing for significance of having *oblast'* status did not reveal a statistically significant relationship (Table 10.6). Another finding that supports the hypothesis that democracy is the key factor guiding aid choices is that EU donors apparently show a preference for working with *non-state* over *state* actors in regions with high levels of democracy and openness. The regression model in Table 10.4 shows that stronger levels of regional civil society negatively correlate with share of projects conducted with regional bodies as key partners. Even so, the regression data below hint at the fact that institutional pluralism existed, at least at the level of local governments, in regions where in the absence of strong civil society, regional bodies accounted for a large share of project activity. Similar logic applies to work with federal actors: regions in which the EU conducted a large share of projects with federal bodies as key partners were also those with low levels of democracy. Federal actors got engaged by default

Table 10.4   Factors Affecting the Likelihood of Regional Bodies Serving as Key Partners in Regional Projects[a]

Variable	Coefficient	Standard error	t	sig.
Distance from Helsinki	−0.279	0.165	−1.515	0.140
Exports to non-CIS states	−0.285	0.133	−0.670	0.508
GRP	0.125	0.250	0.270	0.789
Foreign investment	0.042	0.051	0.186	0.854
Civil society ratings	−0.369	0.415	−2.129	0.042
LSG ratings	0.269	0.488	1.651	0.109
Constant	1.721	2.846	0.008	
Adjusted R sqr.	0.118			
N = 88[b]				

[a] *Source*: See note 23. Dependent variable: logged, share (percentage) of all projects conducted with regional bodies as key partners in a given region (all independent variables in this and Tables 10.5 and 10.6 also are logged).

[b] Chechnya has been excluded from analysis because of missing data.

Table 10.5   Factors Affecting the Likelihood of Federal Bodies Serving as Key Partners in Regional Projects[a]

Variable	Coefficient	Standard error	t	sig.
Distance from Helsinki	0.162	0.246	1.043	0.316
Exports to non-CIS states	0.112	0.186	0.404	0.693
GRP	−0.463	0.366	−1.489	0.160
Foreign investment	−0.107	0.077	−0.519	0.612
Civil society ratings	−0.392		−2.359	0.035
LSG ratings	−0.389	0.732	−2.377	0.033
Constant		3.069	3.528	0.004
Adjusted R sqr.	0.606			
N = 88				

[a] *Source*: See note 23. Dependent variable: Logged, share (percentage) of all projects conducted with federal bodies as key partners in a given region.

as the most trusted partners in regions that lacked transparency and openness among regional elites and an active non-governmental sector (Table 10.5).

All these results point to the conclusion that the factors directing aid-flows were not primarily regional independence vis-à-vis the centre nor regional institutional strength – either of which might be perceived as facilitating the pursuit of EU strategic or economic objectives. Instead, that factor was greater levels of regional pluralism and democracy.

Why did the EU tend to allocate aid to regions that were already more democratic to begin with? Shouldn't concern for democracy have led it to channel money to regions that were *less*, not *more*, democratic? The above paradox suggests that the hypothesis related to bureaucratic factors also is valid. This hypothesis is difficult to test statistically; however, field research and in-depth interviews with EU officials in Brussels and TACIS local support offices in Russia's regions, as indeed other studies of Western aid, strongly support it. Bureaucratic considerations in allocating aid are linked with democratic factors. Regarding Russia, the EU preferred to award money to local partners that were open, trustworthy, reliable, and transparent.[34] This process went both ways, however, as more democratic regions also were more open to external cooperation. Such regions showed greater willingness to commit to project activity for reasons of public, rather than narrow, private, gain. An EU pledge to contribute up to 25% of funding often required the local partner to make co-financing contributions in kind.[35] According to TACIS officials, many regions simply did not show any interest in such project activity as a result, and these were usually the more closed regions. Others, however, did, and their initiatives for cooperation with external bodies were often crucial in attracting TACIS aid, as was apparently the case in Kareliya. Elsewhere, where regional bodies had no interest or 'concept' for external cooperation, the 'huge potential' of non-governmental organisations accounted for success in building many partnerships, as, for example, in St. Petersburg.[36]

Critics on the ground often dismissed local recipients of large volumes of aid as passive actors in the whole process. They alleged that their Western counterparts, in the know about the kinds of projects the EU was likely to choose, prepared applications and even took on the lion's share of co-financing. Such criticisms, however, are simplistic. Western consortia had a reputation at stake, which could be undermined by allegations of mismanagement or simple failure to fulfil assumed responsibilities. They therefore relied on established local partnership contacts that possessed the interest, commitment, expertise, and infrastructure for EU-type project cycles, which often lasted several years from the day of application to the final reporting requirements. As one EU official in Brussels in charge of relations with Russia put it, 'in some towns it is easier to find good reliable partners than in other ones, so I think there is a kind of natural selection there, because of course it will be [a] big risk'.[37] In supporting such projects, the EU therefore rewarded both the normatively developed (open and outward-looking) and bureaucratically acceptable partners.

It is also logical to assume that bureaucratic acceptability was related to corruption practices, which, according to the latest report of the highly respected, Moscow-based INDEM Foundation, were on the rise in Russia in general.[38] Moreover, we know from a joint Transparency International-Russia (TI-Russia) and INDEM study that there were substantial regional variations in levels of corruption as perceived by local citizens.[39] With some interesting exceptions – including Bashkortostan, which appeared as the least corrupt region – the general trend was that regions in the Far East and the 'Southern Belt' were more corrupt than those in the North.[40]

These regional and geographic patterns suggest that corruption is a product of deeper structural factors peculiar to the various regions, some of which are related to our hypotheses. Analysing TI-Russia data, Dininio and Orttung find that in addition to factors related to the size and structure of the local economies, there is another important predictor of regional corruption: the level of democracy, as measured by the competitiveness of regional electoral processes.[41] These findings bring us back to our own research results showing that democracy and pluralism were significant predictors of aid choices. In rewarding high democratic achievers, the EU therefore simultaneously ensured that there would be less likelihood that its money would be squandered, and greater likelihood that regional actors' decisions to cooperate would be related to consideration of public rather than private gain.

The final hypothesis, 'culture', is the most difficult one to test because of well-known methodological complications. The map of aid density does suggest that the European parts of Russia, if we define Europe as an entity stretching from the Atlantic to the Urals, were over-represented, with the EU conspicuously *not* interested in the Far East or the Northern Caucasus. Another striking aspect of project activity suggesting the possible role of cultural factors was the weak representation of the ethnically defined entities, the republics and autonomous areas, in EU aid choices. Did being a 'Russian', and hence, ostensibly, a more 'European' region, actually affect its likelihood of getting more aid? In fact, being a 'Russian' region did not affect regional aid in a statistically significant way, as revealed when a dummy for *oblasti* was added to the regression. A closer look at the data reveals that entities most under-represented were the Muslim republics of the North Caucasus and Volga areas, and not ethnic regions *per se*. However, the data should be interpreted with caution. The Muslim entities were known to be less democratic than the non-Muslim ones, suggesting that it was not cultural factors, such as religion, that affected aid choices, but regional openness.[42] Ethno-cultural factors did appear to influence aid choices in republics that were also relatively open and democratic. Some of the non-Muslim republics had ethno-linguistic groups that shared linguistic, historical, and cultural heritage with the EU's Nordic states or their indigenous minorities. Kareliya, for example, a non-Muslim entity that is also one of the most open regions, accounted for a large share of EU projects conducted in the republics, and most of these (49 projects in which it was key beneficiary region) were conducted by Finland, an EU state with strong cultural ties to Kareliya. With the exception of St. Petersburg, which served as key partner in 57 projects involving Finland, the country was not nearly as active in other regions as it was in Kareliya. Still, Finland is but one player in the EU, albeit an important one, and the regression does not reveal a statistically significant relationship between ethnic factors and aid. Statistically, democracy and distance from the West were clearly the strongest predictors of aid choices (Table 10.6). So the culture hypothesis is valid only to the extent that various geographical areas appeared to *belong* to Europe, or

Table 10.6   Model, Factors Affecting Aid Volumes Per Region[a]

Variable	Coefficient	Standard error	t	sig.
Democracy ratings	0.532	1.260	4.327	0.000
Distance from Helsinki	−0.218	0.333	−1.947	0.057
Foreign investment	−0.032	0.091	−0.204	0.839
Exports to non-CIS states	−0.170	0.164	−0.959	0.342
GRP	0.240	0.328	1.233	0.223
Population	0.158	0.284	1.350	0.183
Oblast' status	−0.037	0.609	−0.319	0.751
Constant		6.204	−1.225	0.226
Adjusted R sqr.	0.375			
N 88				

[a] *Source*: See note 23. Dependent variable: Logged, total funding in euros for projects in which region was listed as first or key partner.

had cultural ties to Europe. This factor may influence aid choices, but it was not the only or the most important factor of influence.

One last common-sense factor is the possible influence of demographic factors on aid choices, which is suggested by looking at the geographical map of aid density. The lightly shaded regions in Eastern Siberia and the Far East, so conspicuously under-represented, were also those with very low population densities and regions experiencing rapid population decline.[43] So one possible explanation of the *Western* thrust of EU aid could be that 'this is where the people are.'[44] In fact, as noted above, another conspicuously under-represented area is the North Caucasus, which has one of the highest population densities in Russia.[45] In order to test statistically for the possible impact of population on aid volumes, I added regional population numbers to the regression with aid volumes as the dependent variable. The regression showed no statistically significant association between the respective variables (Table 10.6).

A 'Proximity Agenda' and democratic-bureaucratic or 'dereaucratic' interpretations of aid patterns

Pragmatic considerations led EU actors to channel much of the project funding to areas close to the EU's borders. I used the broader label 'strategic' to test this hypothesis. However, issues of concern to Western actors accounting for such aid patterns were more 'soft' security in nature than the word 'strategic' might imply. Yet even controlling for proximity, the normative factors of democracy and civil society emerged as the strongest predictors of aid choices. Cooperating with local actors was not seen as an instrumental means to strengthen channels of Western influence in the regions in the context of deteriorating EU-Russia relations at the federal level. Regions with more powers vis-à-vis the federal centre, or with stronger municipalities, were not necessarily recipients of larger volumes of aid. Considering that these actors often made key trade or investment decisions, this reinforces the conclusion, reached from regressing data on foreign investment, trade and GRP, that economic calculations did not guide aid choices.

Another non-instrumental factor apparently affecting aid and cooperation choices was the shared culture or historical heritage of donors and local partners, although some such areas also overlapped with border regions that were areas of soft security concern. Kareliya and Kaliningrad were examples of the interest of Finland and Germany, respectively, in involvement in areas with a historical record of being part of these states, or, as is the case for Finland, those also having similar ethnic and linguistic groups.

However good their intentions, the EU donor agencies did encounter the same pitfalls as their donor counterparts in this and other settings. Bureaucratic factors led aid money to regions that already had higher achievements to begin with. The EU's notoriously monstrous application and reporting requirements ensured that only the most reliable partners, tested over time, with a high level of professionalism and, usually, English-language skills, got to serve as key local partners on EU projects. Co-financing requirements likewise ensured that local aid recipients already had a developed infrastructure and resource base. Finally, it was local actors that often showed initiative in project cooperation. This ensured the self-selection of regions that not only had greater capacity for EU partnership but were also more outward-looking and open.

Our findings did not bear out the oft-heard criticisms of the EU that its policy towards Russia was 'lacking visionary grand designs', pursuing 'roadmaps to nowhere', or that it was an entity involved in the 'proliferation of the fuzzy'.[46] Whatever declaratory statements at high-level summits proclaimed, the fact is that EU technical assistance to Russia had a strongly pronounced, geographically focused regional dimension. While largely concentrating aid in European parts of Russia for 'soft security' and (less so) cultural reasons, the EU was also true to its declared objective of supporting democratic institution-building in Russia's regions.

In 2007, substantial changes were introduced to the regional component of EU aid to Russia. Against the background of the 2004 accession of new member states to the European Union, among which were several bordering Russia, the EU adopted the European Neighbourhood and Partnership Instrument (ENPI) to replace TACIS. The policy sought to ensure that the latest round of accession did not bring new 'dividing lines' to Europe. There was also a bureaucratic rationale, as funding and project implementation procedures were simplified in response to earlier criticisms of the cumbersome bureaucracy of past *Interreg* and cross-border cooperation programmes.

The ENPI also altered the formal arrangements specifically dealing with EU-Russia cooperation, leading to changes in the regional dimension of EU aid. In 2003, the EU and Russia agreed on the so-called four 'common spaces' in security, justice and home affairs, economic matters, and education and culture. Russia's insistence on such arrangements reflected its desire to maintain a special status, or 'strategic partnership', in its relations with the EU. The result streamlined or narrowed areas of EU aid to the 'roadmap' of these four common spaces and the northern dimension. It also, however, injected a degree of ambiguity into EU aid objectives towards Russia. This was obvious even in the key EU document dealing with regional aspects of EU aid. Just one example of a tautology revealing an apparently deliberate ambiguity from an ENPI document will suffice. The document reads: 'The ENPI covers Russia because the European Union and Russia have decided to develop their strategic partnership through the creation of "four common spaces", as agreed at the St. Petersburg Summit of May 2003, rather than in the framework established by the European Neighbourhood Policy.'[47]

So, did the ENPI cover Russia or did it leave Russia out in the cold? The answer is that for those Russian areas bordering the EU, this policy meant a substantial increase in funding. According to TACIS representatives in Russia's regions, the ENPI aimed at greater 'fairness' and 'equality' of funding allocations along the EU's eastern frontier. Border areas along the western CIS were broken down into several regions, with each region assigned set amounts of funding. Earlier, no clear criteria existed as to how much funding would be allocated in a given year per broader neighbourhood region in the context of the earlier cross-border cooperation programme (CBC). After 2007, however, there were set quotas designed to make the process more predictable. For example, prior to the 2007 policy change, 20–22 million euros in aid would be allocated for the *entire* western CIS frontier 'from Moldova to Murmansk', and often one region, such as Kareliya, would manage to obtain the lion's share for reasons mentioned above. After 2007, however, the goal was for a more 'equal treatment' policy. At the very least, it ensured that regional authorities would be competing against regions within their own country for funding, and not against those in other countries.[48] The extent to which the same crucial factor that guided TACIS aid-flows to Russian regions from 1991 to 2007 – namely, the region's level of pluralism and democracy – has continued to direct *ENPI flows* to Russia is an interesting question.

Notes

1 An earlier and different version of this paper was published in *Post-Soviet Affairs*, 21, 4 (2005): 309–34. The editors are grateful to V. H. Winston & Son, Inc, for permission to print this revised version in the present volume.

2 A large portion of the research for this article was carried out while I was a Woodrow Wilson Fellow at the Woodrow Wilson International Center for Scholars in Washington, DC. I am very grateful to the Center for awarding me the fellowship and its staff and scholars for providing support for the research. I would like to thank Rachel Treffeisen for her research assistance, Lullit Getachew and Christian Haerpfer for their help with data analysis, Archie Brown, Alex Pravda, Bill Tompson, and Álvaro Morcillo-Laiz for comments on the article, and the staff of the EC RELEX and EuropeAid offices in Brussels, and TACIS Local Support Offices in Kareliya and St. Petersburg, for facilitating field research. For comments on my data and findings during earlier stages of data analysis, I am also very grateful to Joan DeBardeleben, Jonathan Fox, Dmitry Gorenburg, Arman Grigorian, Pal Kolstø, Jeff Kopstein, Bill Tompson and Ira Straus. I am also very thankful to George Breslauer for his helpful comments and suggestions for improving the article. Any errors are of course solely my own.

3 Peter J. Schraeder, Steven W. Hook, and Bruce Taylor, 'Clarifying the Foreign Aid Puzzle: A Comparison of American, Japanese, French, and Swedish Aid Flows', *World Politics*, 50, 2 (January 1998): 294–323.

4 Ibid.

5 On efforts to promote the Nordic identity consisting of concern for environment, welfare, and civil society, see Pirjo Jukarainen, 'Norden Is Dead – Long Live the Eastwards Faced Euro-North: Geopolitical Re-making of Norden in a Nordic Journal', *Cooperation and Conflict*, 34, 4 (December 1999): 355–82.

6 Clive Archer, 'Nordic Swans and Baltic Cygnets', *Cooperation and Conflict*, 34, 1 (March 1999): 47–71; Christine Ingebritsen, 'Norm Entrepreneurs: Scandinavia's Role in World Politics', *Cooperation and Conflict*, 37, 1 (March 2002): 11–23; Schraeder et al, 'Clarifying the Foreign Aid Puzzle'.

7 Erika Weinthal and Pauline Jones Luong, 'Environmental NGOs in Kazakhstan: Democratic Goals and Nondemocratic Outcomes', in Sarah Mendelson and John Glenn, eds, The Power and Limits of NGOs: A Critical Look at Building Democracy in Eastern Europe and Eurasia (New York: Columbia University Press, 2002).

8 European Commission official Jan Peter Paul, as cited in Christopher S. Browning, 'The Construction of Europe in the Northern Dimension', *Working*

Paper No. 39, Copenhagen Peace Research Institute (COPRI), Copenhagen (December 2001), p. 28.

9   Michael Emerson, 'The Wider Europe as the European Union's Friendly Monroe Doctrine', *Policy Brief No. 27*, Centre for European Policy Studies, Brussels (October 2002).

10 Viatcheslav Morozov, 'Russia in the Baltic Sea Region: Desecuritization or Deregionalization?', *Cooperation and Conflict*, 39, 3 (September 2004): 317–31.

11 Teemu Palosaari and Frank Möller, 'Security and Marginality: Arctic Europe after the Double Enlargement', *Cooperation and Conflict*, 39, 3 (September 2004): 255–81.

12 Joseph Nye, 'The Decline of America's Soft Power: Why Washington Should Worry', *Foreign Affairs*, 83, 3 (May/June 2004): 16–20; Robert O. Keohane and Joseph Nye, *Power and Interdependence*, 2nd edn (Glenview, IL: Scott, Foresman, 1989).

13 Thomas Carothers, *Aiding Democracy Abroad: The Learning Curve* (Washington, DC: Carnegie Endowment for International Peace, 1999); Margaret Keck and Kathryn Sikkink, *Activists Beyond Borders: Advocacy Networks in International Politics* (Ithaca, NY: Cornell University Press, 1998); Helmut Anheier, Marlies Glasius and Mary Kaldor, eds, *Global Civil Society* (Oxford: Oxford University Press, 2002; Laurence Whitehead, *The International Dimensions of Democratization: Europe and the Americas*, rev. edn (Oxford: Oxford University Press, 2001).

14 Sarah E. Mendelson and John K. Glenn, 'Introduction: Transnational Networks and NGOs in Postcommunist Societies', in Sarah Mendelson and John Glenn, eds, *The Power and Limits of NGOs: A Critical Look at Building Democracy in Eastern Europe and Eurasia* (New York: Columbia University Press, 2002).

15 Kees Biekart, *The Politics of Civil Society Building: European Private Aid Agencies and Democratic Transitions in Central America* (Utrecht: International Books, 1999); Sarah L. Henderson, *Building Democracy in Contemporary Russia: Western Support for Grassroots Organizations* (Ithaca, NY: Cornell University Press, 2003).

16 Biekart, *The Politics of Civil Society Building*.

17 Kevin F. Quigley, 'Lofty Goals, Modest Results: Assisting Civil Society in Eastern Europe', in Marina Ottaway and Thomas Carothers, eds, *Funding Virtue: Civil Society Aid and Democracy Promotion* (Washington, DC: Carnegie Endowment for International Peace, 2000).

18 Henderson, *Building Democracy in Contemporary Russia*.

19 Philip Hanson, 'Federalism with a Russian Face: Regional Inequality and Regional Budgets in Russia', in Peter Reddaway and Robert Orttung, eds, *The Dynamics of Russian Politics: Putin's Reform of Federal-Regional Relations*, Vol. 2 (Lanham, MD: Rowman and Littlefield, 2005).

20 Aleksandr Berdino, Director, TACIS Regional Support Office, interview with Author, Petrozavodsk (5 July 2004).

21 Martin Eisenbeis, Project Manager, TACIS Cross-Border Cooperation Small Project Facility, EuropeAid Cooperation Office, European Commission, interview with author, Brussels (14 April 2004).

22 Information on TACIS can be found on 'Europa,' the website of the EU (http://europa.eu.int/comm/external_relations/ceeca/tacis/). On the European Neigh-

borhood Policy and funding instruments that replaced TACIS, see: European Commission, 'The European Neighbourhood Policy', 'Europa' website, European Union, Brussels, 2005, online at http://europa.eu.int/comm/world/enp/ components_en.htm.

23 A note on the data: The EU TACIS LSOs website http://62.38.207.105/tacis/en/ index.asp) contains lists of projects conducted under the umbrella of each of the nine LSOs. The data were not always complete. Where several regions were listed as participants, I identified the region listed first as key participant. In many projects, multinational companies served as key contractors. In this case, I listed them as 'consortium' without specifying a country. In calculating volume of aid in euros per region, I used the region listed first in a given project. This is an imperfect solution, but in the absence of data on what exact share of a given project each region obtained, it is the only possible one. The variables I included in the dataset are project numbers per region, total volume of aid in euros, and additional population and economic data from the 2003 *Goskomstat* compilation of regional statistics for 2002: Goskomstat Rossii, *Regiony Rossii: Sotsial'no-ekonomicheskiye pokazateli 2003 [Russia's regions: socio-economic indicators 2003]* (Moscow: Goskomstat Rossii, 2003). I also borrowed regional scores for democracy, civil society, and local government from Nikolai Petrov's study: Nikolai Petrov, 'Regional Models of Democratic Development', in Michael McFaul, Nikolai Petrov and Andrei Ryabov, eds, *Between Dictatorship and Democracy: Russian Post-Communist Political Reform* (Washington, DC: Carnegie Endowment for International Peace, 2005). The data in all tables come from these sources.

24 Numbers of projects conducted by year are as follows: 1992: 31; 1993: 49; 1994: 81; 1995: 88; 1996: 90; 1997: 108; 1998: 135; 1999: 91; 2000: 53; 2001: 119; 2002: 124; 2003: 89; 2004: 58; 2005: 2. These figures were compiled by the author from project data available from the TACIS LSOs website.

25 Vladimir Skorokhodov, Head of the Office, TACIS Local Support Office, interview with author, St. Petersburg (13 July 2004).

26 Goskomstat Rossii, *Regiony Rossii: Sotsial'no-ekonomicheskiye pokazateli 2003 [Russia's regions: socio-economic indicators 2003]* (Moscow: Goskomstat Rossii, 2003).

27 These encompass environmental concerns, public health, judicial affairs, and other areas: Hanna Lehtinen, RELEX , Directorate General for External Relations, European Commission, interview with author, Brussels (14 April 2004).

28 Mendelson and Glenn, 'Introduction'. They estimate that in 1990–1999, the US government devoted 2.8% of its total aid funding to democracy promotion, while the EU allocated 9%.

29 Carothers, *Aiding Democracy Abroad*. For comparisons of donor cultures, see Quigley, 'Lofty Goals, Modest Results', Dan Petrescu, 'Civil Society in Romania: From Donor Supply to Citizen Demand', in Marina Ottaway and Thomas Carothers, eds, *Funding Virtue: Civil Society Aid and Democracy Promotion* (Washington, DC: Carnegie Endowment for International Peace, 2000); James Richter, 'Evaluating Western Assistance to Russian Women's Organizations', in Sarah E. Mendelson and John K. Glenn, eds, *The Power and Limits of NGOs: A Critical Look at Building Democracy in Eastern Europe and Eurasia* (New York: Columbia University Press, 2002).

30 Nikolai Petrov, 'Regional Models of Democratic Development'. The time-frame of his study is 1991–2001. It was part of the Moscow Carnegie Center's project on socio-political monitoring of the regions. His methodology and rankings were modeled on Freedom House surveys of democracy.

31 Thomas Risse-Kappen, 'Introduction', in Thomas Risse-Kappen, ed., *Bringing Transnational Relations Back In: Non-State Actors, Domestic Structures, and International Institutions* (New York: Cambridge University Press, 1995).

32 Tomila Lankina, *Governing the Locals: Local Self-Government and Ethnic Mobilization in Russia* (Lanham, MD: Rowman and Littlefield, 2004).

33 Jeffrey Kahn, *Federalism, Democratization, and the Rule of Law in Russia* (Oxford: Oxford University Press, 2002); Daniel S. Treisman, 'Russia's "Ethnic Revival": The Separatist Activism of Regional Leaders in a Postcommunist Order', *World Politics*, 49, 2 (January 1997): 212–49.

34 For details, see http://europa.eu.int/comm/europeaid/evaluation/methods/index.htm.

35 For large projects with an investment component, the share could be 25%; for smaller projects, such as for universities participating in the Tempus programme, it could be as small as 5%. Usually, it ranges between 10% and 20%. Although the Western partner could assume the whole share of co-financing, the EU did not recommend it Valentina Chaplinskaya, European Commission Delegation, interview with author, St. Petersburg (13 July 2004).

36 Skorokhodov, 'Interview'.

37 Lehtinen, 'Interview'.

38 Fond INDEM [INDEM Foundation], 'Vo skol'ko raz uvelichilas' korruptsiya za 4 goda: rezul'taty novogo issledovaniya Fonda INDEM [What is the rate of increase in corruption over a four-year period: The results of the INDEM Foundation's new research]', press release, Moscow (July 2005), available at www.anti-corr.ru/indem/2005diagnost/2005diag_press.doc.

39 Fond INDEM/TI-Russia, 'Regional'nyye indeksy korruptsii [Regional indices of Corruption]', Moscow (October 2002), online via www.anti-corr.ru/projects.htm.

40 Elena Chirkova and Donald Bowser, 'Corruption in Russian Regions', in Robin Hodess, ed., *Global Corruption Report 2004* (London: Pluto Press/Transparency International, 2004), p. 295; online version: www.globalcorruptionreport.org/gcr2004.html.

41 Phyllis Dininio and Robert Orttung, 'Explaining Patterns of Corruption in the Russian Regions', *Working Paper No. 727*, William Davidson Institute, Stephen M. Ross School of Business, University of Michigan (Ann Arbor, MI, 2004), available online at www.transparency.org.ru/CENTER/c_publications.asp.

42 Nikolai Petrov, 'Regional Models of Democratic Development'; Kelly McMann and Nikolai Petrov, 'A Survey of Democracy in Russia's Regions', *Eurasian Geography and Economics*, 41, 3 (April/May 2000): 155–82.

43 Fiona Hill and Clifford Gaddy, *The Siberian Curse: How Communist Planners Left Russia out in the Cold* (Washington, DC: Brookings Institution Press, 2003); Michael Bradshaw and Jessica Prendergrast, 'The Russian Heartland Revisited: An Assessment of Russia's Transformation', *Eurasian Geography and Economics*, 46, 2 (March 2005): 83–122.

44 I am grateful to Ira Straus for this point.

45 Fiona Hill, 'Russia's "Tinderbox": Conflict in the North Caucasus and Its Implications for the Future of the Russian Federation', *Occasional Paper*, Strengthening Democratic Institutions Project, John F. Kennedy School of Government, Harvard University, Cambridge (September 1995), available online at http://bcsia.ksg.harvard.edu/BCSIA_content/documents/Russias_Tinderbox_1995.pdf.

46 Gänzle Filtenborg, Mette Sicard, Stefan Gänzle, and Elisabeth Johansson, 'An Alternative Theoretical Approach to EU Foreign Policy: 'Network Governance' and the Case of the Northern Dimension Initiative', *Cooperation and Conflict*, 37, 4 (December 2002): 387–407; Vadim Kononenko, 'A Road Map to Nowhere', *Moscow Times* (14 May 2005); Michael Emerson, 'EU-Russia: Four Common Spaces and the Proliferation of the Fuzzy', *Policy Brief No. 71*, Centre for European Policy Studies, Brussels (May 2005).

47 European Commission, 'Proposal for a Regulation of the European Parliament and of the Council Laying Down General Provisions Establishing a European Neighbourhood and Partnership Instrument', COM (2004) 628 final, European Union, Brussels, (29 September 2004), online at http://europa.eu.int/comm/world/enp/pdf/getdoc_en.pdf.

48 Berdino, 'Interview'; Eisenbeis, 'Interview'.

Index